THE HIDDEN MAYA

Other Books by Martin Brennan

The Boyne Valley Vision (Dolmen Press, 1979)

The Stars and the Stones (Thames and Hudson, 1982)

The Stones of Time (Inner Traditions, 1994)

T·H·E
HIDDEN MAYA

MARTIN BRENNAN

BEAR & COMPANY
PUBLISHING
SANTA FE, NEW MEXICO

LIBRARY OF CONGRESS CATALOGING-IN-PUBLICATION DATA

Brennan, Martin, 1942-
   The hidden Maya / Martin Brennan.
      p. cm.
   Includes bibliographical references and index.
   ISBN 1-879181-24-X
   1. Mayan languages —Writing.   2. Inscriptions, Mayan.   3. Manuscripts, Maya.
I. Title.
F1435.3.W75B74 1998
497'.415211—dc21
                                                          97-42434
                                                            CIP

Bear & Company, Inc.
Santa Fe, NM 87504-2860

Text and cover illustrations: Martin Brennan
Text and cover design: Melinda Belter
Editing: Sonya Moore
Printed in United States of America by R.R. Donnelley

9 8 7 6 5 4 3 2 1

CONTENTS

DEDICATION &
ACKNOWLEDGMENTS

For well over a century epigraphers have been working on the truly monumental task of deciphering the Maya hieroglyphs. After making initial breakthroughs in rereading glyphs largely concerned with recording time, these researchers arrived at insurmountable impasses. Despite intensive work by such brilliant epigraphers as Sir Eric Thompson, Maya texts remained for the most part mysterious and unfathomable. In the early 1950s a major breakthrough occurred mainly due to the insight of Yuri Knorozov, who recognized that key elements in the writing system had phonetic values. As spoken Maya is a living language, a vast road had been opened which penetrates deeply into the meaning of the enigmatic ancient texts.

Although at first Knorozov's idea was ridiculed as being quack speculation and many of his initial translations proved to be incorrect, many epigraphers applied his ideas, and by the 1960s some texts were beginning to be deciphered in their entirety. In the subsequent decades as the phonetic approach became widely accepted enormous strides were made, a process that continues presently; and as a consequence most of the ancient hieroglyphs can now be understood and are being reread with confidence and accuracy. This is one of the most exciting, revealing, and penetrative decipherments in the history of epigraphy.

In contrast to the famous decipherment of the Egyptian hieroglyphs, which were interpreted mainly through the diligent work of a single person, Jean-François Champollion, the meaning of the Maya hieroglyphs has come to light through the systematic solutions of numerous scholars. In *The Hidden Maya* I have not attributed the particular decipherments of the various glyphs presented to individual epigraphers. That would be a separate study in itself, and in most instances it is not the meaning of a glyph that is disputed but exactly who was the first to have recognized it. Besides, the process of deciphering Maya script has become so productive that often two or three epigraphers arrive at accepted rereadings simultaneously.

I have specialized in the interpretation of the handsigns in the ancient art, and in doing so I came to realize that the meaning of the handsigns is coordinated to the ideas expressed in the accompanying texts. I am therefore extremely indebted to the work of the epigraphers in the field. A list of some of them, and researchers in related areas, includes: Anthony Andrews, Anthony Aveni, Heinrich Berlin, Janet Berlo, Hermann Beyer, Victoria Bricker, Arlen Chase, Diane Chase, Ernie Chase, Michael Closs, Michael Coe, Clemency Coggins, Constance Cortez, Jack DuBois, Munro Edmonsson, Fedrico Fahsen, Barbara Fash, William Fash, Vilma Fialko, Daniel Finamore, Linda Flores, Tomas Flores, James Fox, David Freidel, Peter Furst, Eric

Gibson, Ian Graham, Nikolai Grube, Donald Hales, Norman Hammond, Stephen Houston, Christopher Jones, Grant Jones, Tom Jones, David Joraleman, Dr. Josserand, John Justeson, Terrance Kaufman, David Kelley, Yuri Knorozov, Jeff Kowalski, Ruth Krochock, George Kubler, Manfred Kudlek, Ben Leaf, Carl Lehrburger, Matt Looper, Floyd Lounsbury, Bruce Love, Barbara MacLeod, Joyce Marcus, Peter Matthews, Judith Maxwell, Jeffrey Miller, Mary Miller, Virginia Miller, Werner Nahm, William Norman, Jorge Orejel, Gary Pahl, Esther Pasztory, Tatiana Proskouriakoff, Dennis Puleston, Robert Rands, Dorie Reents, Berthold Riese, Jack Roberts, Merle Greene Robertson, Francise Robiscek, Ralph Roys, Linton Satterwaite, Linda Schele, Michael Sellon, Robert Sharer, Leslie Shaw, John Sosa, Andrea Stone, David Stuart, George Stuart, Carolyn Tate, Karl Taube, Dennis Tedlock, and Evan Vogt. I am a dwarf standing on the shoulders of giants. Although it is inevitable that the names of many valuable contributors have inadvertently been omitted from this listing, it is to these scholars that this book is dedicated.

The Hidden Maya was completed in Great Barrington, Massachusetts, in 1996. During the germinating years many members of the community, notably Arthur Gregory, Bruce Kelly, and Bob Magadini, were extremely helpful in enabling its completion to become a reality. Others whose contributions I gratefully acknowledge and without whom the work could not be accomplished include Bob and Bonnie Benson of Yellow House Books, Sheila Faxon, Michael Houlihan, Margaret Murdock, Douglas Savage, Helen and Michael Selzer of Farshaw's Bookshop and Bibliofind, Inc., Natalie Smith, and Leonard Weber. The final preparation was done in Boulder, Colorado, where Alisha Michell and Elizabeth Lee Cantrell helped organize the material and Theo Ehrhardt, Charles Grant, and Louise Randolph kindly provided work space.

A NOTE ON THE
ILLUSTRATIONS & SOURCES

The figures in this book have all been created by the author in order to reveal the specific iconographic contents of the works of art discussed in the text. The intention is to disclose as clearly and accurately as possible the various forms, motifs, handsigns, and glyphs that were present in the original art. There is no attempt to represent the current condition of the art, which is frequently marred by various flaws including cracks and abrasions. As much as possible these have been eliminated and therefore a certain amount of restoration and reconstruction has been employed in order to illuminate the original contents of the compositions.

The techniques the author used subjected the original art to careful analysis and magnification for clarification, and the intensity of the lines is restored in a process known as line enhancement. Reconstruction is employed cautiously and with reserve, only being used when solutions are blatantly obvious. If there is any reasonable doubt to a resolution, the author has opted to allow the flaw to remain in the interest of accuracy.

The clarified renditions arrived at have an artistic charm of their own; they sometimes unveil configurations and aspects of the art that have been previously obscured, and they allow a deeper appreciation of the originals. However the reader is reminded that they are considered to be more or less schematic diagrams, and they are in no way intended as substitutes for the originals which are often bathed in brilliant radiant colors impossible to match in black-and-white reproductions.

Most of my formal training in art took place at Pratt Institute in Brooklyn, New York, during the early 1960s. I distinctly recall the guest lecturer who appeared at the introduction of the intensive art course; he was the famous mythologist, Joseph Campbell, who had recently written *The Hero with a Thousand Faces*. In explaining that the myths of many cultures include a theme which he referred to as the hero's journey, Campbell made a lasting impression on me. In these universal scenarios, the hero suffers a separation from his (or her) world, sets out alone to confront mysterious forces, and finally returns in glory, carrying the knowledge gained to a magnificent reunion. The Greeks express their appreciation of the benefits of fire in the Prometheus myth: Prometheus goes to heaven, steals the secret of fire from the gods, and presents it as a gift to humankind. In ancient India, Gautama Buddha renounces the comforts of his princely world to go on the hero's journey that leads to his nirvana. He triumphantly returns thence, bringing with him the noble truths of the Eightfold Way, the path to enlightenment. The hero of the Jews, Moses, seeks his God on Mount Sinai, receives the Ten Commandments and returns with them to unite his people. In each case, the reunion brings forth a teaching of integration—a new way to manifest the spirit in the experience of ordinary life.

I see the myth of the hero's journey being played out again in our main source of Maya mythology, the *Popol Vuh*, which chronicles the exploits of the Hero Twins in the Otherworld. As can be expected from the Maya, here we get a highly elaborate and fantastic treatment of the basic universal theme. The Twins do not simply return to humanity; they revisit the gods to confront them with their acquired knowledge and cunning. They do not present us with a rigid set of rules or a preordained formula for enlightenment, which would be totally out of character with Maya religious thinking. Rather, their actions on the supernatural plane of existence establish a model of ideal behavior and their epic story is a wonderful monument relating an episode in humanity's perpetual endeavour—the eternal quest for a triumphant overcoming and final solution to the enigmatic problem of the human condition and the eventuality of death.

The four main categories of documentation used in this book to provide knowledge of the Maya civilization and its religion are: archaeological remains, including painted pottery; Native books in hieroglyphic writing; early accounts in Native languages written in Latin script by learned Indians; and books in Spanish by conquerors or priests. Only a few Maya-painted manuscripts of pre-Conquest date have survived the ravages of the Conquest and the systematic extirpation of Native "idolatry" pursued during the sixteenth century by the fanatical authorities of the Inquisition. From the lowland Maya region, three calendrical and ritual screenfolds—the codices Dresden, Madrid, and Paris—are the only pictorial manuscripts extant.

A key Maya source is *Popol Vuh*, which comes to us as a work compiled in the Quiché Maya dialect shortly after the Spanish Conquest and written in Latin script. We also have annals of the Cakchiquels, neighbors of the Quiché tribes and a collection of chronicles known as the *Chilam Balam*, which deals with the history of the Yucatan; however, it is widely recognized that nothing can compare to the *Popol Vuh* in the introduction it affords to the mythical and religious thought of the Maya. Regardless of the fact that the work is dated many centuries after the fall of the Maya empires, there is little doubt that it is rooted in ancient traditions. For example, in the genesis episode at the very beginning of the epic, seven gods form a council and between them arises the "word," which is the manifestation of Creation. Precisely the same event is beautifully portrayed in an ancient vase painting entitled *The Vase of the Seven Gods* (see figure 2.13 on page 77). The painting can be accurately interpreted as a veritable illustration of the episode, enhanced by specific dates and visual material which potently breathes new life into the antiquated pages of the *Popol Vuh*. The myth interrupts the genesis episode and inserts the legendary cycle involving the Hero Twins, the creators of magic, a couple found in numerous other

Mesoamerican mythologies and whose brilliant phantasmagoric exploits adorn the surfaces of many ancient Maya vases.

Only a few pre-Columbian Aztec sacred books have survived—such as the Codex Borbonicus, the Codex Borgia, the Codex Fejérváry-Mayer, and the Codex Becker. Only a few of them, such as the Borbonicus, are truly Aztec, while others, such as the Borgia, seem to emanate from the priestly colleges and temples of the "Mexica-Puebla" area, between the Oaxacan mountains and the central highlands.

The Codex Nuttall is a pre-Conquest screenfold that originated in western Oaxaca. It is believed to have been sent by Cortés to Charles V in 1519 together with the Codex Vienna. After a rather adventurous and extensive tour of Europe it finally was acquired by the British Museum in 1917. The Selden Roll appears to be pre-Columbian but it originated from sixteenth-century western Oaxaca and now is in the Bodleian Library, Oxford. The Codex Ríos is painted on European paper ascertained not to have been manufactured until at least 1569.

T·H·E
HIDDEN MAYA

Figure 1. **We Went North**, *rock painting. Valley of the Tule River, California*

INTRODUCTION

I developed an interest in early writing systems at a very young age while growing up in Brooklyn, New York. I lived in close proximity to the Brooklyn Public Library and distinctly recall my first trip to the children's section. The book I selected was entitled *The Children's Book of Chinese Characters*. It demonstrated how the simplest characters are pictorial representations of the objects they stand for. I had already developed a firm commitment to being an artist, and this book revealed a relationship between writing and art that profoundly fascinated me.

Near the library stands the Brooklyn Museum, an institution that was also to have a strong influence on my early development. My first encounter with Maya culture occurred in the exhibits on the first floor. Here large-scale models of the ancient Maya temples were constructed. What were these structures built for? Who were the people who used them, I asked myself, and what secrets did these particularly

3

strange, perplexing hieroglyphs that adorned the ceramics possibly contain? Later on in life I was to find the answers to the questions I had originally posed to myself as a child.

The first of seven trips to Mexico occurred soon after I studied visual communication at Pratt Institute in Brooklyn, and lasted for a year. For many months I lived with an Indian family deep in the mountains of Jalisco. From there I ventured out into even more remote areas by foot and on horseback. In Nayarit I encountered the Huichol and made a detailed study of their wonderful art and religion. Near obscure villages where no white man had ever been I beheld spectacular petroglyphs and magnificent rock engravings on boulders and cliffs, which reinforced my lifelong interest in the ancient art of Mesoamerica.

In the later 1960s, fulfilling an ambition I had held for many years, I left Mexico for Japan. I took residence at Shotokugi Zen Monastery, which has a historical tradition as an important art center, and undertook a study of oriental calligraphy under the direction of Reverend Ogata. I later moved to the outskirts of Kyoto where I continued exploring oriental art and the development of Chinese characters. Here I met the aged Kimitaro Kitamura, Japan's foremost scholar of Irish culture and the Gaelic language. He was also a recognized authority in Buddhist literature and Shintoism, which he introduced me to. A central feature of Shintoism is ancestor worship and one of the most important symbols is the mirror. I was later to find out that this is also true of Maya

religious beliefs. Kitamura explained to me that the oriental studies I had immersed myself in were only secondary; my real purpose in coming to Japan was looking into the mirror and seeing myself. He urged me to go to Ireland, the ancestral land of my parents.

On June 3, 1970, I arrived at Dublin airport and made a beeline for New Grange, one of the principal prehistoric mounds in the Boyne Valley. At that time the mounds were thought to be gigantic burial places. Any attempt to decipher the profusion of petroglyphs in these mounds was considered futile. I couldn't accept any of this and so began my first major project in epigraphy.

I first determined that the chambers of the mounds were astronomically aligned and the meaning of the petroglyphs was related to this. I was able to recognize in them an abundance of lunar and solar images, the earliest known fully worked out calendars and functional sundials, which preceded anything previously known by thousands of years. This of course overturned many apple carts but I published a preliminary work entitled *The Boyne Valley Vision* (1979) and a culminating book, *The Stars and the Stones* (1982), which was reissued in the United States as *The Stones of Time* (1994). In these works I had tapped into some of the earliest methods of recording numbers and indeed the very fundamental beginnings of writing itself.

In June of 1982 I returned to Brooklyn. The thrill of realizing the potential of archaic writing to transmit information was now an obsession. To me there is no greater intellectual pleasure

in life than to decipher an ancient inscription and reveal a hidden message
that has not been reread for hundreds or
perhaps thousands of years. When I first
saw the ancient stones of Mexico in my
youth I looked at them with awe and
wonder but I had made no attempt at
interpreting them. I now had experience, ambition, and confidence. I was
curious to see if another look at the ancient stones of the North American continent would perhaps instigate another
investigation, so one Saturday afternoon
soon after my arrival I was once again in
the rooms of the Brooklyn Public
Library. By the end of the day I came
across a book that I knew was to be the
starting place for my next major project
in epigraphy. *Picture Writing of the
North American Indians* by Garrick
Mallery first appeared in 1893 as *The
Tenth Annual Report of the Bureau of
American Ethnology*. In a section entitled "Gesture and Posture Signs
Depicted" I was stunned to see one of
the clearest and most perceptive interpretations of pictographs on stone that I
had ever encountered.

In figure 1 I have redrawn this
stone. Mallery's approach in interpreting the art is rooted in his knowledge
of American Indian Sign Language, of
which he was easily one of the foremost
students. It is amazing how easily the
images on the stone can be explained by
utilizing Mallery's initial interpretations. I have labeled the main actors A,
B, and C. The headline or main message
conveyed is in the sweeping gesture
made by character A who is central in
the composition. It means "we went
north" as north is the direction indicat-

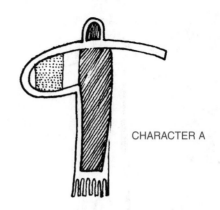

CHARACTER A

ed by the right arm of this figure. All the
other information is subordinate to this.
The basic technique of using the hand
to indicate direction is natural and universal.

Character C explains the reason
why they went north. The natural and
universal handsign expressing "nothing,
nothing here" is made by throwing one
or both hands outward from either side
of the body. This gesture is reiterated by
subordinate figures above and to the left
of this figure. According to Mallery the
extended toes represent an emphasis of
this gesture.

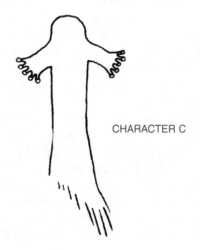

CHARACTER C

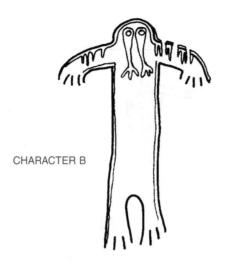

CHARACTER B

Character B expresses feelings. Mallery invokes another handsign to explain that it depicts sorrow. To sign "rain" the Shoshoni, Apache, and other Indians hold the hands at the height of and before the shoulder, fingers pendant and palm down, then push downward a short distance. Here "eye rain" —tears—is expressed and reinforced by the graphics surrounding the eyes. (I suggest that rather than trying to grasp the procedure cerebrally, you perform these signs with your hands. We humans handsign every day; handsigns are the great mother of communication. I will describe this in detail later.)

Subordinate pictographs between A and B explain the reason for the sorrow. Mallery uses yet another handsign to explain these. They are apparently making the universal gesture for hunger by passing the hands toward and back from the sides of the body, suggesting a gnawing sensation. He notes that the man in the horizontal position may possibly denote a "dead man," a pictograph adopted by

the Ojibway, Blackfeet, and other tribes as a common device representing a dead body.

Using Mallery's approach I have interpreted the figures between C and A as the shamans of the tribe. The two figures making the "hunger" gesture are pictographs derived directly from the Plains Indian handsign for "shaman." The forefinger is placed on the forehead, which indicates "brain," and moved upward signifying "big." They evoke the nonhuman spirit form that hovers behind the right arm of the main figure, confirming and reassuring to the viewer that the move north is approved by the Great Spirit.

Mallery noted that similar drawings occur at a distance about ten miles southeast of this locality in the Tule River Valley as well as other places toward the north. It seems probable that the pictograph was made by a portion of a tribe that had advanced for the purpose of selecting a new camping place. They had failed to find the quantities of food necessary for sustenance, and therefore erected this notice to inform those who followed of their misfortune and determined departure toward the north. (In figure 2 I have redrawn a landmark used to aid winter travelers in finding their way across the practically featureless frozen tundras west of Hudson Bay. Its meaning is blatantly obvious.) It became immediately apparent to me that Mallery's convincing explanation of these petroglyphs could not possibly be accomplished without a well-grounded knowledge of handsigns and their applications in forming communicative symbols. He states his basic

Figure 2. **Go That Way**, *stone cairn. Level country west of Hudson Bay, Canada*

premise: "When a gesture sign had been established and it became necessary or desirable to draw a character or design to convey the same idea, nothing could be more natural than to use the graphic form which was known and used in gesture sign." Subsequently I began my own research in this area and found that not only were Mallery's assertions correct, but graphic signs which are derived from hand gestures played an extremely significant role in the development of writing and this fact had since been overlooked or ignored.

I termed these signs "manographs," of which the ancient Egyptian ruler illustrated in figure 3 is a typical example. The Egyptian ell, containing twenty-eight "fingers," is a measure that clearly arose from the ordinary lives of the

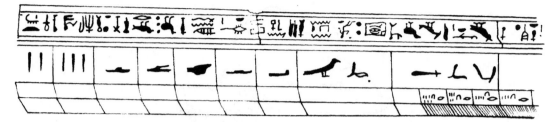

Figure 3. Ancient Egyptian ruler, about 10 inches in length

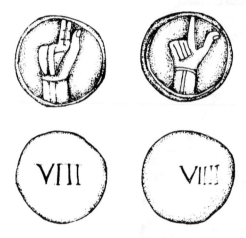

Figure 4. Two Roman counters showing the numbers eight and nine formed by finger gestures, and numerals eight and nine, probably first century A.D. *British Museum, London*

common people. In this ruler the segment of the number one is missing but the numbers two and three are easily discernible. A handsign, the thumb closed over the palm, is substituted for the number four. Another manograph with the thumb extended away from the palm represents the number five. Similarly, the numbers six, seven, and eight are all indicated by renderings of corresponding handsigns. It is extraordinary that on the same ruler are the "true" Egyptian number symbols for thirteen, fourteen, fifteen, and sixteen, which appear with a symbol that indicates fractions of the ell.

Another remarkable use of manographs is shown on the two ivory Roman counters shown in figure 4. Roman numerals themselves were widely used not only because they could easily be carved but because they were readily formed on the hands by common people. The numeral eight for example was easily formed by the V-sign on one hand representing "five" and three upraised fingers on the other hand indicating "three" according to an ancient method of number computation done on the hands, by which complex calculations could be made. On the reverse of the counters are the numerals eight and nine.

It is not surprising that sculptors used these finger signs on their art. We are informed by Pliny the Elder, who died in A.D. 79, about a statue in the forum of ancient Rome that depicted Janus as God of the Sun. Janus, the two-headed god of time, the year, and all beginnings and endings, lends his name to the first month of the year. He was shown forming the number 300 with

Figure 5. Chinese coin, Han Dynasty, around 200 B.C. From the collection of R. Scholsser, Hannover, Germany

ear seal forms of the characters wherein numerous hands are depicted in both stationary and moving aspects. When the scribes adapted these to the brush, forming the characters as they are still known today, they most often eliminated the clear delineation of the hands in the more ancient forms and thus erased the true origins of the character.

An example of this is clear in the Chinese coin depicted in figure 5. On the left is an inscription meaning "series nineteen." The cross above is the number ten; below this a nine is represented by a manograph depicting a moving left hand. This number gesture is still used in southern China to this day. The more modern form of this character is an abbreviation that suggests the movement only and eliminates the hand.

Handsigns are more prominent in Maya art than in any other art in the world. I had long been intrigued by them but had not been able to gain access to their meaning. Although Mallery's initial attempts at explaining the Maya handsigns were a failure I saw in them possible avenues of approach that would not only lead to a comprehension of the handsigns but would open portals into the very essence of Maya spiritual thought.

Regardless of his rather clumsy start, Mallery in fact anticipated and pioneered a uniquely effective field of inquiry and so I became curious about his background, which is included in appendix one. In the process of continuing Mallery's work and exploring its full implications in relation to the mystery of Maya handsigns, I at once confronted the problem of the origin of Plains

his right hand and the number 65 with his left to symbolize the days of the year.

Mallery states a universal principle: that the pictograph develops simply as a graphic rendering of an object but when there is an attempt to convey subjective ideas it is likely that a graphic representation of a handsign, or what I term a manograph, will be employed. In applying Mallery's ideas to the study of the development of writing I came to the conclusion that for this reason those cultures that had a highly developed system of handsigning were the ones most likely to develop a system of writing. For example, I noted that there was very little evidence of handsigns in Inca art and consequently little or no writing.

I found the close relationship between handsigning and the development of writing played an exceptionally important part in the formation of Chinese characters as was suggested by Mallery. To fully appreciate this however one must go back to the ancient lin-

Indian Sign Language. Naturally my first sources of information were the Indians themselves. The Blackfeet, whose territory covered parts of Alberta and Saskatchewan in southern Canada and parts of Montana and North Dakota, have a mythological explanation for the origin of the signs. In the myth, two brothers who are twins fall in love with the same woman. One is overcome by jealousy and devises a plan to get rid of his rival. He lures his brother on a canoe trip to a tiny island on a large lake and abandons him there. He feels sure his brother will die of starvation in the oncoming winter. Instead the twin is taken into a beaver lodge for the winter where he is sheltered, fed, and taught the Beaver Medicine—supernatural power—and the divine art of handsigning. When summer comes the twin returns to the village and teaches the people handsigning.

A pipe bowl (figure 6) from near this area shows a bear spirit giving instruction to a shaman. Pipes were decorated with mythological and religious scenes as smoking was usually a ceremonial activity. This could easily be a variation of the myth with the bear replacing the beaver as instructor.

A tradition of the Arapaho, whose territory extended through parts of Nebraska, Kansas, Colorado, and Wyoming, tells us that the creator of all things, the original Arapaho, taught the Indians how to "talk with their hands." Captain W.P. Clark, Second Cavalry, U.S. Army, questioned Iron Hawk, an Arapaho chief, on the origin of the handsigns. Iron Hawk replied, "The sign language was the gift of the Great Spirit. He gave us the power to talk with our hands and arms and to send information to a distance with the mirror, blanket, and pony." To the Indian the sign language is a sacred thing.

When white men, mostly soldiers,

Figure 6. **The Shaman and the Bear**, red stone pipe bowl, East Dakota

traders, and hunters, first began to learn the Indian sign language they were amazed at its communicative power. A skillful signer could transmit information two and three times faster than a person speaking. Sign language became famous. An early film was made of Buffalo Bill handsigning with Chief Iron Tail, the Indian who was memorialized on the infamous five-cent coin. The Indians' proficiency was so great that it was assumed that they invented handsigning themselves.

Statements from serious students of Indian affairs and skillful interpreters farther south painted a very different picture of the origins of the sign language. Colonel Richard Dodge, U.S. Army, stated, "The Plains Indians believe that the sign language was invented by the Kiowas." Kiowa territory covered parts of Oklahoma, Kansas, Colorado, New Mexico, and Texas. They were generally recognized as the most adept in handsigning. Ben Clark, an interpreter at Fort Reno reported, "The Cheyennes think the sign language originated with the Kiowas, who brought it from Mexico."

Dr. William H. Corbusier, U.S. Army, said, "The Plains Indians did not invent it. The traditions of the Indians point toward the south as the direction from which the sign language came. The Comanches acquired it in Mexico." Comanche territory was parts of New Mexico and southern Texas. The handsign for Comanche is made by extending the index finger outward with a slow sinuous motion. Its meaning is "snake," the name they were known by to the Indians. It is widely believed that the word "Comanche" is derived from the Spanish words "Camino Ancho" or the wide road, referring to a famous ancient trade route from New Mexico into Casas Grandes in Mexico and thence on to points south. In his book *Indians of the Southwest,* M. Jourdan Atkinson states that the sign language made "communication possible from the Mohawk Valley to the Valley of Mexico and on through the empires far south."

Conventional scholarship has for long asserted that at best only casual connections existed between the Southwest and Mesoamerica, but the transmission of a sign language represents a significant cultural exchange, which would only suggest systematic contact. Other evidence produced by modern scientific examination and archaeological studies proves that a highly structured formal trade system developed. Some of this evidence is included in appendix two.

My approach to the problem of the Maya handsigns now had another dimension. These developments presented a new way of access; a back door opened by their distant cousins: *If the sign language of the Plains Indian, which is known, well documented, and currently in use, originated from Mexico as the traditions of the Indians affirm, then it could be possible to use this language to penetrate into the meaning of the unknown handsigns of the ancient Maya.*

I began by learning everything I could about American Indian Sign Language and its relationship to their pictography, using Mallery's ideas as a launching pad. Signing is a precise communicative device and also an art. A

Figure 7. **Young Elk Receives a War Report**, *drawing after Kurz, 1851. Smithsonian Institution*

skillful American Indian signer performs with the grace and eloquence of a dancer. The system is refined to such an extent that an individual's signature can be detected in the way the embellishments of a sign are rendered. It seems that, having inherited the art from Mexico, the Plains Indian not only mastered it but perfected it. The vast stretches of the Great Plains provided the ideal environment to do so. On long hunting vigils requiring absolute silence the Indians could joke, gossip, tell stories, discuss strategies, or delve into any matters of human interest whatsoever, all through the medium of the silent language.

I am a great admirer of some of the drawings produced during the last century which realistically depict the daily life of the Plains Indians. Some of these sketches vie with modern photography in their capacity to convey detailed information. I have redrawn one of these, shown in figure 7, because it is highly instructive.

We see Young Elk, a major chief of the Omaha, whose territory included parts of Nebraska, South Dakota, and Iowa, receiving a report from one of his captains. This is very serious business. The handsigns shown in the illustration are tiny fragments of an intricate conversation. They cannot be translated in the way we can reread a sacred handsign as presented in Maya art. What is revealing is that although these are members of the same tribe who share a common oral language, the preferred medium of communication is the sign language.

Interestingly, Young Elk is not the warrior in the elaborate feathered war bonnet and buffalo robe decorated with pictographs recording his martial exploits. Simply attired, Young Elk appears on the left. A single feather in his headband contains enough information to convey who he is. He carries only his bow and arrow. As a true chief he is not concerned with his own material advancement but with the welfare of the tribe. Only on ceremonial occasions would he wear his full regalia. Otherwise, contrary to Hollywood versions, he dresses simply.

In some Indian villages on the plains, two or three tribes whose languages were radically different lived together. As a matter of pride an Indian would refrain from ever using an uttered word from the language of a different tribe. Instead the sign language was employed and Indians would grow up and live together in the same village throughout their lives, never verbally exchanging a word with one another. How would such people, deeply rooted in a tradition of handsigning, transmit a written message?

In figure 8A on the left is the pictograph of a Dakota named Afraid of Him, taken from Red Cloud's Census. To sign "afraid" the index finger is crooked and the other fingers are closed as the hand is drawn backward. The meaning is "shrinks back from." The handsign for "trade" is shown in B and means "exchange." In the pictograph

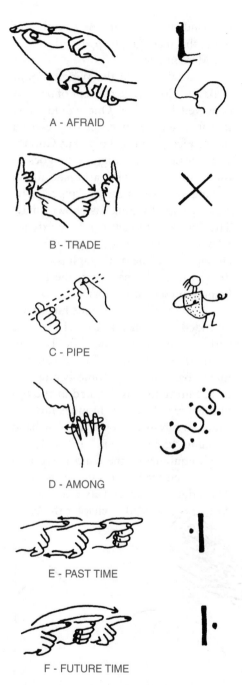

A - AFRAID

B - TRADE

C - PIPE

D - AMONG

E - PAST TIME

F - FUTURE TIME

Figure 8. *Some Plains Indian handsigns compared with their pictographic equivalents*

the hands become bars. As a symbol of trade, this manograph appears throughout Mesoamerica.

C is taken from the Winter Count of Batiste Good. The concept of peace is conveyed by a pipe. One would think that it would be far easier to present a simple pictograph of a pipe but Good is so immersed in handsigning he goes to the trouble of drawing a human figure making the handsign for "pipe." The handsign for "among" is shown in D. The fingers of the left hand are extended and the right index finger is waved among them. The pictograph is directly derived from the handsign, the fingers being represented by dots.

To sign "time" the index fingers are extended as the hands are held parallel and moved toward the left. To sign "past time" the right hand quickly moves back meaning "time behind" as in E. Future time is denoted in the opposite way in F. The right index finger is suddenly advanced before the left hand meaning "time in front." In the pictograph equivalents, the hand is reduced to a bar and the finger is shown as a dot. The origin of this and its relevance to writing is discussed in chapter three.

Plains Indian pictography consists largely of histories and calendars. Events are unfolded in a time setting that is a spiral emanating from a center and evolving outward from right to left. In the same way time is visualized graphically as moving from right to left in depiction of the *tonalmatl*, the 260-day Mesoamerican calendar. Thus the pictographs in E and F replicate the motion of the hands expressing time. The device of using a dot to indicate the finger and a bar to represent the hand can be traced far back to the Olmec civilization, and it is used throughout all of Maya history. This too is discussed in detail in chapter three.

If a people's usual mode of conversation is oral language, their prayers will tend to be spoken. If a people's usual mode of conversation is sign language, their prayers will tend to be handsigned. Hence, the pictograph for "prayer," figure 9B, shows a hand. The pictograph actually represents a fundamental ritual as is described in chapter one. In figure 9A is the pictograph meaning "the spirit above." Figure 9C is taken from a Navaho ceramic; in it the artist has combined these two pictographs demon-

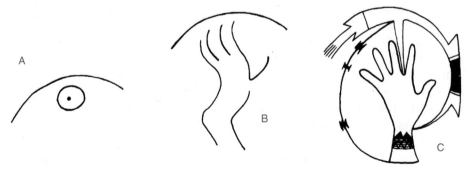

Figure 9. Pictographs and art of the Navaho

Figure 10. Correction glyph, Xochicalco, Mexico

strating how art can be deeply influenced by pictographic writing.

Figure 10 is a calendrical correction glyph from Mexico. When a calendar maker has made a miscalculation this glyph overrides the error. The main sign is *pop*, which means "mat" and denotes authority. Below this is *chak*, which here means "great." The four circles probably symbolize the four directions that segment the Mesoamerican calendar and imply that the correction applies everywhere for all time. The correction itself is shown by the movement of the hands. The right hand discards the incorrect daysign "Reed" and it is replaced by the left hand drawing in the correct daysign "Eleven Vulture" by means of a rope.

Manographs are abundant in Nahua pictographic writing from which the pictographic writing of the Plains Indians is probably derived. The principles of both systems are the same. Interestingly, some Nahua pictographs can be traced back to Olmec hieroglyphic writing and these also appear in the Plains Indian system. This is demonstrated in chapter one.

Some highly abstract pictographs are in fact directly derived from hand-

Figure 11. The number ten, Nahua handsign and pictograph

signs. Figure 11A shows one of the ways the number ten is expressed on the hands. Figure 11B is the Nahua pictograph *matlac* meaning "ten." A Nahua pictograph in figure 12 bears the inscription "Andrés Tilmatlaneuh" or "Andrew, the cloth lender." The handsign depicted actually means "give." To

*Figure 12. **Andrés Tilmatlaneuh**. Mexican manuscript, number 3, Bibliothéque Nationale, Paris*

express "lend" a Plains Indian will sign "give" followed by "future time" and then "give" again.

Plains Indian pictography is not considered true writing because by definition writing represents words, but pictographs are accepted symbols, manographs, and pictures of the objects or verbs they stand for. (Maya hieroglyphics are true writing because while the system retains its origins in pictographic writing, the artist uses phonetics capable of rendering the sound of any word required.) In the same way handsigning systems that do not represent the sounds of spoken words are not considered to be true sign languages. American Indian Sign Language is an exception to this. It is generally considered a language because of the enormous number of handsigns it employs. In that respect there is no other handsign system in the world that even remotely compares to that of the American Indians. I have been told that this intertribal system contains over 100,000 signs.

By comparison the Chinese characters number some 80,000; no one can possibly learn all of them in a lifetime. In Japan their use in some areas is restricted by law, lest a Tower of Babel arise. Newspapers can only employ 1200 of them. An eighth-grade scholastic requirement combining these with their phonetic signs is more than ample to convey any information necessary regarding everyday events.

It has long been recognized that in their writing the Maya deified time, and the principal actors in their drama of time are the deified embodiments of the numbers they represent. Known as the *Oxlahun Ti Ku,* or The Thirteen of God, these deities will singly or in combination form substitutes for numbers. What has not been recognized is that the Maya also deified their sounds in their writing system. To them writing is a sacred thing; the act of writing is considered magical, and it is prayer. The artist will usually present the god of a particular sound, rather than merely depicting a phonetic.

A Maya hieroglyph for writing itself is instructive. Figure 13A shows the way a Plains Indian signs "writing," which is natural and self explanatory. It can be a verb or a noun depending on the context in which it is used. Its equivalent is the Maya hieroglyph shown in B. That can readily be understood as a mere pictograph but it also contains another dimension. These hands speak, they carry phonetic values that evoke sounds rendering the word *yich,* which literally means "surface" and refers to the writing or painting on the surface of vases, on which this glyph will frequently appear.

The left hand when inverted carries the phonetic value *ye.* I think that when the fingers are upright it becomes *yi.* To reinforce this the curlicue phonetic symbol for the sound is inserted in the left corner of the hand. This is even clearer in the glyph shown in B. To evoke the *ch* sound for the right hand the artist borrows from a handsign that carries the phonetic value *chi.* The reader is supposed to know that the full sound is not intended. Only the *ch* is read to finally arrive at *yich.*

To evoke the same word the artist

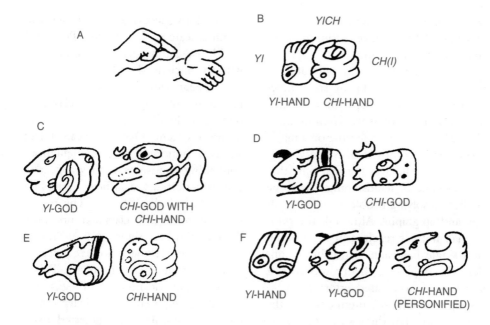

Figure 13. Plains Indian handsign "to write" (top left) and the Maya hieroglyph Yich, (top right)
"writing surface," "the writing"

may use two or three glyphs. In C and D, instead of using merely the phonetic *yi* sign the artist invokes the god of the sound. Likewise to arrive at *ch* the Deer God is invoked. In the Cholan Maya language *chiih* is the word for deer and the Deer God, formally known as *Zuhuy Zip*, presides over and represents this sound. In depicting the deer head in C the *its'at* (artist) combines a hand with the deer image. The hand itself denotes sacredness. That writing is an act of prayer is readily apparent in E and F. In E the god of *yi* is paired with the *chi*-hand. In F, the hand of the god of the sound *yi* is shown, then the god in head form, and finally a deified personification of the *chi*-hand.

In his book *Mannerisms of Speech and Gestures in Everyday Life*, Sandor S. Feldman, M.D., a clinical professor of psychiatry, states, "For thousands of years scientists have been interested in the exciting subject of gestures. It may not be an exaggeration to say that knowing everything about the expressive movement of human hands and fingers means knowing everything about the origin and development of man as an individual and as a social being."

It became apparent to me just from studying some of the hieroglyphs for "writing" that the Maya had a highly developed and refined sense of gesture and its applications to writing and nonverbal communication. In the sanctification of both sound and gesture they had achieved levels of attainment far beyond similar applications in any other culture.

Moreover, work in this field, which I felt was bound to produce astonishing results, had not yet begun.

For nine years I was only able to work on the project in my spare time. However, in Los Altos, California, during the summer of 1991, circumstances allowed me to work full time on a major investigation. Outside of Mallery's initiatory work this was the first time that a knowledge of handsigning was to be applied to solving problems in archaeology and epigraphy. Although the project had not yet resulted in the reading of a single handsign I was fully confident that the basic theory was correct and with concentrated effort a breakthrough would be imminent. At the time I knew that there was a profusion of handsigns in the art and therefore they must be important. I was yet to realize that they are central to and provide access to the very core of Maya thought.

It was very encouraging that a few miles away a breakthrough was being made in another new application of handsigning. Francine Patterson was teaching Koko, a lowland African gorilla, Standard American Sign Language. Koko was using some three hundred handsigns at the time and forming sentences. This research had immense implications, for previously we had defined ourselves as the sole language users on the planet. Also British zoologist Jane Goodall, having observed African chimpanzees in the wild more attentively than anyone else, reported numerous uses of gesture and their meanings, suggesting a continuity linking ape and human language. At the same time, researchers in Florida were having

tremendous success using handsigns to communicate with dolphins. Perhaps I could use handsigns to communicate with the ancient Maya.

I began with the classical standard procedure of epigraphy, the classification of all the forms of a given communication system. Over the years I had amassed hundreds of documentations containing handsigns as they appear in Mesoamerican art, a sufficient sampling for a general classification. The results were surprising. I classified no more than a hundred signs in use, and of these no more than twenty appeared with a high degree of frequency. This is far less than the number of signs that would be required for ordinary everyday communication. It suggested a system of gestures called "emblems" by students of nonverbal behavior.

Cultures that have a highly developed system of sign language are prone to develop a special set of handsigns that are considered sacred and used in rituals. This is true of the Plains Indians and is most obvious in India, where a sacred handsign system known as *mudra* developed, eventually spreading over wide areas of Asia. It is still practiced today. I had become interested in this system while living in Japan. Considering that practically all of the Maya handsigns appear in a ritual context, I began to get an inkling of what I was dealing with.

Of the twenty signs that appeared most frequently, two were prominent and these often appeared together. In one, the thumb touches the ring and middle fingers. The index finger and the small finger may be extended or closed but analysis showed it was the same

Figure 14. **Zero Days**, *Palenque Palace tablet,* A.D. *702. Palenque, Mexico*

sign. This sign was bewildering. In the other, the thumb and the index finger touch or nearly touch, forming a disc. Late one evening it occurred to me that a Plains Indian would immediately recognize this sign as representing the Sun and that it would not be at all surprising if a handsign meaning "sun" was prominent in Maya art. The next morning I would investigate this further.

I woke up early, took out my notebooks, and sat at a table in the backyard. For a long time I gazed with amazement at the two full-figure forms of glyphs from the Palenque Palace tablet shown in figure 14. The tablet commemorates the accession of the ruler Kan Xul to the throne in A.D. 702. It begins by giving the exact date of his birthday in A.D. 643. To express any given date the Maya count all the days starting from August 13, 3114 B.C., the beginning of the present era. They do this in five groupings, the largest being the *baktun* of 144,000 days. The tablet counts nine of these, accounting for 1,296,000 of the days. The smallest grouping is the single day, *kin*, which is represented as *chikin*, the Sun. In this particular count there are no single days as all the days have been accounted for in the higher groupings. To express this the artist has used the full-figure form of the God of Zero embracing the Sun God in his monkey aspect.

The Sun God makes the handsign for "sun," which immediately suggested that the God of Zero would reciprocate with the handsign indicating "zero." This turned out to be the case.

Only three cultures arrived at a concept of zero independently: the Maya, the Babylonian, and the Hindu of India, from whom we inherited it by way of the Arabs. The Maya concept of zero is imbued with deep spiritual meanings and is very different from ours. By zero, we mean "there is nothing." Their zero, *mi* or *lub* in their language, does not mean there is nothing but has much broader implications. It means the count has evolved or spiraled up to higher levels. Hence, the God of Zero is shown gazing upward. The godsigns on his upper arm and forearm are emblems of the *tonalmatl*, the sacred cycle of the 260-day calendar, suggesting the idea of a completion of a cycle of time.

Embedded in the Maya concept of zero and its various symbols is a philosophy central and fundamental to the Maya vision of the cosmic and the divine. Number was among the chief tools used in the Maya quest for the meaning of time, which they considered an attribute of the gods, here portrayed as living personified powers. In their search through the ever-changing stages of past, present, and future time they perceived it as coming from the divinity, as part of its very being, permeating all and limitless. In this magnificent obses-sion they counted zero as both a termination or completion and a portal which continually raises the reckoning of time to higher levels in infinite cycles of limitless ages.

Reflected in this continuous ascent to higher levels is their concept of sacrifice, regarded as the chief means of human spiritual evolution. The termination or completion of a time cycle is equated with death, not a finality but a portal of evolution. The God of Zero wears his hair bound in the manner of a sacrificial victim. The symbol of zero in the codices is represented by the snail-shell symbol of ever-spiraling evolution. The handsign for zero, and by extension human sacrifice, is represented by a snail. When a Plains Indian signs "snail," the tentacles are mimicked by extending and contracting the index and small fingers in unison. Thus both of these forms of the sign appear in Maya art.

The Sun God in his monkey aspect appears making the sacred sign of zero in figure 15A, which is taken from the Dresden Codex. The Monkey God has manifestations both as a day god and a god of the night. He is the god of the syllable *ku* or the god that forms *kul*, "holy," which his glyph can represent. It appears as a divinity mark which labels images as "holy things." He is named in the three glyphs in the upper register, the first of which is *hoy-i*, "blessed." In the third glyph his solar aspect is expressed as Great Pure Craftsman. The main sign here is *men*, the eagle, which here means "fashioner" or "artisan." In the Nahua system wherein the twenty daysigns are related to parts of the

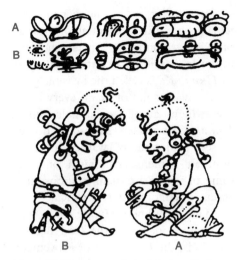

Figure 15. **Itzamna and the Monkey God**

human body, the eagle is the right hand. The Sun is the maker of days and time itself; all possible time cycles are built of or fashioned by this fundamental unit, the single day. One of his many functions is as a patron of knowledge and the arts. Above the *men* sign are glyphs reading *ah-po* meaning "lord" and affixed is the glyph *sac*, "white," which by extension means "pure."

The glyph in the center refers to his role as *Xaman Ek*, the North Star, or *Ah Chicum Ek*, the Guiding Star. *Ek*, the second syllable in the glyph, is "black," and by extension "night." As the North Star he mirrors the function of the Sun, which is seen as central in the daytime sky just as the North Star appears at the core of the heavens at night, all other stars revolving around it. In Mesoamerica the North Star is considered a portal. One of the Maya glyphs for *xaman*, "north," has the glyph for *caan*, "sky," altered to show an opening on top. The Monkey God

is an enterer and first in many series and cycles. Curiously it was through his image that I recognized the first meaning of a Maya handsign.

One of his many glyphs refers to the Monkey God as *Yaxan Chuen*. *Yax* means "new," "fresh," and "first." In figure 15A *Chuen* means "monkey," the name of his daysign. Frequently he wears a "blessed" or "holy" headdress prefixed by a bone symbol, here referring to his function as the core of the night sky. The twenty daysigns are regarded as lords who guide the Sun on its daytime journey across the sky. The *Bolon Ti Ku*, Nine of God, are the Lords of Night responsible for guiding and bearing the Sun in its perilous journey through the underworld in an unbroken succession. *Xamen Ek* is the first Lord of Night. The delivery of the Sun at dawn to the Lord of the Day is seen as an allegory of birth. These and related signs are explained in chapter two.

The twenty daysigns representing the Lords of the Day have a standard sequence in both Nahau and Maya cultures but there are also other cycles within the sequence that have various beginnings. In one variant, the Day of the Monkey, *Chuen*, is the first created day of the series, when the creator, *Hunab Ku*, brought forth divinity from himself or herself creating heaven and Earth. Among Maya daykeepers to the present time the Day of the Monkey is an important ceremonial event and a day of celebrations.

In his many manifestations and roles *Chuen* certainly presents himself as a complex deity. When it is considered that there are numerous even more complex gods performing on the vast stage of Maya art, it is easy to see how, without a grasp of the fundamentals of Mesoamerican religious thought, some students of the subject can become entangled in a labyrinth of interlocking mazes. As one researcher succinctly put it, "I could never understand pre-Columbian Mexican history until I realized that every character was his own grandmother." By contrast I find that when the underlying principles are understood, a unified field emerges that is not only comprehensible but admirably cohesive, penetratingly perceptive, and ultimately wholly logical. Any problem lies within the mind of the viewer and probably has its roots in the perception of the identity of the supreme being and creator of the universe, *Hunab Ku.*

Since the Maya belief in a single, supreme, creator deity emerged in post-Conquest mythological literature, it was never fully accepted by scholars. Rather it was thought to be a borrowing from Christianity artificially fused with authentic ancient Maya myth. Reinforcing this is the fact that the art presents an extensive entangled pantheon of gods wherein no supreme being can be seen. The reason is that the supreme being is conceived of as embodying all time, all space, and all that exists in it. As the oneness in all and the all in one, *Hunab Ku* is the primal unity, a totally undifferentiated being. As the Maya themselves say, "All that exists is only movement (time) and measure (space) in the memory (mind) of *Hunab Ku* (*Hun*, one, *ab*, state of being, *ku*, god)." The *its'at* would not even think of trying to portray such a totally

supreme being, who is neither male or female, young or old, but all of these at once. Any attempt at a personification in the art would be a contradiction and so *Hunab Ku* is called the invisible god. Ironically, in spite of being everything, everywhere, at all conceivable times, *Hunab Ku* is hidden. Instead we do get to see, somewhat by way of substitution, an immense panorama of gods some of which are manifestations, creations, or children of *Hunab Ku.*

The Maya know *Hunab Ku* by various names including the God Behind the Gods, the One Giver of Movement and Measure, *Zamana*, Creator of the Universe, and the Great Hand. The extension of his or her total realm is unknown except that it consists of all and the Pole Star is a portal to it.

In figure 15B a son of *Hunab Ku*, *Itzamna*, presents the *chi*-hand to the Monkey God. Both of them perform many roles as both astral and solar deities. Of the two, *Itzamna* is far more complex, having both celestial and terrestrial aspects, being Lord of Day and Night, inventor of writing and books, and intimately associated with his brother *Kinich Ahau*, a solar manifestation of *Hunab Ku*. His name, Lizard House, is in B, the register below those of the Monkey God. The third glyph is the syllable *na* meaning "house" and refers to yet another role he plays as Lord of the Milky Way; symbolizing this he sometimes wears a conch shell. Our solar system of course is in the Milky Way, which is, like the conch shell, in the shape of a spiral. This has immense implications because our understanding of this did not come until

A

B

C

D

the late eighteenth century, long after the development of astronomy as a science. Since *Itzamna* as a celestial deity makes many appearances throughout the chapters of *The Hidden Maya*, it is hard not to conclude that the Maya

Figure 16. The Mesoamerican gesture indicating prayer and reverence

knew the Milky Way was our "house" in the cosmos. The problem of *how* they knew it remains as one of the most mysterious and challenging in the study of ancient astronomies. (Recently I was informed by a contemporary Maya day-keeper that they arrived at it through the careful observation of movement and the application of measure.)

Once the first two handsigns were reread the rest followed in rapid succession. The next obvious step was to look for the Moon handsign in depictions of the Moon Goddess. These correlated perfectly not only with the handsigns of the Plains Indians, but they also could be compared, with interesting results, with Moon handsigns used by the contemporary Maya in the Guatamalan highlands who use variations to describe different aspects of the Moon. These handsigns in turn furnished more detailed information about variations as they appear in the ancient Maya art.

I now focused my study of Plains Indian handsigning on ritual usage. In his book *The Old North Trail or Life, Legends, and Religion of the Blackfoot Indians*, Walter McClintock describes taking part in rituals and gives detailed accounts. He provides highly informative photographs in which the participants are all shown to be dramatically handsigning in unison. In the many different rituals described, handsigning plays a significant or central part. In a ceremony confirming and formalizing his adoption by Mad Wolf, McClintock describes a gesture frequently seen in Mesoamerican art as their manner of blessing. Some examples are shown in figure 16.

Although these signs were created by different cultures in widely varied time periods they retain the same fundamental form and meaning, a crossing of the heart. The figurine in A is Olmec. The effigy in B is of a man prepared for burial rites (and the form is confirmed in archaeological finds). The circles at the navel are a simple but powerful invocation of life. In C the chieftain One Deer kneels before the enthroned warrior priest Eight Deer (as shown on page 45 of the Codex Nuttall). D is a Nahau funerary urn in the form of *Chicomecoatl*, Seven Snake, the goddess of the Earth and of agriculture. In the same or similar contexts, the gesture is seen in rituals performed by both humans and gods in scenes painted on Maya vases. This is one of the positions in which the Maya kings traditionally held the Double-headed Serpent Bar.

I found the system of handsigning to be so consistent and uniform that if the meaning of a sign could be established in any Mesoamerican culture it would be likely to carry the same meaning in all of them. This greatly accelerated the translation process and produced some major rereadings. The Maya were by far the master handsigners of Mesoamerica but most of their signs had to be accessed by means of the advanced intact system of the Plains Indians.

The emergence of a basically unified means of communication came about in Mesoamerica probably for the same reasons it did later on the Great Plains. Mesoamerica was another Tower of Babel with hundreds of different dialects being spoken. (When I was in Mexico centuries later the government

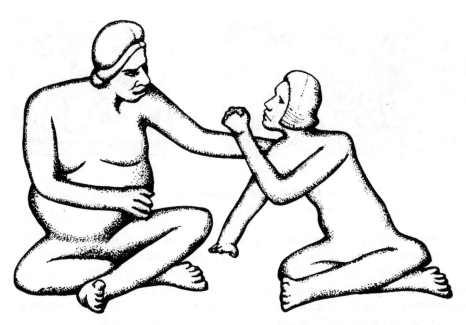

Figure 17. Pottery figurine group, before 1200 B.C., from Xochipala, Mexico.
Princeton University Art Museum

was engaged in a major campaign to get everyone to speak Spanish, with little or no success!)

Shortly after 1300 B.C. important regional capitals or cities made their appearance in various parts of Mesoamerica. These participated in a solidly structured network of interregional commerce requiring some means of communication other than verbal. Of course a sign language could have been formulated much earlier but it leaves no evidence. Some of the very earliest pottery, such as the figurines shown in figure 17, shows a prolific use of handsigning.

Once the regional centers developed into large city-states they became truly cosmopolitan. Entire sections of the great city of Teotihuacan were occupied by peoples from widespread re-

gions, including the Maya. In turn, archaeological evidence shows that Teotihuacanos were physically present in the great cities of the Maya. In figure 18 a scene from a vase found in Tikal shows Teotihuacan emissaries arriving after a journey of one thousand miles from the north. They are greeted by handsigns. As this mode of communication had for centuries been previously established, it

Figure 18. **Emissaries Arriving from Teotihuacan**, *detail, carving on a black cylindrical vase. Deposit 50, Tikal, Guatemala*

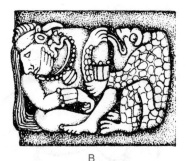

A   B

Figure 19. **The Day Ten Ahau, Eight Cumhu**, *details of an initial series written with full-figure glyph,* A.D. *736. Stela D, Copan, Mexico*

is doubtful if visitors or even many long-term residents would take the trouble to learn another language. The diversity of the oral languages was retained in spite of systematic contact, while the systemization and unification of the sign language was intensified.

Using the methods outlined there were very few handsigns that could not be explained. These few appeared only once in my documentations and in situations wherein the context in which the sign is presented could not be determined. As American Indian handsigning relies heavily on context, the problem is that more than one explanation is possible. In only one instance the context was quite clear while the meaning of the sign eluded me, but for this another approach presented itself.

A stela at Copan uses ten panels to record a date that occurred in A.D. 736. The first six panels record the 1,405,000 days that have passed since the starting point of the calendar and then typically the day arrived at and the Lord of Night as shown in figure 19A. The day is Ten *Ahau*. The god of the number ten is *Cimi*, the God of Death.

For the most part, he behaves in a beneficial manner as he appears here. Sometimes he can be quite mischievous. He appears in human form here, with only the skeletal features of his head sufficient to reveal who he is.

Cimi embraces a cartouche in which we see *Ahau*, lord of the twentieth, and last, cycle of days. Always benevolent, he is an embodiment of the radiant presence of light and a lord who encompasses the cycles of time. Next is *Yum Caax*, the sixth Lord of Night. His vegetal headdress alone is enough to identify him. As Lord of the Harvest he represents life, prosperity, and fruitfulness, never death. He also functions as the fourth Lord of Days. We see these gods at the moment when *Cimi* and *Ahau* have completed their duty in guiding the Sun through the day and now *Yum Caax*, burdened with the Sun on his back, will carry it on its journey through the night. The jaguar skin covering is a symbol of the night sky.

Ahau shows his respect by saluting *Yum Caax* with the abbreviated single-arm version of the reverence gesture shown in figure 16. This gesture appears frequently in the ancient art and is still in use today. Obviously *Yum Caax* is performing a reciprocal gesture of reverence and it can be classified as such, but American Indian signs and gestures also carry meanings and to know a sign is to know its meaning.

Some of the early Spanish friars had written in detail, although not in depth, about the Native American culture they were encountering. At the time of the Conquest and for a considerable time afterward, handsigning must have played a conspicuous part in the daily lives of the Indians, and I was very curious to read these comments. Surprisingly, in this rather extensive literature I found only *two* observations but one solved this problem of the gesture of reverence. The other proved to be of major significance in explaining a completely perplexing ritual involving handsigns that was portrayed on numerous Maya vases. The results of this research appear in chapter five.

In his book *The Aztecs: History of the Indies of New Spain*, Fray Diego Duran refers constantly to the "eating of the earth," a Native custom of lowering the middle finger to the Earth and then placing it on the lips as a gesture of courtesy and reverence. *Yum Caax* is seen in the act of performing the first part of the gesture in A. In B, the Frog God has completed the first part and is performing the second part.

In the original panel, the Frog God is "above" in the fifth panel, which shows the count of days in groupings of twenty called the *uinal*. The Maya calculated the actual length of a month with precision, but these calculating periods were referred to by the Maya as a *uinal* or a month because they roughly resembled an actual month. As the sound of the word *u*, "moon," approximated the sound *uo*, "frog," the Frog God represented this period of *uinal*. The God of Zero can be recognized by his headdress and the hand placed on his jawbone, which represents a particularly gruesome human sacrifice.

Besides the classification of the handsigns, I had embarked on another standard procedure used by epigraphers: the careful review of all previous studies on the subject. Outside of Mallery's initial work, I could find only a single attempt made to interpret a handsign in the Codex Nuttall (p. 70). It was misguided, but probing it led to a solid rereading.

In the codex, Eight Deer is depicted engaged in a ritual with Four Tiger. I have redrawn the scene in figure 20D. On the right Eight Deer raises his right hand extending two fingers in a handsign that had been interpreted to mean that this was their second meeting. My first impression, as explained further in chapter three, is that this method of indicating a number on the fingers is a very strong cultural imprint. We would automatically and naturally express "two" this way. American Indians both north and south of the Mexican border would just as naturally do otherwise. (See p. 107.)

Also note that this is not even the second time they meet. Their first encounter (in the codex p. 52) is shown in A. At the top, in the center is the year-sign Seven House, which would be

Figure 20. **Eight Deer's Encounters with Four Tiger**, *from the Mixtec Codex Nuttall, centering on events around* A.D. *1000, Oaxaca, Mexico. Museum of Mankind, British Museum, London*

about A.D. 1045. This is followed by the daysign Thirteen Alligator, some 200 days before their meeting in D. Eight Deer's name is written above him, Four Tiger's name extends from his foot. In D, Four Tiger is attired as a priest and holds a bird for ritual sacrifice and an incense burner, *tlemaitl*, literally "Hand of Fire." (I am using Nahuatl terms here as the Mixtecos, The People of the Clouds, inherited the Nahua culture.) His nose ornament, *nariquera*, indicates that he is a member of a warrior cult of the highest status. He is in fact a chieftain. In A, Eight Deer is applying for initiation into the cult. On the previous pages of the codex, we learn that he was born in the year A.D. 1011 and began his military career at the age of eight. He has conquered many towns and performed the necessary rituals. Now at the age of thirty-four he is claiming his right to wear the nariquera. He comes to this preliminary ritual attired as a warrior complete with a spear—*tepuztapilli*, javelins—*mitl*, and shield—*chimalli*.

On the following day—One Wind —Eight Deer is invested in the order of knights, his nose being pierced by a priest. This was at a place named Tulixhuaca in Jiyacan. Three days after the event, on the day Four Snake, he meets with Four Tiger for the second time as shown in B. He now wears the nariquera. Handsigns are used to show an exchange. The pointing finger in this context means "to take." Four Tiger takes a bird of sacrifice and Eight Deer takes what is probably a *xonecuilli*, the staff of fertility. The ritual exchange apparently confirms the initiation.

Eight Deer then conquers five towns and leads a giant war conference at Tilantongo with 111 named warriors. Four Tiger is conspicuous by his absence. The conference ends in the year Eight Rabbit, A.D. 1046, on the day Four Wind.

On the next day—Five House— Eight Deer embarks on a major military campaign, overcoming important regional capitals including Chiyo Canu, Ocotepec, and Teposcolula and its subject villages. Four Tiger takes no part. On the day Nine Snake, Eight Deer returns to Tilantongo where a struggle for political power with Four Tiger ensues at the third meeting shown in C. This has been interpreted as a mock battle but while it is not a real fight, the artist is symbolizing an actual struggle for power. Facial expressions denote aggression and the emblems on the shields are indicative of conflicting political interests. Eight Deer is in all probability challenging Four Tiger's leadership.

At a meeting held on the day Two Movement, thirty-two days later, the conflict has been resolved and Four Tiger and Eight Deer are shown sealing a treaty pact in D. The action in their fourth meeting is shown by means of handsigns. Eight Deer signs "friend" or "ally" precisely as a Plains Indian would by holding the right hand in front of the face with the index and middle fingers extended. The hand is then raised upward. The sign means "brothers growing up together," and it appears in a similar context on a Maya vase shown in chapter two, figure 2.15.

Four Tiger's handsign is commonly seen in Maya monumental art, vases, and codices. It is usually accompanied by the glyph it forms and means "to sow, to scatter." It forms the Nahua pictograph, *tlatepehua,* which carries the same meaning, referring to the scattering of sacrificial blood on the paper shown above the *teocalli—tiotl,* god, *calli,* house—where it is burned. (These and other handsigns and their related glyphs are discussed in chapter nine.) In E one of Eight Deer's chief aides, Twelve Vulture, further seals the pact by going to a cave in the mountains. He is dressed in the guise of a priest and bears ritual implements.

After this the key regional center Tulancingo falls, followed by over forty other towns. I have identified some of these as Sachio Putla, Acatepec, Tataltepec, and lastly Cholula far away in the state of Puebla, where we finally learn who the actors are in this extensive campaign. Four Tiger and Eight Deer are seen together in a boat crossing a river to subdue Cholula. On the return journey to Oaxaca they retake Sachio and conquer other towns. At Coixtlahuaca they are shown fighting side-by-side in a large battle where they take many prisoners. Throughout the rest of the codex they are continually seen together in battles, rituals, and games.

In doing a detailed study of this extraordinary codex, I realized that the Nahua artist, in order to transmit an enormous amount of information concisely, is using a hidden formula: An event is described in a scheme reducing the action to factors of when, who, what, and where in that order. We shall see that the Maya artist uses the same fundamental approach to recording events and underlying Mesoamerican art. There is a school, a learning tradition, that is deeply rooted and whose tenets are shared by both the *tlacuilo* (Nahua artist) and the *its'at* (Maya artist).

The human hand indeed possesses immense communicative power. It is not a mere coincidence that the motor areas of the human brain controlling speech and hand movement are adjacent. It is believed that communication by handsigning preceded the development of spoken language. I began my study having become interested in the role sign language played in the origin of writing which eventually blossomed into an entirely new approach to interpreting Mesoamerican art.

Anyone who studies American Indian Sign Language is immediately impressed by the rationale inherent in the system. The logical basis upon which the handsigns are formulated is directly transferred to the process of creating pictographic writing and continues on in the development of hieroglyphic writing. The same logic is inherent in painting, which the Mesoamerican artist does not distinguish from writing. To approach the art in this manner is to understand its underlying principles of which one, the sign language, is deeply hidden in its origins. When these inner sources are tapped, Maya art is transformed radically from mystery to revelation, from enigma to a source of enlightenment.

We begin with the most basic fundamental hand symbol on the North American continent: the "sun-in-hand"

motif. This emblem was known to practically all Indian tribes and must represent something deeply entrenched in
their consciousness. A primordial motif,
its domains stretch from the icy regions
of Alaska; across the Great Plains and
over to the Atlantic; throughout Mexico
where it emerges as a Maya hieroglyph;
to the Inca of Peru; and as far south as
the Cave of the Hands in Argentina,
consistently retaining its meaning wherever it appears.

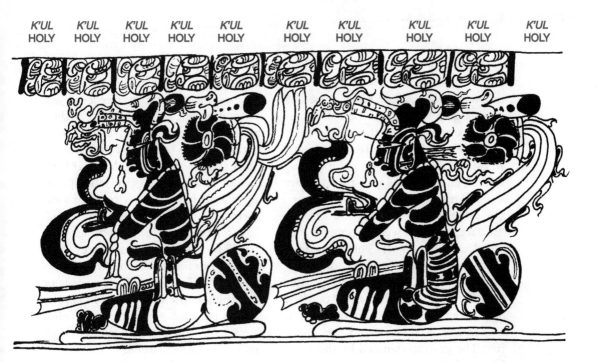

| K'UL | K'UL | K'UL | K'UL | K'UL | K'UL | K'UL | K'UL | K'UL | K'UL |
| HOLY | HOLY | HOLY | HOLY | HOLY | HOLY | HOLY | HOLY | HOLY | HOLY |

Figure 1.1. **Holy, Holy, Holy**, *cylindrical vase*

THE GREAT HAND

*Now the wizards vie with one another in taking
the shapes of the Blue Heron and of the Hummingbird.
Then white flowers descend from the Source of All and
from the folds of the Great Hand. When the hearts of
the flowers appear, the priests place four branches of flowers
on the burning Altar of the Sun.*

This quote is taken from "Ceremonies Performed by the Itza" in the books of *Chilam Balam. Chilam* means "priest" or literally, "interpreter of the gods" and *Balam* means "jaguar." The Maya term *its'at* also implies much more than either "artist" or "scribe." It means both and more—one who is clever, ingenious, artistic, scientific, and knowledgeable. The personage depicted on the vase illustrated in figure 1.1 is a master *its'at*.

We know this from several telltale factors revealed in the painting on the drinking vessel. A vase of this type was used largely for the ceremonial imbibing of cacao in a ritual that can be compared to the Japanese Tea Ceremony. In the Maya ritual the utensil itself was central, and admiring it as a work of art was an important part of the ceremony. On a Maya vase the painting or *yich*, "surface," also served to sanctify the vessel as a holy object. This function is usually performed by a set of hieroglyphs written around the top. Referred to as the Primary Standard Sequence (P.S.S.), these are repeated in a chantlike fashion around the upper rim. The gesture assumed by the actor has a counterpart in the Nahua pictograph that means "to bless." In the formation of the hieroglyph the *its'at* demonstrates being more than merely a rote learner of glyphs. Mastery enables the *its'at* to freely adapt and modify a glyph with creative ingenuity and freedom while retaining the clarity inherent in the system.

A hieroglyph is created using the Monkey God head as a mainsign meaning *k'ul*, "holy." Two primary godsigns are infixed in the head. Above is the sign for "mirror" or "brightness," below is the *akbal* or "darkness" godsign. To write a prefix this artist inserts two mirrors in front of the Monkey God head. Here the allusion is to the introductory glyph of the P. S. S., *a-ya*, which usually has a mirror as a mainsign and means "it came into being" or "it came into the light." The glyph is repeated nine times, nine having the meaning of "innumerable" or "infinite."

The painting exudes what is known in Sanskrit as *prana*, in Chinese as *chi*, in Japanese as *ki*, and in Gaelic as *gal*. There is no one word for this in English, but it means something like "vital force spirit." It has a central function in Indian yoga and Chinese t'ai chi ch'uan. In texts on the tenets of the tao of painting, the Chinese artist is constantly exhorted to wield the brush with "chi". The *its'at* depicted has no shortage of it; it is illustrated as spiritual energy emanating from the hand. The Maya equivalent of "chi" is referred to as *coyopa* or "lightning in the blood," which enables one to perceive within the body messages from the external worlds—both natural and supernatural.

The artist shows the manifestation of the vital energy as pouring forth in bifurcated smoke scrolls in which appear blood-bead–drop signs. In much the same way the Chinese artist in drawing the character for "chi" describes it as an emanation of steam. The *its'at* echoes the action of the smoke scrolls in the light or brightness emblems in the glyphs.

As well as painting and writing, the training of an *its'at* required deep spiritual cultivation. It is probable that this painting is a self-portrait, a tour de force demonstrating the artist's spiritual and artistic attainments. No signature would be required by an *its'at* of this stature. More than likely his or her works were widely known and eagerly anticipated. There are only subtle differences in the presentation of the two figures. In one the headdress bears a Smoking Mirror image and in the other a Blue Heron. The net-bag headdress is a symbol of an artist while other features of apparel such as the muan bird feather identify a priest. The eyes are focused on the mudra, which manifests the blessing. The formation of the hands represents a highly refined cultural development, having its roots in a cult of the hand, a powerful shamanistic symbol in the Americas for over 2000 years.

In the predawn eastern sky of A.D. July 5, 1054, near the tips of the horns of the celestial bull, Taurus, a nebula of great beauty—called "the crab"—suddenly exploded in a supernova, ejecting most of its mass. It was the brightest object, other than the Sun and Moon, ever seen in the sky in recorded human history. About five times brighter than any of the planets we see in the night sky today, it could be seen even in the daytime for about three weeks before slowly fading in brilliance.

It is interesting to compare how this event was perceived and recorded by various cultures at the time. Europeans were terrified of a sign that portended that the world was coming to an end. The star appears prominently as a sinister and malicious object on the famous Bayeux Tapestry, a narrative of the events leading to the Norman conquest of England. The Chinese typically took a more restrained attitude; court astronomers of the Sung Dynasty considered it "honorable" and recorded it as a "guest" star. The North American Indians revered it, leaving a number of recordings of the phenomena in the American Southwest.

It is known that the passing seasons were measured by many of the tribes in the Southwest from the position of sunrise on the horizon. One of the best documented of these rudimentary solar calendars is that of the Hopi Indians. Important horizon positions were noted for agricultural events and festival days. Points on the horizon had names such as "corn may be planted" or "work in the fields begins." Altogether some thirteen horizon landmarks were significant when the Sun rose above them; the two extreme points, the solstices, were known as "houses of the sun."

Figure 1.2A shows petroglyphs from California, Oklahoma, and New Mexico that appear at various sites that were occupied at the time of the supernova. Calculations show that the Moon was in its crescent phase on the morning of A.D. July 5, 1054, and the supernova should have appeared just above or very near the Moon, as shown in the drawings.

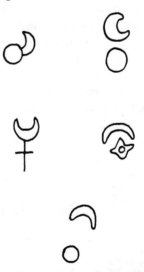

Figure 1.2A. Petroglyphs in the American Southwest, showing the supernova that appeared A.D. July 5, 1054

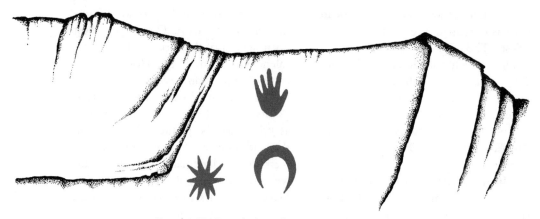

Figure 1.2B. Petroglyphs in the U.S. Southwest, A.D. *July 5, 1054*

Among the most avid skywatchers were prehistoric basket makers and cliff dwellers, the Anasazi Indians, whose civilization thrived in the Four Corners region of the American Southwest nearly two thousand years ago. They were the ancestors of the present-day Pueblo Indians of New Mexico and Arizona. Their remarkable Chaco Canyon ruins feature solar constructs and intricate patterns of cross-kiva alignments by which rays of celestial objects illuminate specific wall niches of the Great Kiva at unique astronomical times.

It is highly likely that the rock-wall painting in Chaco Canyon, shown in figure 1.2B, tells the story of the supernova event of A.D. 1054. It is certain that an astronomical event is depicted. The handmark denotes the spot's sacred status among the Anasazi of the area. Throughout North America the appearance of a hand at a site is symbolic of that site's use in sacred ceremonies. It denotes a place where spiritual forces manifested themselves in visions, and it bears evidence of the spirit contacts of past generations that ensured growth, prosperity, and harmony for future generations.

The enactment of sky worship in ritual is clearly shown in the Pueblo petroglyphs illustrated in figure 1.3. A cross is composed of apparent phases of the Moon surmounted by the cross-in-the-circle emblem of the Sun. Below the cross a hand is extended. Left and right hands are shown raised in supplication to the Sun and Moon, the triangles being symbolic of emanations of spiritual powers.

The stone disc shown in figure 1.4 is from the Hopewell culture, mound

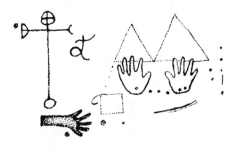

Figure 1.3. Pueblo petroglyphs in the Southwest

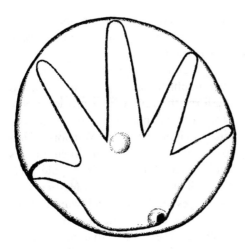

Figure 1.4. Fine-grained stone disc with incision, Illinois, Hopewell culture

alry in a raid on a Cheyenne village in Wyoming's Big Horn Mountains took a grim trophy. They found a necklace of human fingers consisting of eight left-hand middle fingers, obviously considered a source of strong "medicine" or spiritual power by its owner. (Interestingly the fingers taken were from Custer's Crow and Arikara scouts. Apparently the white soldiers' fingers were not valued much for spiritual power.) The American Indian handsign for "Cheyenne" consists of extending the left index finger with the right index making as though to cut or slash it. It means "Finger Choppers."

The shell carving from Oklahoma in figure 1.6 shows an Indian praying to the Sun with hands extended and a speech scroll extending from his mouth. The same gesture is seen in the picto-

builders who flourished from about 300 B.C. to A.D. 700. The right hand incised on the disc is symbolic of a hand raised to the Sun in supplication. The disc implies the Sun or the Sacred Circle of the Sun. Such depictions obviously had a deep ritual significance. An image cut from sheet mica of a hand over ten inches in length was found buried with a Hopewell Indian in Ohio, over 400 miles from the nearest source of mica.

Along with a cult of the hand there was a widespread reverence for the pointing finger, also a symbol derived from ritual use of the hand in ceremonies. A seven-inch-long thumb carved from cannel coal is also from Hopewell culture (figure 1.5). Cannel coal burns with an intensely bright flame, and such objects were probably intended as burnt offerings.

A cult of the finger was existent on the Great Plains until comparatively recent times. Five months after the famous Custer "massacre," the U.S. cav-

Figure 1.5. Thumb, carved from cannel coal, eastern woodlands, Hopewell culture

Figure 1.6. Shell gorget, Craig burial mound, Oklahoma

graphic drawing of the Sun Dance ceremony shown in figure 1.7. With slight variations from tribe to tribe, all Plains Indians performed the Sun Dance, the purpose of which was to secure the Sun God's protection. If it was not per-

formed exactly as the originators had prescribed, great calamity might come to the tribe.

The drawing provides a vivid, concise graphic description of the ritual. To perform the ceremony a medicine pole was erected at midday when the Sun was at its height in the sky. Warriors taking part ran skewers through their breasts and attached them to the pole with rope. Slowly circling the pole, they fixed their eyes on the Sun, following its path across the sky for the rest of the day while leaning back so that almost all of their weight was hanging. Their suffering was offered to the Sun and the sky spirits. Those left standing at sunset became medicine men. In the pictograph, "prayer" is indicated by the warriors' hands extended toward the Sun.

One of the largest Sun Dances ever recorded took place in June of 1876 near Little Bighorn in Montana. A gathering of Sioux and Cheyenne led by *Tatanka-Iyotanka*, Sitting Bull, was said to be eight thousand strong and the camp was three miles in length. Sitting Bull had prepared himself spiritually and

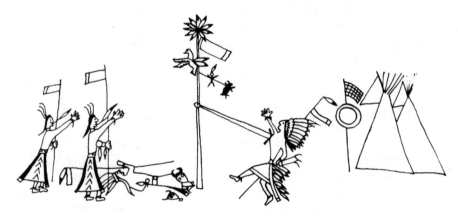

Figure 1.7. Pictograph of the Sun Dance Ceremony, Dakota Sioux

physically for some time before the ritual. On the commencement of the sacrifice he sat down at the base of the medicine pole as Jumping Bull knelt before him brandishing a finely ground knife blade. Within a half hour he cut fifty pieces of flesh from each of Sitting Bull's arms.

During this time Sitting Bull showed no sign of pain while blood gushed from his arms. He sang to *Wakan Tanka* asking for protection for his people; he prayed for a vision. Such a procedure has close parallels to ritual bloodletting among the Maya: Divine guidance from guardian spirits of deified ancestors is sought through a massive physical jolt to the system caused by bloodletting, or by an ecstatic trance or alternate state of consciousness, or both. Apparently the vision seeker is oblivious to the pain that such a procedure would normally involve.

After initiating the ceremony in this way Sitting Bull danced for the rest of the day, all through the night, and into the next day until he collapsed, in a trance, into the arms of Black Moon to whom he whispered his vision. He saw soldiers falling down like grasshoppers, their heads down and hats flying off, followed by triumphant Indians on horseback. When Black Moon announced the vision to the people he said that *Wakan Tanka* would protect them, and the people were filled with resolve and fighting spirit. The fulfillment of Sitting Bull's vision occurred at the famous Battle of Little Bighorn wherein General Custer and the entire Seventh Cavalry were annihilated.

Although that Sun Dance lasted

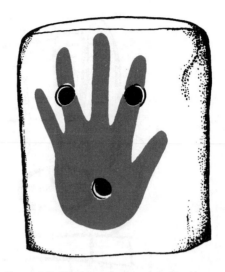

Figure 1.8. **Kachina**, *leather mask, Zuni Pueblo. Brooklyn Museum, New York*

only two days it was never forgotten by the people who attended. Years later warriors who participated in the dance and in the battle produced drawings of the events on ledger paper. What is remarkable about the drawings is that apparently all of the warriors, including Sitting Bull, were skilled artists. The style employed, in which a figure or object is depicted by denoting its most salient features, is directly derived from pictographic writing. Exactly the same process is used in handsigning, so a skilled handsigner will naturally be adept at applying these techniques to artistic endeavors. The same process is evident in Mesoamerican art.

The role of the hand in American Indian art and ritual is demonstrated in the leather kachina mask shown in figure 1.8. This Zuni Pueblo mask represents the Anahoho Kachina who is the Messenger of the Gods. In order to

Figure 1.9. Cult object, Craig burial mound, Oklahoma

symbolize communication with the spirits the Indian artist uses the hand. Of course it should be noted that, as in handsigning, pictographic writing depends largely on context to transmit meaning. In a pictographic story, when members of a friendly tribe are encountered, a hand would simply mean, "we said hello." In a fighting scene or on a war horse it records, "I killed an enemy barehanded." On a cliff wall or ritual

Figure 1.10. Design motifs, eastern woodlands

object such as the kachina mask shown here it implies ritual communication with the spirit world.

A prime example of this can be seen in figure 1.9, another cult object made of shell and found at the Craig burial mound in Oklahoma. Displayed by a shaman, the sun-in-hand motif has a powerful ritual significance. It represents an appeal to the "sun-power" that safeguards all life. The hands are shown displaying the cross-in-circle design associated in old Indian lore with the cardinal directions of the rising and setting Sun at the summer and winter solstices. The Sun's cycle of apparent movement through the year and its daily rising and setting are all part of the Sacred Circle, which dictates times of certain rituals.

The design motifs in figure 1.10 appear in the southern part of the eastern woodlands during the Temple Mound II period, which has been termed the Southeastern Ceremonial complex or the Southern cult. The iconographic elements shown in these motifs as well as those displayed on the cult objects in figures 1.9, 1.11, and 1.12 pertain to religious ritual. They have long presented a great mystery, especially the eye-in-hand motif, largely because in these designs ritual precedes art. The art cannot be understood without knowing the basic ritual it symbolizes.

Prayer or communication with the potent metaphysical forces governing and regulating everything in the Indian's world was done primarily through the use of the hand. Before imploring the Sun's protection the Indian first goes through rites of purification by cleansing and penance. At dawn, on the first appearance of the Sun's disc on the horizon, the arms are extended toward the Sun while exposing the palms to the Sun's rays. Pleading worthiness to commune with the Sun, the Indian chants something to the effect, "Lord Sun, or Great Mystery in the Sun, see my hands, they are clean. . . ." The sun-in-hand is the emblem of the Sun God's recognition and protection. The eye-in-hand is the confirmation that the Sun God has indeed seen that the worshiper's hands and, by extension, his or her actions, are pure.

Not only is this ritual so basic that it was used by practically all American Indian tribes, it is still in use today among the Mescalero Apache. For example, on the last day of a girl's coming-of-age ceremonies she sits in a ceremonial tipi that faces the east. A shaman enters the tipi; with a sun symbol painted on his palm he blesses her with his hand,

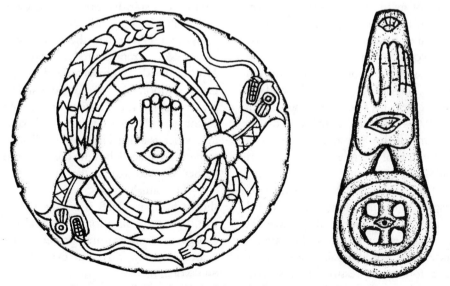

Figures 1.11 (left) and 1.12 (right). Cult objects, Moundville, Alabama

chanting, "The Sun has come down to the Earth, it has come to her. . . . Long life! Its power is good." We shall see that the same set of symbols, with elaborations, appears in Mesoamerican art, as well as in far northern regions of the continent.

Figure 1.13 is a drawing of the centerpiece of a carved wooden headdress known as *The Mystery of the Sea*. It was made by a member of the Tlingit tribe, master wood-carvers of Alaska. This and similar headdresses represent mythological beings and were worn by members of the Northwest Coast tribes in ritual reenactments of scenes from their myths. The design motifs are not superficial "decorations"; each element is imbued with spiritual meaning. The sun-in-hand motif displayed reveals the divine nature of the being portrayed and the presence of spiritual power.

The Haida woven hat (figure 1.14) was also used in ceremonial reenactments of myth. The sun-in-hand motif distinguishes the image from an ordinary killer whale and reveals it as the mythological sea being, *Tieholtsodi*. Dance and ritual played an important part in appeasing sky, earth, and sea spirits especially at critical times during the year—observances marked by the positions of the Sun and stars, governing the time of the migration of the caribou or the appearance of fish shoals.

The northern tribes impersonated seasonal spirits in ceremonies. A wooden dance mask representing *Negafok*, the cold-weather spirit, is illustrated in figure 1.15. He is usually shown wearing a forlorn expression because with the breaking of the ice in spring, he must leave the people. The prominent sun-in-hand motif identifies him as a protector of the people. The mask has seal and fish effigies and feathers representing the flight of the shaman.

Figure 1.16 is a detail from a Tsimshian storage chest. The Tsimshians were fishermen and hunters living near the Tlingits in what is now British Columbia. The chest was filled with a shaman's supernatural paraphernalia. The sun-in-hand motif serves to reveal the presence of potent spiritual treasure; it means "protection," and warns that the chest should not be carelessly opened.

The shaman in American Indian societies serves the tribe in many capacities. He or she communicates with the gods and also performs in the role of healer. Navaho sand paintings (created by carefully applying sand by hand to make a specific design) are visualizations of religious rituals in which the hand is a symbol of spiritual power, protection, and healing. The sand painting shown in figure 1.17 is called the Hail Chant. Father Sky is represented by stars and Mother Earth is characterized by the maize symbol. Their hands held aloft in prayer display the emblem of the Sun. In the act of constructing a sand painting, which is a ritual in itself, medicine is sometimes placed beside the hands of Father Sky and Mother Earth.

The Tsimshian ceremonial crest hat shown in figure 1.18 is highly instructive. It is a visualization of a ritual that evokes the supernatural power of the bear; indirectly this is an extension of Sun worship.

The Great Spirit, or Great Mystery,

Figure 1.13. **The Mystery of the Sea**, center-piece, carved wooden headdress, Tlingit tribe, Alaska

Figure 1.14. Woven ceremonial hat, Haida tribe, British Columbia, Canada

Figure 1.15. Wooden dance mask, Tlingit tribe, Alaska

Figure 1.16. Detail from a Tsimshian storage chest, British Columbia, Canada

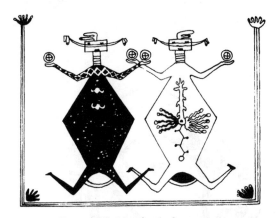

Figure 1.17. Navaho sand painting

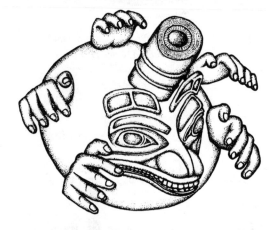

Figure 1.18. Wooden ceremonial hat, Tsimshian tribe. National Museum of Canada, Ottawa

Figure 1.19. Detail, Mixtec manuscript, the Bodley Codex

or Good Power is thought to be everywhere and in everything—mountains, plains, winds, waters, trees, birds, and animals. All animals are thought of as receiving their endowment of power from the Sun. Some, such as the grizzly bear, buffalo, beaver, wolf, eagle, and raven, are worshiped because they are considered to possess a larger amount of the Good Power than others. They are naturally prayed to for assistance and this is done largely through the use of sacred handsigns.

The grizzly bear is admired for its strength and ferocity. In the ceremonial hat, shown in figure 1.18, five hands display the sacred sign of the Bear. Partly closed hands are held alongside the head to indicate the bear's ears; added to this is a clawing motion with the hands in front clawing downward. What is truly remarkable is that although this hat originates from far northern regions of the American continent, its meaning would be instantly recognized by most Indians on the Great Plains.

In *The Old North Trail*, Walter McClintock describes a number of these ceremonies and he includes photographs. In the Ceremonial of the Beaver Medicine, Beaver songs are sung accompanied by marking time with the forefinger. He explains that the Beaver Chief made this sign when giving instruction to *Akaiyan*, the founder of the Beaver Medicine. To evoke the spirit of the Beaver, its handsign is used: The flat left hand is held in front of the body, the flat right hand is below same, and the back of the right hand strikes up against the left palm sharply. The meaning is that the tail of the beaver strikes mud or

Figure 1.20. Panel from the Codex Fejérváry-Mayer, City of Liverpool Museum

water. The tail is its most salient feature and represents, *pars pro toto,* the beaver itself. Making the sacred sign of the beaver lodge in unison the participants pray to the spirit of the Beaver, "Pity us! Grant us your wisdom and cunning that we may escape all dangers. May your medicine provide us with food. May all of us be blessed."

In the Buffalo Ceremony the fingers are closed with the two index fingers curved toward each other in imitation of buffalo horns, the sign of the Buffalo. Similar techniques are employed in the Elk Song, the Swan Song, and in the songs of all the animals invested with Sun Power.

McClintock supplies valuable information regarding the use of the extended index finger in ceremonies. This is an extremely important handsign, the ritual use of which is widespread throughout North America and Mesoamerica. As we shall see, its usages are numerous, depending on context.

In Nahua pictographic writing the extended index finger is called *tlamahuizo* and is used to express admiration or marvel at something or simply to call attention to an object. In Mixtec codices its use is extensive and diverse. In the detail from the Bodley Codex shown in figure 1.19, Four Tiger uses the handsign in a context in which it means "to take" or *tlatlanehuia* in Nahua pictography. Four Tiger takes a prisoner from Eight Deer who speaks stony words as he signs *tlancuhtia,* "to give." These two signs are explicit in the panel from the Codex Fejérváry-Mayer shown in figure 1.20. Here we see the patron god of merchants, *Yacatecuhtli,* Lord Nose, with his cross symbol, which we have seen is derived from the handsign meaning "trade." With his right hand he gives and with his left he takes, succinctly expressing the activities of the merchant. The entire sign is known from Plains Indian sign language wherein the index finger is extended toward an object and quickly pulled back toward the body while curving the finger into a hook.

In the pre-Toltec stele in figure 1.21 the pointing finger is used in an act of worship. Pointing the index finger to the zenith and the Earth was an oath with many tribes of the plains. Here a ball player offers a human heart to the Sun. Another ball player impersonating the Death God points to the Sun as an act of worship while a speech scroll indicating prayer emerges from his mouth. Hovering above the Sun is a god frequently confused with *Quetzalcoatl,* the Plumed Serpent, although I can find no substantial reason for this association. The god is clearly *Xiuhcoatl,* the Fire Serpent, who conducts the Sun on its

Figure 1.22. Detail from the Codex Nuttall

Figure 1.23. **Coatlicue, Lady of Serpents**, statue from Tenochtitlan, the Aztec capital. National Museum, Mexico City

Figure 1.21. Pre-Toltec stele from Santa Lucia, Cozumahualpa, Mexico

daily journey from the eastern horizon to the zenith. He is an avatar of *Xiuhtecutli*, the Old God of Fire. He wears a headdress identifying him as a *Bacab*, supporter of the skies.

The Fire Serpent appears in a similar scene in the sun disc illustrated in figure 1.22, which is a detail from the Codex Nuttall (p. 19). From his mouth

he belches out *Citlaltachli*, the ball court in the sky which is made up of the constellations Cancer and Gemini. Symbolically this indicates that the Sun is leaving these constellations. The reverse of this symbol appears (p. 17) where the Fire Serpent is shown eating or "entering" the ball court in the sky. The temple at Texupan in the Apoala

Figure 1.24. **The Goddess Coatlicue,** *basalt statue from Caliztlahuaca, Mexico,* A.D. *1321-1521*

Figure 1.25. **Coatlicue, Goddess of the Serpent Skirt,** *basalt statue from Coxcatlan, Tehuacan*

Figure 1.26. Statue, Aztec priest

Valley, Oaxaca, is shown with a Venus staff in front of it. Stars on the roof of the temple indicate that it is a place where astronomical observations are made. Inside is a sacred bundle surmounted by implements for the ceremonial making of the new fire. An impersonator of the Goddess One Death or One Death herself is shown worshiping the Sun as she emerges from the jaws of the Earth. I think this goddess is or is closely related to *Coatlicue,* the goddess of the Earth, life, and death. In any event the red headdress, the plants, and her emergence from the Earth identify her as a fertility goddess.

In art, the most consistent characteristic of *Coatlicue* is her display of hands. In figure 1.23 her hands are covered by jaguar paws. (A more detailed treatment of this engrossing statue appears in appendix three.) She wears a necklace consisting of hearts, hands, and the skull of a sacrificial victim. In figures

1.24 and 1.25 her more typical gesture is shown. According to tradition her display of hands is symbolic of her embodiment of both life and death as aspects of a single unity. The display of hands shown by the Aztec priest in figure 1.26 signifies that he belongs to the cult of *Coatlicue.* The volutes hanging from his necklace represent flames of fire symbolizing sacrifice. His *cactli* or sandals are writhing rattlesnakes.

In the images of *Coatlicue* the cult of the hand reaches perhaps its most extreme limits but imagery in the Moche ceramic vessel drawn in figure 1.27 vies with it in bizarrerie. The Moche lived below the Andes Mountains in present-day Peru. The vessel is in the shape of a hand in a gesture that simulates five sacred peaks of the mountain range and is probably meant to invoke the powers of mountain-dwelling spirits. Awestruck mortals huddle below the Andean peaks along with an enthroned fanged god

Figure 1.27. Moche ceramic vessel

who wears a feline totem in his head-dress. They gaze up to the heavens while enacting a human and animal sac-rifice. The various hand gestures depict-ed are apparently those employed in sequential stages of the ritual.

It is in Mesoamerica that the cult of the hand emerges as the dominant sym-bol of religious ritual. The hand in these cultures represents the equivalent of what the cross is to Christianity or the Star of David is to Judaism. It is a prominent motif in ritual cult objects such as the hand staffs used in cere-monies as seen in the Dresden Codex, illustrated in figure 1.28.

Ritual implements invoking the spiritual power of the hand, similar to those found in the Dresden Codex, can also be seen in the Codex Nuttall as shown in figure 1.29. In A, Three Reed, a priestess participating in a fertility rite, is holding a *xonecuilli*, the staff of fertil-ity, in the form of a human hand. B is a detail from the burial ceremonies of Seven Rain. He is shown standing but, as is the case with Maya dignitaries, a stone placed in his mouth indicates a burial rite. He is elaborately attired in

Figure 1.28. New Year cere-monies, detail from from the Dresden Codex

A

B

Figure 1.29. Details from the Codex Nuttall

Figure 1.30. **Camachtli**, *a speaker*, Nahua pictograph

Figure 1.31. **The Hand of God**, Teotihuacan fresco

regalia that includes attributes of both *Xipe Totec*, Lord of Liberation or Spring and the supreme penitent hero of the blossoming war, and *Tlaloc*, the Rain God. As with the Maya, death is viewed as a voyage fraught with dangers. Foremost for this perilous journey will be his walking staff surmounted by a hand signal that serves as a holy sign and a warning to both the gods and demons encountered on his path.

Both the hand and the staff are symbols of communication to the American Indian. A speaker's staff, known as the *kwakiutl*, Chief's Talking Stick, was used by the Plains Indians. The Nahua pictograph for *camachtli*, "speaker," shown in figure 1.30, depicts a hand emerging from the mouth. The two concepts are merged in Seven Rain's staff in figure 1.29B.

As the Indian communicates with the gods through use of the hands, the gods often manifest themselves in the form of a hand or its equivalent, a bird's claw. In the Codex Rios, now in the Vatican, a text in Italian reads, "When the devil becomes visible to them they cannot see all of him, but only the claw of an eagle." Of course the "devil" being referred to in this commentary was the god of the Aztecs.

Teotihuacan, City of the Gods, the oldest metropolis in Mesoamerica, is thirty miles north of Mexico City. Literally the name of the city means "the place where people become gods." The hand is the central motif found in its magnificent ruins. The fresco shown in figure 1.31 is called "The Hand of God." A symbol meaning "wind," and by extension "spirit," is enclosed in a circle. Above this is its material manifestation, the hand that indicates the presence of god. If we can imagine a Plains Indian visiting this ancient holy city, he or she would immediately recognize the meaning of this symbol.

What if our imaginary Indian came across the Nahua pictograph shown in figure 1.32A? It would of course be instantly recognized as the sun-in-hand motif symbolizing the protection of the Sun God. The pictograph is *temac* and does mean protection. Its direct opposite in B is *teixnequitl*, meaning "destruction" or "he who destroys." The glyph shown in C is from the second column of glyphs in the Bazan Slab from Monte Alban, Oaxaca. That the glyph carries the same meaning as the pictograph is quite evident from the context in which it appears. Directly above it is a glyph containing an ax. Above that is a glyph in which the main-sign is Venus, a planet closely associated with war in Maya culture. Directly below the destruction glyph is a head glyph with a speech scroll denoting "stony words." In this context the ex-tended finger sign that appears on the

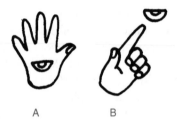

top of the head is a clear sign of aggres-sion. Concluding the text at the very bottom is a Venus sign symbolizing the blossoming war. Starting the text in the upper right-hand corner are two manographs, the second being a hand holding a flint knife. Of the two foot glyphs in the first column, the second indicates traveling. The slab probably commemorates an attack on a town named in the last two glyphs of the col-umn. The personages shown were prob-ably the leaders. The first one impersonates the Jaguar God, symbol of the warrior spirit.

The slab is from Monte Alban's third phase, A.D. 300 to 900. Judging from the style of the glyphs, I would place this slab at the earlier part of the period. There is a pronounced Olmec influence in the writing. The appearance of the "destroyer" glyph assumes knowledge of the sun-in-hand motif. Its appearance here is astounding! It has deep implications, suggesting that the sun-in-hand motif had its origins in Olmec culture. A comparison between the sun-in-hand motifs in Nahua pic-tography and those of the Mound Builders of the Mississippi Valley and the Southeastern states (see p. 40) re-veals similarities both in form and mean-ing so specific that they could not have been arrived at independently. Cultural exchange between the two areas had been suggested since at least the begin-ning of the twentieth century. I would advocate that the possibility be revived.

At the time of European coloniza-tion, land access between the two areas would have been extremely difficult be-cause large swamps had formed around

Figure 1.32. The Bazan Slab, Monte Alban, Period III

the Mississippi drainage areas. Previously, however, the terrain was quite different and land access was certainly feasible. Access along the coast by sea was always possible.

Very recently archaeological evidence has been found uncovering enormous trading sites along the Mexican coastal areas. In 1986 workers were building a dock at the Acula River not far from Veracruz on the eastern coast of Mexico. (Another version has it that villagers from La Mojarra were digging a fish pond. In any event a most extraordinary stone emerged out of the mud.) They uncovered an eight-foot stela with texts recording the dates A.D. May 21, 143 and A.D. July 13, 156. They had found the earliest writing yet deciphered in the New World. On the face of the stone there is a full-figure portrait of a richly attired warrior-king and 465 glyphs telling of his rise to kingship through years of warfare and

elaborate accession rites presided over by a shaman. The writing is called epi-Olmec because it was used by people living in former Olmec territory, at least some of whom were probable Olmec descendants.

Because of their early achievements in art, religion, economics, and politics, the Olmec are regarded as a sort of "mother civilization" to certain cultures that came after. Manographic writing appears in Mesoamerican writing systems with meanings unchanged for over a thousand years. I was astounded to find some of the principal ones on the Mojarra stela, fully developed and with their meanings unchanged. It seems we are beginning to rediscover a new panorama of pre-Colonial America.

I have redrawn some of these glyphs in figure 1.33. In A is the *tzuk*-hand, a verb of fundamental importance in ritual, meaning "to present" or "to display." Also central is the inverted hand

Figure 1.33. Glyphs from the Mojarra stela, Olmec, A.D. 159

Figure 1.34. Panels from Mixtec codices

shown in B, the *dz'a*-hand, also a verb, meaning "to give." The *ch'am*-hand shown in C represents a basic bloodletting rite which remains at the core of Maya religious activity throughout its history. The glyph in D is the second glyph in the second column of the Bazan Slab. Here it means "harvester" and forms part of the warrior-king's name.

In E is the hand of the warrior-king from his full-figure portrayal, the central focus of the entire stela and succinctly summing up the entire text. It is the *tzuk*-hand, which displays an emblem asserting and confirming kings of the Nahua, Mixtec, and Maya, who flourished along Mexico's Gulf Coast between 1200 and 400 B.C. From their ancient heartland they traveled and traded throughout Mesoamerica on a vast scale: From the highlands of central Mexico to the western reaches of El Salvador signs of Olmec culture have been found. Their glyphs reflect fundamental patterns later to be seen in Maya art, such as the use of the calendar,

number, the bar and dot system used to record it, religious motifs, the political "poster" dealing with the accession to power of the personage portrayed, and most importantly, the development of writing.

As a specialist my primary concern was with the manographs that were certain to appear on the stela. By the time data on the stone became available I had already recognized certain key manographs in the Maya hieroglyphs and because of their prominence I had given them their probable Maya names. These glyphs represented a considerably refined "right to rule."

It is truly amazing that when we find the earliest examples of these manographs, as well as many of the hieroglyphics, they are already highly refined and fully developed. It is normal in studying a writing system to be able to trace the slow development of a character over a period of hundreds of years as we can with our own letters or with Chinese characters. These can be traced back to very primitive origins and then be seen to evolve into their present forms. The great mystery about Mesoamerican hieroglyphs is that in many cases the earliest examples known are already fully developed; they appear to materialize suddenly from out of nowhere.

In spite of the fact that the Maya enlarged upon and developed the Olmec hieroglyphs to an ultimate state of refinement, the basic tenets of the methodology were already quite sophisticated and the major breakthroughs required for the development of true writing were already in place prior to the Maya inheriting the system. A prime example of how the Maya developed a glyphic idea to its full capacities can be seen in the sun-in-hand motif itself.

We have seen that the sun-in-hand motif represents a fundamental Sun ritual and carries the same basic meaning practically wherever it appears. For emphasis let us look at examples of the ritual it symbolizes from two Mixtec codices. The scene shown in figure 1.34A is from the Codex Colombino and shows a worshiper in a jaguar costume sitting on a stone that denotes his authoritative status; the hill is designated "Spiral Hill." He prays to the Sun God by displaying his palm. In B, from the Codex Becker, we see the same hill with its spiral motif placename. A person named Four Reed, who is partially obliterated in the drawing, is being installed as a lord, which in this culture means the representative or living manifestation of the Sun. An attendant at the ritual displays one or both palms to the Sun God. The Sun God responds to this supplication by pointing to Four Reed, affirming the accession. A Plains Indian will sometimes point to the Sun in a gesture that boasts, "I am like the Sun." Here is its opposite: The sign means, "Yes, he is me or my representative." With his other hand the Sun God bestows his blessing.

Examples of Maya sun-in-hand glyphs are shown in figure 1.35 and as can be expected they are refined developments and have variations. These are not ordinary hands but sacred holy hands that have been blessed by the Sun. The power of the glyph is so revered it may become the subject of a sculpture in itself, as shown. Just how rooted the ritual is in Maya conscious-

Figure 1.35. Maya sun-in-hand hieroglyphs and hand in stucco

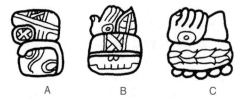

A   B   C

Figure 1.36. The Maya hieroglyph for dawn

ness is demonstrated in the hieroglyph for "dawn," three versions of which are shown in figure 1.36. The association of the rising Sun with the open palm (in B) is so strong that the mere presence of the hand in association with the Sun indicates "dawn," the time that the ritual takes place. The mainsign in A has the sun emblem within a sky emblem, presumably on the horizon. In C the mainsign shows the headband of the Sun God meaning *pars pro toto*, the Sun itself. Here again the juxtaposition of hand and Sun is sufficient to imply "dawn." The Maya use the same reasoning in glyphs for "east."

The Maya could actually express the sun-in-hand ritual in writing. The illus-

tration shown in figure 1.37 is a detail of a jade earflare. The first glyph is a development of the sun-in-hand motif wherein it becomes a verb. When the ritual is expressed as a verb the hand is shown grasping the Sun. The subject of the verb is the hieroglyph below, *Kinich Ahau*, the Sun God. The artist has not merely symbolized the ritual or named it: This is a statement. The earflare was discovered in a Late Preclassic tomb in Belize, which dates it sometime between 50 B.C. and A.D. 50.

With the coming of the Early Classic period about A.D. 120, Maya culture began to blossom. Rituals became far more elaborate. We no longer see the rather simple sun-in-hand ritual expressed but there are numerous extensions of it. The basic idea of imploring the Sun God's protection is retained but its applications are widely expanded and adapted to the needs of the far more complex rituals of an advancing civilization. These developments are reflected in the usage of the glyph.

The glyph shown in figure 1.38A

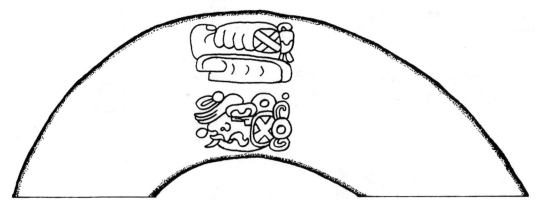

Figure 1.37. Detail, jade earflare, Pomona, Belize, 50 B.C.–A.D. 50.
Trustees of the British Museum, London

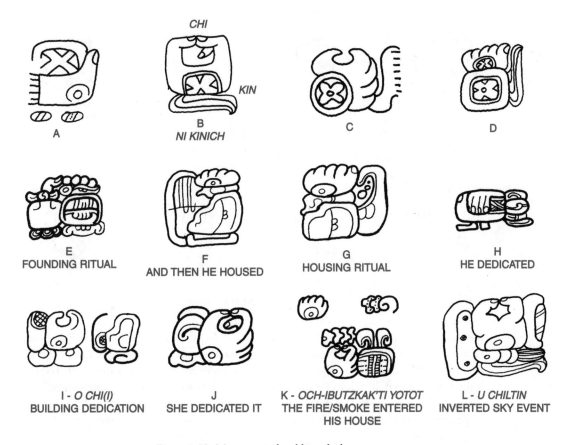

Figure 1.38. Maya sun-in-hand hieroglyphs

dates from A.D. 120 and represents the basic sun-in-hand ritual. Soon after the beginning of the Early Classic period the kingdom of Copan was established and the Tikal dynasty was founded. Along with the establishment of dynastic powers, in the city-states entire schools of artists could be supported. Dated stelae began to be erected. Out of these schools a new and far more advanced sun-in-hand glyph began to emerge as seen in B. This incorporates the sun symbol inside the handsign for "sun" along with the emanating rays of the Sun. As these signs carry sound values, we not only see the sacred symbol of the Sun, we hear the sounds *kin-ni-chi* evoking *Kinich,* the holy name of the Sun God.

Glyphs in C and D are directions, *chi-kin* in C being the east, literally "next sun" in Yucatec and meaning "where the sun rises." The glyph in D is pronounced in a similar way but the closed hand over the Sun here denotes "west," the direction of the setting Sun. The glyph *Mah Kina* or Great Sun, which we shall encounter in subsequent chapters, is a title. The Sun is now firmly in the hand, it evokes a sound, and it

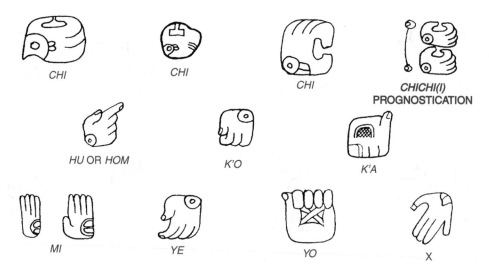

CHI

CHI

CHI

CHICHI(I)
PROGNOSTICATION

HU OR HOM

K'O

K'A

MI

YE

YO

X

Figure 1.39. Maya phonetic manographs

has become a mudra implying that there is an embodiment or manifestation of the Sun. The name of this glyph has for long been known but its full meaning can only be understood in terms of its origin in ritual and its significance as a sacred handsign.

The remaining glyphs shown in figure 1.38 are indicative of complex rituals in which the sun-in-hand symbol serves as a determinative; that is, a glyphic element showing how a mainsign or phrase should be read. In F and G are dedication verbs for massive pyramids. The glyphs in H, I, and J refer to temples and mean "he or she dedicated it." In K there is another variant of a building-dedication ceremony. In L is the hieroglyph *u chiltin*, a ritual called "the inverted sky event." All the elements are read phonetically but the *chi*-hand serves a double function as a determinative that lets us know that it is a ritual.

Besides the *chi*-hand many other manographs carry phonetic values. Some of these are shown in figure 1.39. To render the word *chich*, "prognostication," two *chi*-hands are used. The x-hand (quite possibly "the scattering hand") appears in Landa's famous alphabet, which has proven to be helpful, but it has not yet been found in the hieroglyphs.

Figure 1.40 shows various ways in which an *its'at* might write the phrase, "is its holy name." Perhaps the most interesting is the rendering in C. The Moon Goddess is usually the deity of the sound *na* but here the reader is expected to realize that *u*, the sound of the Moon herself, is intended. The descending squiggly line has the value of *u* and is here used as a determinative, but reading Maya hieroglyphs requires a certain amount of participation by the reader. A Maya term for hand is *kab* and the artist here uses it to encircle the abstract form of *chuen*, monkey, which by

A K'A K'UL BA UK'U K'ABA IS ITS HOLY NAME

B U K'ABA IS ITS NAME

C U K'AB

Figure 1.40. *Maya hieroglyphs,* u k'aba k'ul

extension reads *k'ul*, holy. So we have *u k'ab k'ul*. Where is the *a* in *k'aba*? It is nowhere; the reader is expected to be a little creative and grasp the intention of the artist.

One may think that the wide latitude allowed the artist would lead to confusion. It sometimes does but it is also the saving grace of the writing system. One of the reasons why great strides are being made in the decipherment of Maya hieroglyphics is because the artists substituted one sign for another that carried the same value. Therefore if one sign could be read, two or three of its substitutes could also be read.

The *chi*-hand is used as a phonetic in the vase painting shown in figure 1.41. The theme is a very popular one taken from the mythological *Popol Vuh*. The Hero Twins are summoned to the underworld where they meet one of the chief gods, *Itzamna*, who offers them a drink. The jar, *olla*, is labeled *chih*, which is derived from the *chi*-hand and the phonetic *hi* (shown in A). It contains an alcoholic beverage known as *maguey* or *agave*. It is offered with a hand gesture but *Itzamna* takes none of it himself since it has been poisoned. The artist, using line with extreme economy, beautifully renders the look of apprehension on the face of *Hunahpu*,

A

Figure 1.41. **The Hero Twins with the Frog God Meet Itzamna in the Underworld,** *cylindrical vase*

Y - UCH' AB

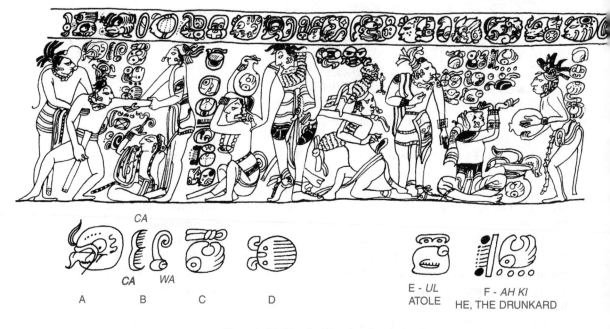

A   B   C   D   E - UL ATOLE   F - AH KI HE, THE DRUNKARD

CA

CA   WA

Figure 1.42. **He, the Drunkard**, cylindrical vase

the first twin, who is obliged by protocol not to refuse the offer. The artist's use of hands in the composition is wonderful.

The hands of *Itzamna*, *Hunahpu* and his twin, *Xbalanque*, are in alignment across the composition. The Frog God, who is an ally of the twins, raises his left hand in the gesture of sorrow. (This sign is found in Mixtec codices. A Plains Indian signs it differently but with the same meaning of "tears.") His right hand is closed in the handsign meaning "death," which is soon to come to the twins. Through cunning and magic the twins are later resurrected and return to the Lords of the Underworld to execute their revenge.

The *chih* glyph can be seen in the vase painting *He, the Drunkard* illustrated in figure 1.42. A jar on the ground holds the fermenting maguey cactus. The artist omits the *hi* phonetic and simply writes the *chi*-hand on the surface of the jar. The same is done on another jar held aloft by a court attendant. The Primary Standard Sequence (P.S.S.) is written on a band around the top of the vase. The text below the P.S.S. in the upper left-hand corner begins with the head of the Cacao God, which is redrawn in A. This is followed by the phonetics *ca, ca,* and *wa* shown in B. The Cacao God was highly revered, cacao being an important ceremonial beverage and the beans serving as a medium of exchange. What is referred to here obviously is fermented cacao, which yields a chocolate liquor. The artist places the text directly below the reference to cacao in the P.S.S., *y-uch'ab ta om cacaw,* "his drinking vase for frothy cacao" followed by the glyph *ta tsih,* "tree-fresh."

Following cacao in the text is *chih* shown in C properly written and below it *cha hom* meaning "to sprinkle" and then a probable version of *ul,* "atole," shown in D, yet another alcoholic beverage. The "sprinkle" verb probably refers to cacao laced with these substances. The assortment of beverages in the text certainly explains the condition of our hero, the drunkard, who lurches below the text, assisted by two attendants. As if he hasn't had enough, a seated courtier offers a narcotic substance in the form of a cigarette. The name of this substance in all likelihood is given in the accompanying glyphs.

The next set of glyphs tells us something about who the drunkard is. At the top is the verb *yilah,* "he saw," followed by *u* and *tzi,* "his brother," then *Ah Cauac,* a title; another title, *Ah Lats,* meaning "he of generations" and indicating that this is a person who is a member of a ruling family; and finally *kelem,* "youth." Following this is the attendant holding a maguey jar and then a figure whose uplifted foot indicates that he is dancing. His accompanying glyphs *chak ch'ok* mean "great lineage member;" he is probably the heir designate. It is he who sees his younger brother, to whom he handsigns. He seems to be under the aphrodisiacal effects of cacao.

In this painting we are getting a glimpse into the daily life of Maya people in antiquity, albeit the noble class. The painting allows us to peer into their world in considerable detail. This is not a mythological scene but a slice-of-life event in the lives of real people. What happens next is truly remarkable. Her left hand held by the heir designate, a kneeling lady handsigns to an attendant, holding a jar, with whom she has eye contact. She uses the *chi*-hand and is obviously calling for more *chih.* The lady, silent for centuries, now speaks to us in meaningful communication. In this moment the painting becomes a living work of art, a celebration of a particularly human potentiality—the ability to transmit ideas.

Of the next group of eight glyphs only two have been reread. The glyph shown in E is the more usual way of writing *ul,* "atole." In F is *ah ki,* "he, the drunkard," *ki* being a cognate of *chi.* Undoubtedly the reference of the text is to the younger brother. The handsign used by the seated courtier is unique. He simultaneously points to the attendant and to the lady. The standing courtier appears to handsign negation, causing the attendant to appear disconcerted and perplexed. Regardless of the ambiguity presented by this situation, the kneeling lady has given us a precious moment in the history of art.

To understand and fully appreciate a work of art like *The Revenge of the Corn God* illustrated in figure 1.43, one must first of all realize that this type of vase painting depicts scenes from the *Popol Vuh,* the mythological exploits of the Hero Twins. Modern researchers

A - YA   HOY - I

MACHAL

MA

CH(I)   (A)L

Figure 1.43. **The Revenge of the Corn God**, *cylindrical vase*

have come to this conclusion comparatively recently. Secondly, it must be understood that in vase paintings of this type, which occur frequently, the artist is not usually attempting to paint the actual events as they were supposed to have occurred. These are scenes as they were ordinarily seen in daily life, as staged in theatrical performance.

Episodes from the *Popol Vuh* were constantly being reenacted in the ancient kingdoms of the Maya. Besides being the state religion, the *Popol Vuh* was the main entertainment for all classes of society. The plays were being continually performed at the time of the Conquest, and they are so deeply rooted in the lives of the people that productions are still created to this day. The ancient artist's renditions of scenes from the *Popol Vuh* irresistibly evoke the idea

of a theater set because that was the medium through which the painter was introduced to its mysteries as a child and it was the most familiar version throughout a person's life.

Not only was it natural for the artist to paint theatrical versions of the episodes, the clients wanted to see actors they could recognize and the scenes depicted as they could recall having seen them on stage. Sometimes an artist does paint a scene visualized as having actually occurred but the vast majority are derived directly from the dramatic entertainment of a staged show.

Thirdly, a work such as *The Revenge of the Corn God* is not even derived from a serious attempt to re-create scenes from the *Popol Vuh* on stage. It is strictly a farce that is being shown. These are comic skits that provide relief from the more serious presentations and fulfill the people's natural need for comedy. They perform a function similar to the Kyogen comedy plays of Japan that are performed between the long and ponderous acts in the Noh Theater. The serious reenactment of the Corn God's revenge was undoubtedly very popular and performed with great extravagance and pomp but here we have a comical version that reaches the heights of absurdity. A comparison between the real god *Pauahtun*, whose glyph appears in the P.S.S. in the upper left corner of the illustration, and the ludicrous *Pauahtun* who is seen in the comic skit directly below his glyph shows just how preposterous Maya comedy can be.

We will become familiar with the P.S.S. in subsequent chapters. It consists of a hierarchy of glyphs. In a complete sequence, gods come first, ending with the God of Cacao, then a person or persons will be named or referred to, and finally a placename, whether it be in this world or a supernatural realm.

The introductory glyph *a-ya* is the most sacred. Nothing can precede it except in rare instances when a glyph denoting time appears. Apparently time to the Maya is the most sacred of all entities. *A-ya* means "it came into being," "it comes into existence," or "it comes to light." Second only to *a-ya* in the hierarchy is a glyph *hoy-i*, meaning "it was blessed," or "it was made holy." *Pauahtun* represents the number five, *ho*, and here supplies a phonetic value. *Pauahtun* is the supreme ordering god of the cosmos, lord of number, patron of writing, and hence of history itself. He is so revered that his head glyph will

stand in for the verb *hoy-i* as it does in this instance. As a *Bacab* holds up the skies, the *Pauahtun* holds up the Earth, the god *Pauahtun* being chief of these two. The scrawny hunchback playing the role of *Pauahtun* in the antics below the P.S.S. is not meant to be taken seriously.

The plot of the story is very simple. The Sun God is summoned down to the underworld where he is killed by the gods who dwell there. His sons, the Hero Twins, revive him and he is resurrected as *Yum Caax*, the Corn God. He then returns to the gods of the underworld to humiliate them. The gods here are played by bald withered old men. They have "god signs" but even these are ridiculous. The "god sign" on the back of the seated god is particularly absurd. Baby Jaguar as usual is played by a dwarf but here as the comic Baby Jaguar he does not don any of his sacred regalia. Very few gods of the Maya pantheon cannot be ridiculed; the Corn God is one of these. He is always played by a handsome youth and his entrance on the stage is cheered by the onlookers. He may be flatulent as he romps across the stage in his comic performance but he will otherwise appear dignified and elegant.

The Corn God speaks to *Pauahtun* who replies, and here the artist employs a device that anticipates the speech balloon of our own comic book illustrators by a number of centuries. A glyph in his speech scroll has been perceptively reread by Richard Johnson in his *Two Vases: Suggested Readings of the Secondary Texts*. Three phonetics are used to render the word, *machal*, meaning "to seize, to grasp." Simultaneously the Corn God hooks his index finger and draws it toward his body in a handsign that we have seen means "to take." The artist has cleverly used both writing and handsign to convey the idea of disrobing the underworld gods of their finery. Again a once-mute oddity is resurrected into a living masterpiece of visual communications that transcends the boundaries of time.

We are beginning to peer into the world of the Maya. It is a realm wherein the theme of resurrection and the means of rescuing the human spirit from its own duality are seminal in the quest for spiritual liberation. In order to understand the mysteries of ancient Maya wisdom we must go inside that world, entering the Iguana House through its foundation. We begin with the Maya conception of the dawning of Creation in the world of duality.

Figure 2.1. **The Resurrection of Xbalanque**, *cylindrical vase*

THE HANDS OF CREATION

After their magical resurrection the Hero Twins, *Hunahpu* and *Xbalanque*, disguise themselves as wonder-working vagabond actors who begin performing miraculous dances of sacrifice in which one twin would decapitate the other and then bring him back to life. The Lords of the Underworld hear of the wonder dramas performed by these new sorcerers and command that they perform their marvels at court.

The reenactment of these particular performances, a play within a play, naturally provides spectacular material for some of the most exciting and popular stage presentations of episodes from the *Popol Vuh*. The theme is of course replicated on numerous vase paintings, *The Resurrection of Xbalanque*, illustrated in figure 2.1, being one of them.

Hunahpu first decapitates *Xbalanque* with his ax. This scene shows the dramatic climax of the performance when *Hunahpu* strikes the altar stone out of which the triumphant *Xbalanque* emerges. The theme easily lends itself to a variety of theatrical settings which influence the artist's depiction of the event. The images used to enact the drama are those of birth and creation. The *tun* or *cuauc* altar stone is the usual prop in the performance; its origins are in Maya cosmogenesis mythology in which the sacred stones are at the core of the mystery of Creation.

In the creation mythology these stones are alive. They are born and deified. Gods and elemental forces reside in them and emerge from them. They are magical essences that can give birth or sprout corn. In the *Chilam Balam of Chumayel,* they exist prior to Creation. In the "Ritual of Angels" section it is stated, ". . . occurred the birth of the first precious stone of grace, the first infinite night, when there was no God. Not yet had he received his godhead. Then he remained alone within the grace, within the night, when there was neither heaven nor earth . . ." Further on in the same section it reads, "This was the first word of God, when there was neither heaven nor earth, when he came out of the stone and fell into the second stone. Then it was that he declared his divinity. Then resounded eight thousand *katun*s at the word of the first stone of grace, at the first ornamented stone of grace. It was the macaw that warmed it well behind the *acantun.* Who was born when our father descended? You know. There was

born the first macaw who cast the stones behind the *acantun* . . .".

In a section called "A Song of the Itza" it is said, "But God the Father was created alone and by his own effort in the darkness. But the stones were created separately. This was the land of *acantun* . . ." . In the section entitled "Creation of the World" it states, " . . . very rightly they worshiped as true gods these precious stones . . .".

There are many kinds of throne or altar stones. Three types are mentioned in the creation text on stela C at Quirigua which concerns the "stone-birthing" of *Itzamna*: a jaguar-stone throne, a "snaggletooth"-stone throne, and a serpent-stone throne. In the vase painting we see *Xbalanque* emerging from a vulture-stone throne. The symbolism underlying this derives from the word *tun,* "stone," being the name of the 360-day calculation year of the calendar, over which the vulture presides.

The handsign used by *Xbalanque* as he emerges from the stone is of immense significance. These are the hands of Creation. My first recognition of this sign came in the classification of these

Figure 2.2. Mixtec placesigns for the town of Teozacoalco

handsigns. It quickly became apparent that the handsign was important; it appeared in Aztec, Mixtec, and Maya art and it always appeared in association with birth or creation. I did not know how to relate this sign to American Indian Sign Language and therefore to arrive at its meaning until I came across a clue in Mary Elizabeth Smith's book, *Picture Writing in Southern Mexico.*

Among many other careful observations and brilliant deductions she had explained the place sign for the town of Teozacoalco shown in figure 2.2. Her methodology was indeed fascinating. She first went to the Reyes list of Mixtec placenames to find that the original name of the town was Chiyo Canu. The name had changed with time but as frequently happens the placesign or logogram of the town remains the same. Smith then consulted a dictionary of Mixtec vocabulary compiled by Captain Pedro de Alvarado at the time of the Conquest. She found that *Chiyo* means "altar," "foundation," or "building site." *Canu* means "large." In the Mixtec language the word "break" is also pronounced *canu*. Since pictographically it is easier to render "break" than it is to depict the idea of "large" the artist used rebus writing by substituting the sign "to break" for "large," the other meaning of its sound.

Smith had successfully explained the meaning of the placesign and identified it in five places in ancient manuscripts—once in the Selden Codex, three times in the Bodley Codex, and also in the Map of Teozacoalco. I very recently recognized it in the Codex Nuttall (p.68) while writing the manuscript for this book. It is the third town captured by Eight Deer after the giant conference at Tilantongo.

Usually the full-figure form of the placesign appears but once, as shown in figure 2.2A. In B the artist lacked space and substituted the handsign meaning "to break" for the full-figure drawing. Unwittingly this *tlacuilo* "putter down of the thoughts" had provided an important key symbol in the language of handsigns.

I immediately saw the interconnected logic of meaning in the handsign "break": the American Indian handsign for dawn, which means "daybreak," and how it extends finally to mean "birth." Just as we express the idea of dawn by using the term "daybreak," a Plains Indian will express dawn by first holding the hands together and separating them in the "to break" sign. Dawn is a metaphor for both birth and creation. More significantly birth is viewed in Mesoamerican cultures as a "break" with an original unity. We are born into the world of duality by separating or breaking away from our original oneness.

A knowledge of the meaning of this handsign alone provides new insights into perhaps hundreds of works of Mesoamerican art. The introduction to the Codex Nuttall shown in figure 2.3 is one example. It begins in the lower right-hand corner with the ancestral hero god Eight Wind emerging from the maw of the Earth. The handsign he displays can be compared with the handsign used by *Xbalanque* as he bursts from the vulture-stone throne in his rebirthing. When the duality decides a god or person shall be born, the indi-

C

(WEST)

D

(NORTH)

B

(SOUTH)

A

(EAST)

Figure 2.3. Page from the Codex Nuttall

vidual consequently is inserted in an omnipotent order, the day of birth in the *tonalpohualli*, the sacred 260-day calendar, or the days of destiny being determining factors. The days form a mandala of time, which is related to space directionally. The maw of the Earth is in the south, as is the day Eight Wind in the mandala. His assistant

Twelve Alligator has emerged from the east. The temple in the west is symbolic of the setting Sun. Their first act is to light the fire in the temple. Twelve Alligator carries sticks in his bundle for this purpose and carries a fertility staff sacred to the Sun.

Above Eight Wind's name is the yearsign One Reed, the first year in a

52-year cycle. Above that is the day One Alligator, the first day of the 260-day cycle. Together these signs indicate a beginning. The ball-court emblem is an extremely clever device that succinctly sums up the Mixtec concept of cosmogenesis. It is divided into four quadrants symbolic of time and space, movement and measure. Red represents the south and below it is blue in the east. Parallel to blue is yellow in the north, above which is green, the west. The spatial order follows the sequence of time in the sacred calendar and the positioning here corresponds to the directional format used in the panel. The ball court indicates movement. The stripes represent stones positioned at the beginning of Creation. The image portrays creation as the establishment of a cosmic order which is then put into motion.

Further symbolism is imbedded in the sun staff, which relates to *Xipe Totec*, God of the Germinating Seed and in the facial markings, which are practically a separate language of visual signs in themselves. In this two-and-a-half-inch high initial panel of the codex the *tlacuilo* has packed an enormous amount of information. The accomplishment is attained through the artist's mastery of symbology and the application of a hidden formula that organizes information into a sequential pattern of when, who, what, and where.

There is another technique employed in the writing that is not immediately perceptible but that becomes apparent through a careful study of the manuscript. The artist first states the most pertinent features of an event and then proceeds to enlarge on the occurrence by supplying further details. The next panel appears above, and in it we step back to view a panorama of the event sweeping across two columns. Here the artist itemizes some of the specifics.

In B, Eight Wind's headdress reveals his acquired name, Flinted Eagle. The birth or creation handsign is now embellished with symbols full of implications: The *ahuehuetl*, the giant cypress tree, and the *pochotl*, the ceiba tree, are merged with the hands. These are the trees from which the Mixtecos mythologically originate, and in the spoken language mentioning these trees evokes the idea of authority. Twelve Alligator now holds the staff of Venus, the Morning Star, the Bringer of Dawn. The possession of such objects confers status, authority, and the right to rule. The sacred maguey cactus emanates from the forehead of Eight Wind.

The now fully emerged pair appear in the guise of hierophants of *Tezcatlipoca*, the Smoking Mirror, protector of wizards. Their bodies are painted with *ulli* derived from latex or *ocote*, pitch pine. Eight Wind wears the jeweled mirror breastplate of the Smoking Mirror; presumably they have come as expounders of its sacred mysteries. With his right hand Twelve Alligator confers a blessing on the four shaman-priests who greet them in C.

Their appearances in the codex follow the order in which their daysigns appear in the sacred calendar. The first is One Reed, a personification of the year One Reed and nameday of the planet Venus. His gesture indicates gratitude. One Rain offers a *xocolli*, the feathered fringed shirt of a high priest, which Eight Wind is seen to be wearing in panel D directly below. Next Eight Vulture displays the sacrificial quail, a sunrise symbol, and points to the temple of the rising Sun, indicating where the ceremony is to take place. Ten Lizard ends the sequel by employing a handsign that throughout the codex means "closing."

The placename given is the Monkey Mountain, shown adorned with spirals and which includes a ball court, a jewel, and a sacred bundle. These symbols will be discussed in reference to the Maya cosmogenesis. The scene in D gives a date of the day One Motion in the year Seven Flint. I have very tentatively and only as a working hypothesis assigned this to about the year A.D. 928 in the Gregorian calendar. Eight Wind is seen crossing the river at Apoala, the River of the Lineages. The placesign is given in the river by showing a hand pulling up plants meaning "roots." Eight Wind is about to engage in a magical ascension from *Tlaloc* Hill, a place dedicated to the Rain God and also associated with the origins of the Mixtecos as the People of the Clouds. Eight Wind's first act of creation is related to the Mixtecos as Descendants of the Trees symbolized by the split tree, the house of birth in *Tamoanchan*, the sacred garden.

The tree from which the individual emerges at birth is a cosmic pillar, a portal uniting various levels of the universe. As he crosses the river at Apoala, Eight Wind is accompanied by Eleven Flower, who will assist him in his ascent. He bears the celestial rope. Fully unraveled (as shown on page 18 of the codice),

Figure 2.4. **The Hands of the Descending God**

the rope—made of *ixtle*, agave cactus fiber and adorned with tufts symbolizing clouds—takes a sinuous journey from Apoala into the heavens through a portal in the sky. The same kind of rope is used in the Huichol ceremony of the magical flight to Wirikirta, the land of divine peyote.

In Mesoamerican art the "breaking" handsign is frequently encountered in association with shamanistic journeys transversing various realms of the cosmos. *The Hands of the Descending God* shown in figure 2.4 are an example. In a remarkable set of eight stelae from Xochicalco, now in the National Museum in Mexico City, these hands are shown in reverse as *Quetzalcoatl* begins his creation from the underworld, exactly paralleling the opening of the Codex Nuttall.

The opening of the Selden Roll, shown in figure 2.5, includes a break in the skies as *Quetzalcoatl* has ascended into the realm of *Ometeotl*, the supreme god who resides beyond the thirteen heavens. Although poorly drawn the scene is revealing as in it we see a rare depiction of this god who is the equivalent of the Maya *Hunab Ku*, the Only Giver of Movement and Measure. The She-He, the one and double at once

Figure 2.5. The opening scene of the Selden Roll, Toltec

who represents ultimate reality, is shown as male and female personages named *Ce Mazatl*, One Deer. The artist deals with the problem of symbolizing an all-encompassing god by cleverly drawing the male figure adorned like a true Indian chief. He wears only a simple *maxtlatl* as he confers his blessing upon *Quetzalcoatl* who is the manifestation of the wisdom of the supreme *Ometeotl*.

Quetzalcoatl is the *nawal* or alter ego, counterpart and natural complement of *Ometeotl*. His mission is to establish communication between Earth and heaven and to unite humanity with god. This aspiration toward the divine is reflected in his ornaments, which not only convey the idea of authority but represent high degrees of spiritual consciousness. The essence of his teachings is that human existence must strive to transcend the world of forms that conceal ultimate reality. The means of advancing along the path to spirituality is purification, the only weapon powerful enough to penetrate matter.

Sitting on the Jaguar Throne, *Quetzalcoatl* holds the staff of fertility and wears the spiral-shell jewel of life. From shinbones in his hat emanates the flowering blood of sacrifice. The hummingbird, which dies during the dry season to be reborn during the rainy season, symbolizes resurrection and imbibes the redeeming blood of sacrifice. *Quetzalcoatl* will return to the Earth through the break in the heavens and emerge from the maw of the Earth to be met by four shamans just as Eight Wind is in the Codex Nuttall.

The essential ideas expressed in these two codices provide us with key insights into Mesoamerican concepts of the right to rule and the meaning of rulership itself. These become invaluable in our perception of the function of the ruler in ancient Maya culture. In both of these tribal histories the ancestral kings are shown as powerful shamans who can interact between spiritual and material worlds. The divine couple in the Toltec Selden Roll are named Deer, which in Mesoamerican shamanistic traditions is the emblem of the god of sustenance and fertility without which rain, crops, health, and life cannot be obtained. Both Eight Wind and *Quetzalcoatl*, whose daysign name is Nine Wind, not only embody a religious doctrine of liberation but they are empowered by the gods with supernatural forces that serve to guarantee the material well-being of the people and the fertility of the land. They also have powers and responsibilities in warrior tasks.

There is a fascinating interconnection between Mesoamerican societies that sometimes becomes apparent in mysterious ways. The date given in the opening scene of the Selden Roll is the day Two Deer in the year Thirteen Rabbit. Interestingly, this would fall on the first day of the sixth month of their calendar. In the Maya calendar the sixth month is dedicated to *Kukulcan*, the Maya name for *Quetzalcoatl*. The same date in the same year in the Mixtec Codex Nuttall (p.4) is connected with a resurrection rite led by the warrior-priestess Nine Monkey, who we will meet in a subsequent chapter, and Two Dog, a primordial divine shaman. This could be a mere coincidence if it were not for the fact that in the Selden Roll, *Quetzalcoatl* emerges from the heavens on the day Seven Reed in the year Seven Reed, which would be the first day of that year and a highly significant date in the Codex Nuttall (p.38) where it closes the entire mythological-genealogical section. We see *Quetzalcoatl* named as Nine Wind and dressed in basically the same attire as in the Selden Roll, leading a procession of masked priests, one of which is One Rain, one of the four shamans shown in figure 2.3. Besides this, the date following Seven Reed in the Selden Roll is the first day of the year Seven Flint, which also appears in the Codex Nuttall and here again we

A   B   C

*Figure 2.6 A and B, Maya glyphs meaning "dawn;" C, **Lord Fire Flame**, Codex Borgia*

encounter Nine Wind, this time in his guise as a warrior.

In the final act of his epic, *Quetzalcoatl*, as master of his inner unity, is transformed into the planet Venus. In Mesoamerican cultures the journeys of the Sun, Moon, and planets through the heavens and the underworld are equated with the voyages of shamans through the same regions. They too are envisioned as accessing various levels of the cosmos through portals. The Maya hieroglyph *na ho chan*, "the place of the sunrise," means "first hole in the sky," and is shown in figure 2.6A. In it we see the glyph *caan*, "sky," and *kab*, "earth," separating to allow the emergence of the glyph of the Sun. In B is the glyph *holchan* or *holkab*, which means "dawn" and by extension could refer to birth.

In the depictions of the nine Lords of Night that appear in the Codex Borgia they are all shown making the "breaking" sign symbolizing the dawn. Shown in C is the first Lord of Night in the Nahua system. He is *Xiuhtecutli*, the year lord known as Lord Fire Flame. The moment depicted is the breaking of dawn as he triumphantly delivers the Sun after its nocturnal journey through the center of the Earth. The same logic used in making the handsign is evident in the construction of the hieroglyphs.

The Maya incorporated their system of sacred handsigns into their dances in much the same way that the *hastamudra* is used as an essential part of Hindu classical dance. There are some five hundred mudras described in Hindu technical manuals but in practice performers usually limit their gestures

or "phrases" (sequences of mudras) to those meaningful and familiar to their audiences. In Maya dance scenes the "breaking" handsign is one of the most frequently encountered as it appears consistently in dances that celebrate the birth of the Hero Twins.

The Dance of Ek Chuah, in a vase painting shown in figure 2.7, echoes elements found in the mythological birthing of the Twins. *Ek Chuah*, the Black Scorpion, is the god of traveling merchants and cacao growers. In Nahuatl he is *Yacatehcuhtli*, Lord Nose, and his symbol is the fan, the emblem of traveling merchants, which he wields in the painting along with a fertility staff.

In the mythology *Xquic*, Blood Woman, a daughter of a Lord of Death, finds the skull of *Hun Hunahpu*, father of the Twins, hung in a calabash tree after he was sacrificed by the Lords of the Underworld. He magically impregnates *Xquic* by saying, "Stretch out your right hand here so I can see it." He then spits on the palm of her hand. The right hand is symbolically male and she will in fact bear male twins. The dance shown in the painting is apparently a celebration of a related episode in the mythology, now lost but in all probability well known to the audience of this performance as a variation of the more typical "birth of the twins" dance theme. While prancing to the beat of drummers, *Ek Chuah* inserts his phallic long nose into the left palm of a woman as she displays the "breaking" sign, which here explicitly reveals that this will result in a birthing. To the Maya, dancing has not only a spiritual significance but also a magical function as it seeks to enchant

*Figure 2.7. **The Dance of Ek Chuah**, cylindrical vase*

the holy powers in a rite of fertility.

The Mesoamerican pantheons are great complexities wherein gods and goddesses may have many diverse attributes and some deities are aspects or different guises of others. *Cuaxolotl*, the Goddess of Duality, is shown in figure 2.8 as she appears in the Codex Borgia. She may be an aspect of the Goddess of Life and Death. Known as She of the Divided Head or She of the Two Heads, she is the female counterpart of *Xolotl*, deity of all dual phenomena. *Xolotl* in turn is an aspect of *Quetzalcoatl* who, "astralized" as Venus, represents spirit but as *Xolotl* is a symbol of matter. The goddess is shown displaying the "break" sign, here meaning the separation from the original unity which is the cause of the coming into being of all dual phenomena symbolized by the twins she bears. She wears a mask of

*Figure 2.8. **Cuaxolotl**, from Codex Borgia*

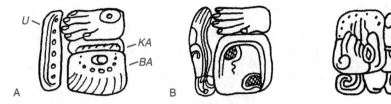

Figure 2.9. Maya glyphs indicating "birth"

Figure 2.10. **The Corn God**, stone sculpture, Copan

Xolotl on the back of her head and on her face is the jawbone of a sacrificial victim.

The word for "birth" in Nahuatl is *temo*, "to come down." The Maya have similar metaphors as shown in the glyphs in figure 2.9. In A the verb is expressed as a hand touching the phonetic combination *ka-ba*, *kab* being the Earth. The entire reading would be *u-kab*, "he touched Earth." B would be read in the same way but the daysign *Caban* is substituted for "Earth." In C there is an up-ended frog's head that as a logograph represents *sih*, a word for "birth." As a phonetic element it represents the syllable *hu* and forms *hul*, "to arrive."

The Corn God is often associated with the "break" handsign of birth as is seen in the sculpture illustrated in figure 2.10. This is considered one of the finest representations of *Yum Caax* or *Ghanan* known. This image has often been compared with meditational depictions of the Buddha, the handsigns being likened to the symbolic gestures of the mudra. Now that we can read this handsign it is clear that the gesture carries an entirely different meaning than the equivalent gestures in the Buddhist system. However we can also now clarify that comparison between the sacred handsigns of the Maya and Asian mudras is quite valid: Both systems act as aids to, or as outward visible signs of, spiritual attainment; both are used mystically or magically to contact or unite with spiritual forces or invisible powers in nature; and both are used communicatively in painting, sculpture, dance, and ceremony in remarkably similar ways.

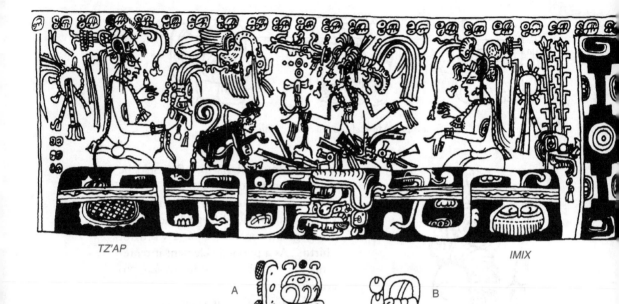

TZ'AP   IMIX

A   B

Figure. 2.11. **The Resurrection of the Corn God**, *cylindrical vase*

The sculpture was originally found by Alfred Maudslay in Copan at the beginning of the twentieth century. The archaeological setting in which it was found bears a close resemblance to the vase painting *The Resurrection of the Corn God* shown in figure 2.11. At Copan representations of *tun* or *cuauc* altar stones ornamented the exteriors of temples. Out of openings in their heads three-dimensional Corn Gods burst forth, this statue being one of them.

What is represented is the rebirth of the Sun God, *Hun Hunahpu*, father of the Hero Twins, as the Corn God. In the *Popul Vuh* his severed head symbolizes the harvested ear of corn and the maize seed planted beneath the surface of the Earth to rise from the underworld reborn and coming to fruition in the fields of this world. The idea is somewhat akin to the Christian Holy Communion. To the Maya corn is the mythological substance as well as the actual sustenance of mankind. The Corn God is known as *Ah Uaxac Yol Kauil*, an idea at the root of Maya religious thought. *Ah* means "he," *Uaxac* is "eight," the number of the Corn God and a reference to the doubling or coming to fruition of the number four which is the Sun God. *Yol* means "heart of," *Kaa* means "abundance" and *uil* is "sustenance."

In other reverential terms *uac*, the number six, is used as an analogy to a bursting forth in the four directions, zenith, and nadir. Notice too that in Maya cosmology the colors assigned to the four directions are red/east, white/north, black/west, and yellow/south. Corn appears in five colors—red, white, black, yellow, and a mottled form. Green, the color assigned to the center, is closely associated to the Corn God. It also happens to be at the center of the color spectrum.

The long wavy hair of the Corn God, representing cornsilk, is adorned with circles of jade. Maize, or corn, is called *tun*, which is also a word for stone in general and jade in particular. Jade symbolizes young maize, being green, and also means "precious." In the vase painting the artist repeats the hieroglyph *U Huntan*, the Precious One, across the top of the vase as a substitute for the P.S.S. For comparison I show other examples of this glyph in A and B. The Corn God in the sculpture wears bracelets composed of the Maya and Nahua graphic symbol meaning "gold," another precious substance associated with maize.

The theme of the dressing of the Corn God for his resurrection appears on numerous vases and was undoubtedly a major feature in theatrical performances of mythological events. The artist makes no attempt to portray the actual event, as the scene clearly takes place on a dais, a regular architectural feature of Maya structures and the probable stage for such performances. The platform is transformed into a panel representing the Earth in which we see the head of *Hun Hunahpu*, known as the First Father, and *Hun Nal Ye*, One Maize Revealed. The emerging foliation reaches fruition on the right as an elaboration of the glyph *Imix*, "waterlily," the first daysign of the calendar, the root

from which all things spring, embodying in Maya thought such concepts as beginning, Earth, water, and abundance. *Hun Nal Ye* is credited with making creation events happen. On the left the vegetation culminates in a glyph, *tz'ap*, which can mean "to place in the ground," "to set up," or "to plant."

Emerging from the head of *Hun Hunahpu* as if it were a seed, the Corn God blossoms forth, dressed for his resurrection by two goddesses as revealed by godmarks meaning "brightness" on their arms. The miraculous act of rebirthing, usually performed by the Hero Twins, is here shown being carried out by a monkey god, perhaps representing *Hun Hunahpu*'s first set of twins who are turned into monkeys in the *Popul Vuh*. The monkey, whose role on stage could be performed by an actual trained monkey, a dwarf, or a child, is shown displaying the "touching Earth" sign with his left hand and indicating "speech" or "talking" with his right as

Figure 2.12. **Chalchihuitlicue**, *panel from the Codex Fejérváry-Mayer. City of Liverpool Museum*

he reads from a codex the magical incantations that will restore *Hun Hunahpu* to life as the Corn God.

The hands of creation are evident in a panel from the Codex Fejérváry-Mayer, redrawn in figure 2.12, which illustrates the growth of the personified maize plant in a particularly favorable year when it is nourished by the fertility goddess of water, *Chalchihuitlicue*, She of the Jade Skirt. She bestows life on the corn plant by filling the fields with water in which the plant is seen to take root. She is adorned with water and rain symbols, notably the stream of water gushing from her head which manifests itself finally as a hand holding an overturned water jar. This is a symbol of the all-important rain gods, of which she is a consort.

In Yucatec and other Maya languages one of the terms for "hand" is *kab*, which is also a verb meaning "to make something with one's hands" or "to create." This is an extremely important symbol that carries the idea of the rain gods as makers of germination or of life in general, and as such will subsequently be discussed in detail. Here the descending waters are contrasted to the ascending flames, which rise from a ball of rubber incense, placed in a vessel containing an offering of a bundle of wood as the codex recommends on certain specified days. The magic plant and the goddess are focused on their offering. The contrasting relationship alluded to is between the incense burner known as the *tlemaitl*, or "hand of fire" in Nahuatl and the hand of water materialized above. The interaction of these venerated elements, fire and water, creates the heart of life itself and forms an underlying hidden substructure that will be seen to lie at the root of the Maya cosmovision.

In a wonderful painting of the Creation entitled *The Vase of the Seven Gods*, illustrated in figure 2.13, the dawning of the first day of this era is brought forth by an action of the hand of a god. The date given in the first two glyphs of the text is Four *Ahau*, Eight *Cumhu* or August 13, 3114 B.C. The next two glyphs, *tz'akahi ek u tan* state that "it was manifested or put in order in the center or place of blackness." In the creation passages of the *Popol Vuh* it is said,

And then came his word, he came here to the Sovereign Plumed Serpent, here in the blackness, in the early dawn. He spoke with the Sovereign Plumed Serpent, and they talked, then they thought, then they worried. They agreed with each other, they joined their words, their thoughts. Then it was clear, then they reached accord in the light, and then humanity was clear, when they conceived the growth, the generation of the trees, of humankind, in the blackness, in the early dawn, all because of the Heart of the Sky, named Hurricane. Thunderbolt Hurricane came first, the second is Newborn Thunderbolt and the third is Raw Thunderbolt.

So there were three of them, as the Heart of the Sky, who came to the Sovereign Plumed Serpent, when the Dawn of Life was conceived:

How should it be sown, how should it dawn? Who is to be the provider, the nurturer?

U-BAH	PLACE-NAME	MAH KINAH	NOMINAL	U-YAHAW-TE	A-YA	HOY-I	Y-UCH'AB Y-UTAL	TA TE'EL	TSIH	CACAO	CHAK CH'OK	KELEM

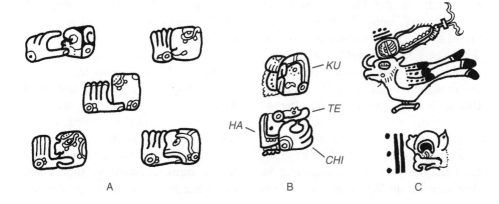

Figure 2.13. **The Vase of the Seven Gods**, *cylindrical vase*

Let it be this way, think about it: this water should be removed, emptied out for the formation of the Earth's own plate and platform, then comes the sowing, the dawning of the sky-Earth . . .

And then the Earth arose because of them, it was simply their word that brought it forth. For the forming of the Earth they said "Earth." It arose suddenly, just like a cloud, like a mist, now forming, unfolding. Then the mountains came forth. By their genius alone, by their cutting edge alone, they carried out the conception of the mountain plain, whose face grew instant groves of cypress and pine . . .

Such was the formation of the Earth when it was brought forth by the Heart of the Sky, the Heart of the Earth, as they are called, since they were the first to think of it. The sky was set apart, and the Earth was set apart in the midst of the waters.

In the painted version of the Creation we see Lord One Death, one of the principal gods of the underworld, sitting on the Jaguar Throne at the foot of which is a sacred bundle containing the glyph "star over Earth" or Venus, the Morning Star. At the unwrapping of the bundle of the Morning Star, the daybringer will bring about the unfolding of the Creation and set it into motion. The god responsible for the first act of creation is the Jaguar Paddler, first in the upper row of gods. He is one of two gods who symbolize the alternations of day and night which creates time. The signal for the dawning of light is given by Lord One Death as he raises his right hand forming a sign that in American Indian Sign Language means

"great star." This sign is usually preceded by the sign "night," which is made by a covering motion meaning "Earth covered over" but here the context is already provided. A brilliant star is signed by snapping the finger against the thumb while holding the hand to the sky, exactly the action shown here.

The paddlers are called *Chan Its'at*, Sky Creators. The Jaguar Paddler of the Night opens the sacred bundle. The Stingray Paddler of the Day is the last god in the lower row. His identity is revealed in two ways: Firstly, in a group setting the paddlers are usually shown positioned at the front and the back. An example of this, from one of the incised bones found in the tomb of *Hasaw-Kaan-Kauil,* is shown in figure 2.14. The ruler is shown in the center of the canoe, in the afterlife dressed as the Corn God. Other occupants, also weeping, are a dog, which usually accompanies the deceased in mythology, a parrot, a monkey, and an iguana lizard. The Jaguar Paddler is in front of the crew in this extraordinary canoe. The accompanying text (not shown) states that "he paddled eighty years to his death." The motion of paddling therefore connotes the movement of time.

Returning to figure 2.13, the Stingray Paddler's identity is most clearly revealed on the vase by the handsign he employs. At first I found this sign extremely perplexing, so its meaning eluded me for a long time. Actually the solutions to problems posed by the handsigns in the art are often the most simple and direct. Besides studying the known signs of American Indian Sign Language it is important to acquire a

Figure 2.14. Incised bone from the tomb of **Hasaw-Kaan-Kauil**

feel for the logic of the system and also one must visualize the signs as they are usually performed, that is, in motion. After some months of contemplating the possible meaning of this sign it suddenly occurred to me that the Stingray Paddler is simply doing what he is supposed to do—paddle. The device used is frequently employed by artists immersed in handsigning. The actual object is omitted and only the action of the hands using the object is shown. Frequently in portraits of *Hunahpu*, as One Blowgunner, that appear in glyphs where space is lacking, the action of blowgunning is shown by the hands, the object is omitted. The same condition exists here, and besides the artist wishes to emphasize the motion of turning. In creation texts it is stated that the sky "began to turn on the north axis." The circles, *pet*, "to turn," and the S-glyphs, *wak*, that appear in the sky band directly below the P.S.S. are the key elements of this phrase. The gods not only create the cosmos, they set it in motion.

Another handsign that initially posed a problem appears as a hieroglyph in the P.S.S. and can be seen in the extreme upper right-hand corner of the illustration and in A. The glyph has been reread by Nikola Grube as meaning *kelem*, "youth." I had been independently agonizing over its possible meaning for some years, sometimes wondering if a precise interpretation would ever come to light. I was not alone as speculation regarding this glyph began at the early part of this century.

Here again, the ultimate solution proved to be extremely simple. One day I was consulting Garrick Mallery's *Picture Writing of the American Indians* in regard to an entirely different matter. Mallery is unaware of the existence of the Maya hieroglyph when he opens a discussion on the relationship between various handsigns and graphic symbols meaning "child." He first points out that the Arapaho handsign for "child, baby" is the finger in the mouth and refers to a nursing child. He then shows that the sign is natural and universal, appearing in the sign language of the deaf and in Egyptian hieroglyphs and their hieratic forms as demonstrated by Champollion.

Both the subject matter and the texts for the most part are readily understood. Following the glyph for the "dark place" in the main text is a list of gods beginning with *Ku Chaanal*, the gods of the heavens, followed by a vertical column listing five other gods or groupings of gods beginning with *Ku Cabal*, the gods of the Earth. Next the god, *Bolon Oc Te*, He of the Nine (or innumerable) Strides, is listed followed by a god that Linda Schele has identified as *Ux-lut*, God Three-Born-Together, who is *Hun Nal Ye*, and whom she places in the middle of the lower row of gods. The last god listed is the Jaguar Paddler.

The glyphs for the gods immediately preceding the Jaguar Paddler still remain a problem. Although the sound of the names can be read as *Ku Ha Te Chi* (as shown in B), the exact identity of these gods has not been determined. I would suggest tentatively, but with some very good reasons, that these are the gods of the twenty daysigns. First of all let us consider the name itself. *Hal* can serve as the phonetic *ha* but it can also be interpreted literally as "twenty." The *te* sign appearing above the hand can mean "wood" but it is also known to serve as a numerical classifier. The *chi*-hand as we have seen is often a substitute for "sun" and by extension "day." The glyphs therefore could easily be interpreted as the Gods of the Twenty Days or the *Uinal*, so let's examine more closely the context in which they appear.

The formation of the twenty-day period is an important part of Maya creation mythology. A section of the *Chilam Balam* entitled "The creation of the *Uinal*" states,

This is a song of how the uinal *came to be created before the creation of the world. . . . This was the count, after it had been created by the day Thirteen* Oc *. . . after they had departed there in the east. Then he spoke its name when the day had no name. . . . The* uinal *was created, the day, as it was called, was created, heaven and Earth were created, the stairway of water, the earth, rocks, and trees; the things of the sea and the things of the land were created.*

On One Chuen *he raised himself to his divinity, after he had made heaven and Earth.*

On Two Eb *he made his first stairway. It descended from the midst of the heavens, in the midst of the water, where there were neither earth, rocks, or trees.*

On Three Ben *he made all things, as many as there are, the things of the heavens, the things of the sea, and the things of the Earth.*

On Four Ix *sky and Earth were tilted.*

On Five Men *he made everything. . . .*

The uinal *was created, the Earth was created; sky, earth, trees, and rocks were set in order; all things were created by our Lord God, the Father. Thus he was there in his divinity, in the clouds, alone, and by his own effort, when he created the entire world, when he moved in the heavens in his divinity. Thus he ruled in his great power. Every day is set in order according to the count, beginning in the east, as it is arranged.*

There are only minor variations between this account of the Creation and that found in the *Popol Vuh*. The *Chilam Balam* emphasizes the creation of the *uinal* as the foundation of the

Creation; *The Vase of the Seven Gods* contains elements of both versions. Adjacent to the glyphs *Ku Ha Te Chi* is the platform upon which the gods of the upper row sit. It consists of a panel of twenty "eye" symbols. Graphically these can be compared to the two disembodied eyes that appear along with crossed bones directly above the right hand of Lord One Death and that are symbols of the god of sacrificial death. If we bear in mind that a title of *Kinich Ahau*, the Sun God, is Lord of the Solar Eye, it is highly likely that the twenty eyes represent the *uinal*.

Furthermore if we follow the artist's line of vision along the panel and extend it beyond the glyphs that I think represent the gods of the twenty daysigns, we come to another bundle resting on the Jaguar Throne directly behind Lord One Death. This bundle contains the daysign *Imix*, the first day in the standard calendrical sequence of daysigns and the day which will immediately follow *Ahau*, the day of the Creation. The gods not only create time as the sky "began to turn on the north (or vertical) axis," they order time on the plane of the ecliptic as "Every day is set in order according to the count. . . ."

An alligator is seen perched on the roof of the temple of the Jaguar Throne and also one is peering out from its base. The alligator is closely associated with the daysign *Imix*. As we have seen in the opening panel of the Codex Nuttall the alligator is the first daysign in the Nahua arrangement of daysigns, which closely parallels the Maya sequence. In creation mythology the Earth is the back of a gigantic alligator that emerges from the primal ocean. In the night sky the alligator is seen in the Milky Way, which may account for the *Imix* signs appearing at the beginning and end of the sky band on the vase.

In this painting the artist has managed to summarize Maya cosmology, at the center of which is the *Wakah-Chan*, Six-Sky or Raised-Up-Sky, the tree at the center of the world. The concept is imbedded in the composition of the painting. The horizontal axis of the Maya world is formed by the four cardinal directions and related to the four extreme positions of the Sun's risings and settings on the horizon. The Sun's movement from east to west along the ecliptic creates the days and forms the horizontal axis of the composition.

In the beginning was the Lying-Down-Sky wherein heaven and Earth were not separated and no light could enter. The miracle of Creation was performed by setting the Raised-Up-Sky, forming the vertical axis relating to north and south, zenith and nadir; thus Six-Sky came into being. The nine layers of the underworld, the plane of the Earth, and the thirteen layers of the heavens are the three basic realms of the cosmos. These are united the *Wakah-Chan*, the World Tree, which unites the three realms by traversing through them at the center. The World Tree is a central portal affording human communion with the divine. On the spiritual plane it is personified as *Hun Nal Ye*, the First Father, who is sometimes referred to as *Wak Chan Uinic*, Raised-Up-Sky Lord. In the human realm the tree is personified as the king.

In the painting, the World Tree is

symbolized by the staff erected at the foot of the throne. At the base the nine layers of the underworld are represented. The upper portion, counting the foliating leaves at the top, represents the thirteen layers of the heavens. A further reference to the thirteen heavens is the muan bird appearing in the headdress of Lord One Death. Another rendering of this remarkable creature and his glyphs are shown in C. He is a horned owl known as *Ox Lahun Chan*, Thirteen Sky, or *Ah Coo Akab*, the Mad One of the Night. He as a personification of the night sky perches over the thirteen heavens.

We can now understand more clearly the visual strategy employed by the artist in rendering the sacred bundle containing the Morning Star. The bundle is shown at the foot of the World Tree and then ascends along the vertical axis to reappear on top of the platform in the hands of the Jaguar Paddler. Also on this vertical axis, appearing directly above the Jaguar Paddler, is the head glyph of *Yahaw-Te*, the Lord of the World Tree. By comparing the head glyph with the face of the deity who occupies the middle position in the upper row of gods, he can be identified as *Yahaw-Te*. Behind him is a god who wears a conch shell in his headdress, the primary symbol of *Pauahtun*, who as the deity who bestows order in the universe would be very likely to make an appearance at the Creation, as would *Cimi*, the Lord of Death and a close associate of the muan bird. He is the first god in the lower row, identifiable by his most salient feature, the fleshless jawbone. He presides over the lowest of the

CIMI   SAK
IK   OL
WAY   A-YA   XU-BAL   HOY-

nine underworlds and the artist refers to this by portraying him pointing to the lowest rung of the World Tree staff. He thus reiterates a fundamental theme that pervades Maya philosophy—life emerges from the seed of death.

All the gods on this extraordinary

Figure 2.15. **The Descent of the Goddess**, *rollout of cylindrical vase*

vase have now been identified. However an account of the Creation would not be complete without a reference to the *Oxib Xk'ub*, "the three hearth stones," which were born or set up as the first act of Creation. It was Matt Looper, a student of Linda Schele, who first saw the

stars in these stones. The Quiché Maya envision a triangle in the constellation Orion composed of the stars Alnitak, Saiph, and Rigel and representing the typical Maya kitchen fireplace. The great nebula M42 is seen as the flame in the center of this celestial analog of the hearth. The Three Stones of Creation are referred to in the *Chilam Balam* as the *Yax Ux Tun Nal*, the First Three Stones Place, and they appear in the painting as three *tun* altar stones set up directly behind the Jaguar Throne. It is astonishing that these stars are found in the Maya constellation *Aac*, the Turtle—what we call the belt of Orion—and that they were at zenith at dawn on the Maya day of Creation.

In Yucatec the verb *ah* means "to dawn" and "to create." The Turtle God is a deity of rebirth who presides over and represents the *a* sound, which, in the vast majority of the world's languages, including our own, is the first or primal sound. The turtle's head denotes the *a* sound in the *ay-a* glyph introducing the P.S.S. on the vase, meaning "It came into existence." Following it is the verb *hoy-i*, "was blessed or made proper." This verb is rendered either by a head glyph of the god *Pauahtun* or a glyph showing a temple or pyramid as seen here. The artist has cleverly incorporated a shell design, the principal symbol of *Pauahtun*, in this version of the glyph, echoing the shell design appearing in the headdress of *Pauahtun* in his portraiture in the painting.

The sequence continues with *y-uch'ab*, "his drinking vessel," *ta y-utal*, "for his sustenance," *tsih te'el cacao*, "tree fresh cacao." The remaining glyphs are descriptive of the person who owns the vase. *Chak ch'ok kelem* describes him as a "great lineage member youth." The verb *u-bah* means "he went" and is followed by what I suppose is a placename. Then there is a title, *Mah Kinal*, "great sun," the person's

name-glyph, and then another title, *U-Yahaw-Te*, Tree Lord. The Tree Lord referred to here is different from but related to the lord of the tree at the center of the world who appears in the creation scene. The genealogical tree of the royal family connects the ancestors at its roots with the contemporary Maya rulers—its flowers—in the same way that the World Tree connects the realms of the cosmos. The artist is aware of this relationship, as the Tree Lord glyph appears directly above the portrait of *Yahaw-Te*.

We can now arrive at a comprehensive understanding of the significance of *The Vase of the Seven Gods*. The apparent placename mentioned in the P.S.S. is not a geographical location but a supernatural place. In these instances the person referred to has passed away. The artist was commissioned to create an object that would be the central focus of a funerary rite. It may have been used only once, then deposited with the remains of the deceased. The *its'at* carefully chose the creation theme to remind the grieving participants in the ritual that the end of one time cycle is the beginning of another, just as the end of an individual's life is the commencement of another in an infinite cycle. In doing so, the artist not only has provided us with a marvelously executed depiction of the dawn of the Creation. We are also given an intimate insight into the most important aspect of any culture: We see the way the ancient Maya perceived the relationship between life and death.

Many parallels exist between *The Vase of the Seven Gods* and *The Descent of the Goddess,* illustrated in figure 2.15. Both scenes apparently take place at a time prior to the emergence of the Earth and the creation of humanity. The mythologies are acted out in a dark place before the unveiling of light in the *Seven Gods* and in a watery place before the separation of the land and the ocean in *The Descent.* Both vases probably served a funerary function.

The setting of *The Descent of the Goddess* is a panoramic view of the primordial ocean divided into upper and lower regions separated by a sky band representing the ecliptic and divided into nine segments. In the illustration the first segment is the Sun followed by probable Mars and Mercury symbols. Next comes Jupiter and Venus and then a repetition of the Mercury and Jupiter signs. The next sign contains bands thought to represent the crossing of the Milky Way with the plane of the ecliptic and finally a sign that I think is likely to represent a phase of the Moon. Interspersed throughout the scene are circular devices called "chalchimites," a word derived from the Nahuatl *chalchihuitl,* the precious jade, symbolic of water. The artist has used these to create a bubbly underwater effect that evokes the dreamtime realm of the gods in which the mythological episode takes place. These are also symbols closely associated with the Moon Goddess who is the central actor in the painting.

Presiding over the upper register are the sky gods: *Kinich Ahau,* the Sun God, and at the opposite end of the sky band, the Moon Goddess, his wife. The polarity expressed here is fundamental to Mesoamerican cosmologies. The direction of east is male and corresponds to the Sun and fire, while west is female, lunar, and related to water. It does not matter at all that the illustration is actually a rollout of a cylindrical vase on which the Sun God and the Moon Goddess are positioned back-to-back. The patterns of spacial organization reflect cosmological principles deeply ingrained in the consciousness of the *its'at* and are remarkably consistent in all forms of Mesoamerican art.

The Moon Goddess has a litany of names and she takes different forms or aspects relating to the various phases of the Moon. As a water goddess she presides over all that is aquatic including the *temazcalli* or "bathhouse," rains, rivers, waterfalls, floods, and lakes, as well as the primordial ocean. The association between the Moon and water is strongly reinforced by the recognition of the lunar effect on tides. After forty years of research into comparative religion, Mircia Eliade concluded that the cycles of the Moon—its birth, growth, death, and rebirth—reflect in a profound way the cycles of human existence. *The Descent* is a prime example of a symbolic narrative that accounts for the lunar cycle in purely mythological terms. In it the Moon is personified in two aspects. In the upper register on the right she is the First Mother whose avatar appears to humanity as the full moon. She is known as the Midwife, the Matchmaker, Our Grandmother, Mistress Mother in the Heart of the Sky, as well as numerous other appellations. In the lower register she reappears in front of the Jaguar Throne in her role as divine matchmaker. In her headdress is a very elaborate *sac* or "white" glyph identifying her as the White Goddess. The descending lunar goddess on the left is a personification of the phases of the Moon. In this aspect she is *Ix Chel*, She of the Rainbow, a consort of *Itzamna*.

In order to fully appreciate this remarkable painting it is necessary to recognize some basic facts regarding the appearance of the Moon in the sky. The first or new crescent of the Moon always appears near the western horizon after being "lost," disappearing in the Sun for one, two, and sometimes three days in each month. We know from the inscriptions that this was carefully observed and recorded by the Maya. As the Moon seems to be drawing continually further away from the Sun, it appears for a longer time in the sky with an ever-enlarging crescent. It gradually enlarges to the shape of a half-moon, then a full moon; then it begins to diminish again to crescent form, rising later and later in the night sky as it approaches the Sun's rising position in the east. In its final phases it rises at dawn just before the Sun, the last glimpse being seen on the eastern horizon before its period of invisibility.

The mythological episode described in the painting accounts for these last phases. The Lunar Goddess is seen in the east embraced by the Sun God before descending into the underworld where her absence is explained by her marriage to *Itzamna*, Lord of the Milky Way, who is known to be her consort. The story begins in the upper right-hand corner where the First Mother, as matchmaker, engages in a conversation with two *Ikil*, wind gods who serve as messengers. The first of these has "god-marks" signifying *ik*, "wind," "life," or "spirit." The other has *Cimi* or "death" markings. These are portal gods. The discussion concerns the descent, as indicated by the action of the First Mother's left hand.

The next gods are aspects of *Pauahtun*. These are clearly identified by *tun*, stone markings, and the waterlily headdresses. The *Pauahtun* is portrayed in animated conversation with the Sun God. The artist creates a cinematic effect by first showing the god displaying a handsign meaning "to talk." In this sign words are "thrown out" as emphasized by the "wind" sign emerging from the deity's mouth. The next handsign is a salutation and the "wind" sign is replaced by glyphs addressing the Sun God. The subject matter of the conversation, the descent, is shown by the next handsign followed by the method through which the descent takes place. The *Pauahtun* makes the "breaking" handsign, opening a portal in the sky-band that allows the Moon Goddess to descend into the underworld. His left hand displays the sacred handsign of the Moon Goddess.

The descent is shown by a juxtaposition of successive phases in the movement of a single body. A descending celestial object, here personified, is portrayed traversing layers of the cosmos in the same way a human shaman would do. The goddess seems to swim or float in an ecstasy of dance closely imitating a universal human shamanistic ritual in which the trance state is accompanied by a sensation of swimming. At the break are the glyphs "sky" and "lady" or "goddess." Above the altar at the foot of her descent is the *Wakah-Chan*, Raised-Up-Sky Place, glyph. The goddess descends into the underworld through the portal of the World Tree, the same path of entry used by both shamans and the dead. Before the altar are jars, the chief symbol of the Moon Goddess and the origin of her glyph, which can be seen between the hands of *Itzamna.*

In depicting the descent the artist has explored visual devices that would not appear in Western European art until 1912 when Marcel Duchamp painted his famous *Nude Descending a Staircase, No. 2.* This work caused a sensation at the Armory Show in New York in 1913, being considered a vision entirely novel in painting. Maya artists had in fact been concerned with depicting movement in such a way for many centuries.

In the marriage scene that takes place in the underworld the artist continues to explore the juxtaposition of successive phases of movement. We see *Pauahtun,* the numen of the interior of the Earth, presiding over the ceremony. He raises his right hand in a gesture of presentation to *Itzamna.* In the Codex Nuttall the offering of a *xocolli* or blanket appears at the ascent of Eight Wind, as we have seen in figure 2.3 and again later in the codex (p. 19) at the marriage ceremony of Twelve Wind and Three Flint. Also presiding over the marriage is the First Mother, Patroness of Matchmakers, shown seated in front of the Jaguar Throne. With her right hand she seals the marriage in

a handsign meaning "alliance," which we saw earlier in the Codex Nuttall (figure 20D). Directly above her handsign are two glyphs that can be read *na-ah-wah. Nawah* in Maya dictionaries is a verb meaning "to dress," referring to a special "dressing" for events such as marriage, which is certainly what is indicated here. These glyphs may also represent the name of the Moon Goddess.

In marriage ceremonies in the Codex Nuttall the bride and groom are frequently depicted pointing at each other. These gestures mean "to take" and they can be seen in the animated dialogue that takes place between *Ix Chel* and *Itzamna.*

The P.S.S. on this vase begins with the introductory *a-ya,* "it came into being," placed directly above the descent of the goddess. Unusually, it is followed by *xu-bal,* "it's writing" or "it's finishing," which allows the next glyph *hoy-i,* "was blessed," featuring the head glyph of *Pauahtun,* to appear above his portraiture in the vase. The next three glyphs are the *u ts'ib nahal* phrase meaning "it was painted" and *y-uch'ab,* "his drinking vessel." Following this is *ta y-utal kakaw,* "for his sustenance cacao." As can be expected the next glyphs are titles, names, and places beginning with *chak ch'ok ah lats,* "great lineage member, he of the generations." The place specified is not presently identifiable, but judging from certain elements in the glyphs it seems to be a supernatural location. One of the glyphs contains the *Cimi* and *ik* signs that appear on the wind gods' markings, and the next glyph contains *sac,* "white," or "pure." This could be a supernatural location called *sac ol way*, "pure spirit of the portal."

The deceased person mentioned in the sequence was obviously respected and loved by relatives and friends. The artist chosen to do the funerary vase was among the most talented of all the great Maya artists, and subsequently we will be reviewing another magnificent work emanating from this painter's brush. The theme presented would have been quite appropriate for a funeral ceremony. The mythology invoked represents a happy event expressing the harmony of opposing forces in nature. *Kinich Ahau* is obviously a fire symbol and *Itzamna* is known as Lord of the Fire. Both are worshiped as sons of *Hunab Ku* and are manifestations of the supreme and only god. Both are married to aspects of the Lunar Goddess who is intimately related to water, so the marriage is a metaphor of the union of opposites. The artist introduces the theme of life in death with the wind gods in the opening of the narrative, which unfolds in an anticlockwise motion around the vase. The cycle of the Moon, like the cycles of the Sun and Venus, is recalled in typical Maya fashion as a metaphor of the eternal cycles of creation, growth, death, and final resurrection.

The narrative ends with a series of eight glyphs that form an *ik* sign behind *Itzamna*. The last glyphs in this format make up the word *its'at* and probably end in the artist's signature. It is obvious that the *its'at* is not a mere painter of decorative pictures but is rather a sage fully versed in and capable of commenting on mythological subjects as well as profound religious doctrine. Skilled in both the arts of painting and writing, an *its'at* also utilized a knowledge of one of the fundamental tools used by the Maya in the exploration of the hidden cycles and process of nature: a mastery of the laws governing the use of number.

Figure 3.1. **Pauahtun Emerging from the Shell**, *vase. National Museum, Mexico City*

THE HANDS OF TIME

A truly great work of art should be simple enough to fascinate a child, yet so profoundly deep in meaning that it is capable of gradually unfolding an inner truth and beauty that becomes more and more apparent to even the most sophisticated viewer throughout the vicissitudes of time. *Pauahtun Emerging from the Shell*, illustrated in figure 3.1, aptly fulfills these requirements. When I first saw this vase at the National Museum in Mexico City in 1966 I was awestruck by its simple and yet marvelously enchanted elegance. After decades of research into Mesoamerican art, I came to realize that this highly imaginative and evocative work is uniquely astonishing. This artist has managed to succinctly enshrine deeply spiritual concepts that form the very basis of Maya cosmology and religious thought.

Among the many extraordinary cultural achievements of the Maya is the infusion of advanced theological ideology directly into a highly evolved mathematical system. Within this development the shell functions as both a primary emblem of divinity and a fundamental arithmetic symbol without in any sense changing its mean-

Figure 3.2. The hieroglyph of the month **Kayab**

ing. The origin of the shell's role in Maya iconography lies in their observation of the apparent motion of the Sun as it changes its positions on the horizon throughout the year.

At spring equinox the Sun's position on the horizon will be due east when rising and due west at setting. From this time the Sun's positions on the horizon will vary widely each day. As the days lengthen the positions move northward until at summer solstice extreme rising and setting positions are reached in the northeast and northwest. Approaching this time the Sun's positions on the horizon vary less and less until during the period around the solstice the Sun appears to slow down practically to a standstill. Hence the word "solstice," meaning "sun still."

To symbolize this time of year the ancient Maya used a universal symbol for slowness, the turtle. We know this because in the ideal 365-day agricultural calendar, the *Haab*, the summer solstice falls in the seventeenth month, *Kayab*. The mainsign for the hieroglyph of this month, shown in figure 3.2, is the head of a turtle. In some Maya languages this month is known as *K'anasi* and in these instances the turtle serves a dual purpose: The sun emblem provides the phonetic *K'an* while the turtle supplies the *ah* sound. The patroness of this month is the young Moon Goddess.

After the summer solstice the Sun's rising and setting positions move southward, again varying until it appears due east and west at the autumnal equinox. At the winter solstice the opposing extreme positions are reached in the southeast and the southwest and the Sun's positions again appear to come to a standstill. To symbolize this period the Maya used another universal symbol of slowness—the snail. The winter solstice falls in the seventh month of the *Haab* known as *Yaxkin* or New Sun. Variations of glyphs for this month are shown in figure 3.3; here again the Maya artist displays an amazing versatility in providing signs that simultaneously have both symbolic meanings and phonetic values. The *Yax* sign in A is clearly a shell but it also provides the sound of the word meaning "fresh" or "new." In B the shell symbol is omitted and another phonetic for *Yax* is used; cords are added symbolizing the strong rays of the Sun which occur during this dry season. These also serve phonetically to emphasize the *n* sound in *kin*. In contrast to the young lunar goddess who is

Figure 3.3. The hieroglyph of the month **Yaxkin**

*Figure 3.4. The hieroglyph **Wayeb***

the patroness of *Kayab*, the patron of *Yaxkin* is the old solar god.

The *Haab* is composed of eighteen months of twenty days ($18 \times 20 = 360$). The last five days are a mysterious period known as *Wayeb*. Among other things *way* means "to sleep" or "to dream." The glyph shown in figure 3.4 has a shell sign above a *tun* or year symbol. The patron of this dreamtime of the year is *Pauahtun*.

The solstices are viewed as portals in both time and space. The corresponding symbols generated become fundamental in the essentially shamanistic Maya cosmovision. The crossband pattern formed by the Sun at its extreme positions on the horizon is not merely an emblem. When the center is added, it becomes the quincunx planigram, the basis for age-old rituals that serve as entrances allowing access to the ancestors and the spirit world. Central to Maya religious ceremony throughout the 3700 years of its existence as a cultural entity, and indeed the focus of the modern Maya shaman, is the setting up of an altar mimicking this pattern.

In modern ceremonies the shaman lays out the solstitial locations with special stones creating an altar. When the central stone is set up, the shaman has

"opened a path" to the Otherworld. The central stone is regarded as the center of the cosmos and it is the equivalent of the World Tree through which the shaman communicates with beings in the spirit world. The center and the solstitial points are divine portals of transformation in both space and time. As such their accompanying symbols, the shell and the quincunx pattern, gain an extended and much deeper range of meanings.

As a portal, the winter solstice is viewed as both an ending and a beginning. Death too is viewed as a portal in the mind of the Maya. In one of the hieroglyphs meaning "death," *och be*, shown in figure 3.5A, the mainsign is the quincunx pattern, which carries the phonetic value *be* meaning "road." The spiral form gives *och*, "to enter" and the shell below is a determinative, but it also could be read here as *och*. Literally, "to die" means "to enter the road," and we are beginning to see how the shell becomes the arithmetic symbol for zero and why it appears in the glyph for the end of the year, *Wayeb*.

Traditionally a central portal of communion with the divine lies at the south end of the Milky Way when it stands erect in its north-south path. It is the road taken by the dead in the afterlife and mythologically it is the path

A   B

*Figure 3.5. The hieroglyph **och be***

taken by the Hero Twins when they go to confront the gods in the underworld. Besides being viewed as the World Tree, the Milky Way is symbolized as a divine serpent. In glyph B (fig. 3.5) the snake's head is substituted for the quincunx pattern and can be either read phonetically as *be* or interpreted symbolically. To be perfectly clear the artist inserts a *be* sign in the eye of the snake. In both instances the shell transmits the idea of a portal.

Pauahtun, Lord of the Shell and all beginnings and endings, is the chief orderer of the Maya cosmos and as such becomes the patron god of mathematics. He manifests himself in a pattern of fourfold beings who rule over the solstitial points or four corners of the world. These are the places that set limitations on the Sun's path and thereby establish order in the universe. Here the old *Pauahtun* and his manifestations are responsible for holding the Earth above the abysmal waters of the underworld. Counterparts are young gods. A *Bacab*, "stood-up-person," holds the sky above the Earth in each of the four cardinal directions. As bearers of the Earth and sky these deities are considered sacred beings who "allow entrance" through portals of space and time. An understanding of their various symbols goes a long way toward a comprehension of the fundamentals of Maya art, science, and religion, which form a unity embodied in the character of *Pauahtun* himself.

In one of his earliest appearances in Maya art, shown in figure 3.6A,

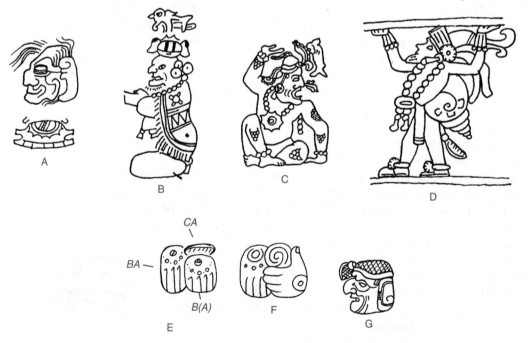

Figure 3.6. Portraits of **Pauahtun** and related glyphs

Pauahtun is readily identified by an accompanying turtle carapace glyph. These glyphs are part of a text engraved on a conch shell trumpet dating from the Early Classic Period, A.D. 300 to 500. The text describes a ritual invoking the Vision Serpent, and the presence of these glyphs assures the reader that "it was in order, it had been made proper." The shell contains a mirror sign meaning "brightness" and hence "holy." Contacting the Vision Serpent requires opening a portal, a primary role of *Pauahtun*.

To the ancient Maya shells, besides functioning as jewelry, were considered sacred objects and religious symbols of key importance. In the creation mythology the first created image was the constellation *Ac*, "turtle," the three stars in the belt of Orion. The hieroglyph *Ac* has the head of a turtle and carries the phonetic value *ah*. In Yucatec the verb *ah* means "to dawn" and "to create."

In the full-figure portrait shown in C, *Pauahtun*, wearing a shell pendant, is covered with god-markings derived from the *Cauac* sign. The glyph for the *Haab* or *tun*—year—is a metaphoric representation of a year as being a combination of a wet and a dry season. The *Cauac* sign symbolizing the rains and the cords is the rays of the Sun. As a stone is ritually erected at the end of a year, by extension the *Cauac* sign can mean "stone." The calculating year of 360 days, a *tun*, is the great base of all Maya time and chronology and can symbolize time itself. In the portrait in B, *Pauahtun* wears a headdress composed of another glyph meaning *tun*, surmounted by a bird symbolizing the passage of time, which he both orders and measures.

In D *Pauahtun* is shown in his Atlantean role of upholding the Earth. There is an amazing parallelism here with the god Atlas of Greek mythology. As punishment for taking part in a war against Zeus, Atlas, a marine creation, was turned into a rocky mountain and condemned to support the pillars that hold heaven and Earth apart.

Pauahtun is not lacking in aquatic features. Besides wearing a seashell in C, he wears the headdress of Maya nobility, the fish nibbling on a waterlily. He is also the patron of *Imix*, the first daysign in the calendar. The glyph of this day is the waterlily, the root from which all things spring, embodying such concepts as beginning, Earth, water, and abundance. It is the glyph that appears most frequently in Maya writing and it is probably the most versatile. In E it is shown functioning both phonetically, carrying the value *ba*, and symbolically in the glyph *bacab*, which can mean a god but also a title bestowed on rulers, priests, and artists in the ancient texts. With a manifesting hand in F, it means "first-born."

The sequence of twenty daysigns beginning with *Imix* contains within it another sequence of thirteen daysigns or daysign patrons who are the *Oxlahun Ti Ku*, the thirteen gods of number. In this sequence the first daysign becomes the fifth and its patron *Pauahtun* becomes the personification of the number five. The Maya system of counting originates from the hand, five being the basic ordering principle, besides being the number generated by the four sol-

Figure 3.7. Variations of the glyph "zero"

stitial points and the navel of the universe at the center. As God of Five *Pauahtun* will be depicted wearing a *tun* headdress, the crown of a master time reckoner, which alludes to the latter part of his name.

In his role as high shaman, *Pauahtun* dons the *pauah* or net-bag headdress of the artists, the first part of his name. His glyph, in G, is a head portrait with the characteristic headdress and shell earflare, the shell being that which opens into the otherworld and the sacred space of the First Father and the First Mother. In texts this glyph can become a verb that is often substituted for by the *hoy-i* glyph meaning "to bless, to dedicate." *Pauahtun* is a unique and special god whose origins arise not from the consciousness of agricultural or hunting societies, but rather from the needs of a literate and learned elite class. In essence he is a master shaman, supreme *its'at*, who by his very presence ensouls people, places, and objects with divinity, thus—"he who makes things holy."

A god even more closely associated with the shell and perhaps a personification of the shell itself is the God of Zero, the embodiment of transcendence. Not being a number, despite having extremely significant numerical

functions, this god is not one of the *Oxlahun Ti Ku*. He is not a bearer of time, rather he transforms it to increasingly higher levels. The glyph "zero" will always be painted red, and it appears in the codices as a shell as shown in figure 3.7. In the mind of the Maya, rather than representing "nothing," zero is a symbol that a count has evolved or spiraled to a higher level. When it appears in the names of gods, people, places, or nodes of time it signifies transformation. As either a numerical sign or a spiritual symbol, it functions as a portal, a gateway to a higher plane. A salient feature of the shell is emptiness.

Since sacrifice is viewed as the means of advancement on the spiritual plane, zero has a dual role, also being the God of Sacrifice. In a portrait taken from an Aztec codex figure 3.8 shows *Quetzalcoatl* wearing the pendant of the spiral wind jewel of life, a shell. In his left hand he holds a sacrificial victim

Figure 3.8. **Quetzalcoatl**, *from an Aztec codex*

while his right hand displays the shell as a symbol of sacrifice.

One of the finest and most informative portraits of the God of Zero is the sculpture of his head in figure 3.9A. The placing of the hand over the jaw indicates a particularly gruesome form of human sacrifice practiced by the Maya, the removal of the jawbone of a living victim, which results in certain death. The god's hair is bound in the manner of a sacrificial victim who has been dressed for this ceremony.

Some of the symbols carved in this remarkable sculpture have phonetic values and can be reread. In the diadem crowning the forehead of the God of Zero there is the spiral-shell form we have already seen in figure 3.5 which may be read as *och*, "to enter." By way of reinforcing this the diadem is mounted on a headband that consists of the rattles, *och* in Maya languages, of a rattlesnake. The diadem is surrounded by a "death-eye" motif. The dismembered eye represents the sacrifice of superficial external vision for the internal vision of reality constantly sought by the Maya mystic. This all-seeing eye can be seen in some of the graphic versions of the God of Zero shown in B.

Of paramount importance is the sacred mudra of the God of Zero which is simply the handsign equivalent of the snail shell; it carries all its symbolic significance as well as being the gesture that indicates *mi*, *lub*, or "zero" in Maya languages. (As I explained in the introduction, I had independently come to the conclusion that this sign must represent zero. Dispelling any reasonable doubts, I have recently been informed by

A

B   C

D   ZERO   DAYS
                  E

Figure 3.9. **The God of Zero**, *stone sculpture and related glyphs*

Figure 3.10. **Buluc Chabtan**, *codex portrait*

the writer Barbara Hand Clow that the handsign is still in current use by the contemporary Maya and it has retained its ancient meaning.) Consistent with the method generally used in American Indian Sign Language, the hand simply mimics the most characteristic attributes of the animal being signified. Here the hand is curved to resemble the snail shell, the thumb touching the middle and ring fingers. The small finger and the index finger are extended and contracted to represent the moving tentacles.

The fire drilling scene shown in figure 3.10 is a rebus for the "act of casting a prognostication." In it, another sacrificial deity, the *Buluc Chabtan*, uses both the *mi*-hand and the *chi*-hand to produce the word *chich*, which means "prognostication," exactly what the accompanying text is about. It should be noticed that in placing his hand over his jaw, the God of Zero will often form the *mi*-hand, strongly reinforcing the meaning of the gesture. It will be found that the interpretation of the meaning of this hand is highly productive and its uses

are logical and consistent throughout all forms of Maya art.

In the ever-fascinating world of Maya art, the hand is used in other ways to produce different words that are the equivalent of "zero." Some samples are shown in figure 3.11. The glyph in A depicts a sun with a closing hand facing downward. The meaning here, "day is done," is quite obvious. The glyph in B is part of a large count of days wherein there are no individual days to be counted as all are accounted for in higher groupings. The hand used is apparently derived from the sign language in which "gone" is expressed by holding the flat right hand in front of the body and raising the fingers to the front and upward. It is also illustrative of the handsign for "no," in which the extended flat right hand is held facing left in front of the body. It is then swung to the right with the back downward and returned to the original position. Again, rather than trying to grasp the procedure cerebrally, it is more advantageous to actually perform these signs with the hands.

Most handsigns move. The manograph is simply the written form of a handsign. The writer transforms a moving sign into a static visible expression so that the written form is in fact a contraction. Handsigns are the great mother of communication. Whether we are aware of it or not, all humans handsign every day, and handsigns played a major role in the origin of writing. The beauty of Maya writing is that in it these origins have to a large extent been retained. The same may be said for Chinese characters, but here again this feature is generally overlooked.

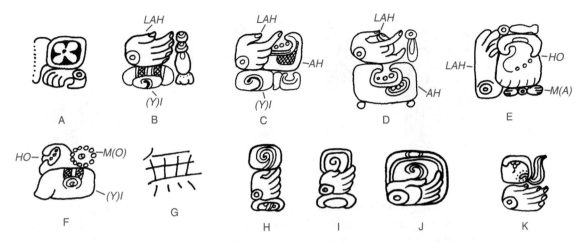

Figure 3.11A-K. Glyphs expressing the ending of time periods; G is the Chinese character MU

The *lah*-hand in B not only express-es the act of discarding but it also has a phonetic value, the *lah* root meaning "to end" or "to finish." The word *lah-i* means "completed," usually referring to a time period. To render the i-sound the artist writes the phonetic *yi* sign and the reader is expected to surmise that the y is not pronounced. A possible hypothe-sis is that the dangling tassel figure may carry a phonetic value of *la*; if so, the addition of the phonetic helps distin-guish the *lah*-hand from the *tzuk*-hand, a hand that presents but is practically identical to the *lah*-hand.

The glyphs C and D translate as "was or were completed." The addition of the phonetic *ah* changes a verb into the past tense. I believe however that the *ah* phonetic in the glyphs in C and D serves a double function. These glyphs exemplify the Maya artist's love of variation and play in glyph construc-tion. In C instead of the expected *lah*-hand, the artist has substituted a *hom*-hand. As we shall see in subsequent chapters, this handsign forms an impor-tant verb in the writing system. In Yucatec and Chol, *hom* means "to end," "to finish," or "to demolish." It is an-other way of expressing the ending of a time period; however, I think that by at-taching the *ah* phonetic to the hand, the artist is cautioning us that although the meaning of the handsign is intended, the pronunciation of the glyph as *lah-i* should be retained. In D, the same pro-cess is even more evident, especially if my hypothesis that the dangling tassel carries the phonetic value of *la* is cor-rect. Here the artist playfully substitutes the *mi*-hand for the *lah*-hand but through the clever use of phonetics in-forms us that the glyph is to be read *lah*.

It is remarkable that all these glyphs refer to various time periods that have "zeroed out" or risen to higher levels or groupings. When the same handsign is applied to spiritual concepts it retains this same fundamental meaning. Sacri-fice is the means of rising to a higher level; it implies "entering" and therefore

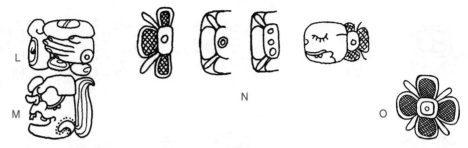

Figure 3.11 L-O. Glyphs expressing the ending of time periods and completion

the shell is the symbol of the sacred portal. I know of no other culture that has achieved such a close integration of spiritual and mathematical thought.

In order to express the time in which a period will end in a date to come, the future suffix *-om* is added to the *lah*-hand rendering *lah-om*, "will be completed" as shown in E. The phonetic values of the handsigns in glyph blocks can be established because they are sometimes conveniently substituted for by using purely phonetic glyphs and these glyphs may appear in exactly the same contexts. *Homi*, a Maya word for "complete," is rendered phonetically in F. The glyph is used at time period endings, anniversaries of rulership, and even life endings.

Whereas there is no controversy whatsoever among epigraphers regarding the translation of the completion glyph into English, considerable confusion arises in providing the Maya word represented by this very important glyph. Equally valid arguments can be presented for a *lah-i*, *tzutzah*, or *homi* pronunciation. In translations the Maya word is usually simply left out or the wrong word *tzuk* is presented (please excuse the pun). The solution to the

problem is quite simple, but it took me a few years to figure it out. The fact is that in the classic Maya world pronunciations of a glyph could vary, but the meaning did not.

A similar situation arises in regard to the Chinese characters. Let us consider for example the character *mu*, "nothing," shown in G. The origin of this character has long eluded scholars, but it actually is a manograph representing a waving hand. It may be pronounced differently in various parts of China or in Korea or Japan, but it will always retain the same meaning regardless of any linguistic variables. The written word becomes a great unifying factor. In the Orient it is wonderful to see people from various countries who speak different languages communicating by indicating Chinese characters on the palm of the hand.

In H, I, and J, the completion glyph is shown as it appears at various sites in the Maya area. All these glyphs refer to exactly the same important ending date marking the close of an era of thirteen *baktun* or 1,872,000 days (5200 calculating years of 360 days). Copan lies far south in Honduras near the southernmost extreme of the Chol-speaking district. Coba is far to the north near the edge of the Yucatan Peninsula. Piedras Negras and Dos Pilas lie between them in a Cholan area but very near the bilingual region. It can be seen at a glance that structural integrity of the glyph remains the same and regardless of how it may have been pronounced it carried exactly the same meaning in all these various districts.

The glyph in K signifies that a *tun* or year had passed, the *tun* sign appearing above the *lah*-hand. The glyphs in L and M essentially mean the same thing expressed in an entirely different way. The glyphs show that a stone or *tun* had been ritually erected or presented at the end of the year. The *tun* has come out of the hand and appears as a personified head in the glyph below. Replacing the *tun* in the hand is the mirror sign, which can be pronounced *tzuk,* emphasizing that this is a *tzuk*-hand in the ritual act of presenting. It should be noted that the fingers of the *tzuk*-hand extend to the left and those of the *lah*-hand are extended to the right. It is by no means a rule, but there is a definite tendency in glyph formation that hands that manifest, display, or present things will extend toward the left while hands that discard or express things gone or past tend to extend toward the right.

In N, the abbreviated glyph *mi* or *lub* meaning "zero" or "complete" is shown. The full glyph is shown in O where it takes the form of a Maltese cross. It is in this formation that the sacred 260-day calendar is presented. The calendar is a combination of the thirteen sacred gods of number with the twenty daysigns, twenty being the number of

the human (ten fingers, ten toes). The symbol expresses the unity of the gods and humankind. It is also symbolic of the unity of time and space. The calendar is written with the day One *Imix* in the east sector, which is the upper right quadrant. It then moves to the upper quadrant on the left, which represents north, and on to the lower left quadrant, where the Sun sets before concluding with the day Thirteen *Ahau* in the south quadrant on the lower right. Thus the sacred calendar represents all possible days in time and all directions of space in a magnificent unity. It is not only a natural symbol of completion, it becomes a symbol of complete illumination. It also contains the concept of zero as a portal.

When an artist uses this sacred map of time as a cartouche framing a pictorial scene in the act, it means that a portal has been created through which the gods are viewing an action on the human plane of existence or the gods or ancestors are being viewed in the spirit world by humans. Also hidden in the cosmogram is one of the best kept and most fundamental secrets of Maya glyph formation and pictorial composition in art. The cosmogram provides the hidden framework upon which the glyphs and the art are built. The eastern and northern quadrants are superior, the western and southern quadrants are inferior. The east is male and the west is female. The north is the future and the south is the past. Everything is unified and everything has its place in a great ordering principle. Now we know why the *tzuk*-hand in L presents the sacred mirror to the left. That is the north, the

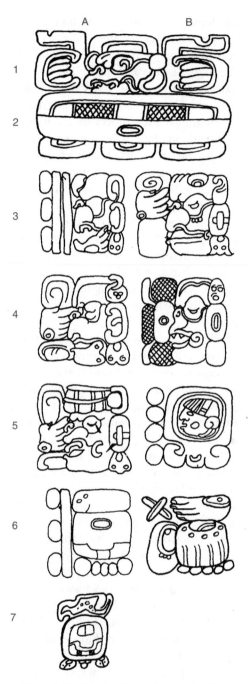

A   B

1

2

3

4

5

6

7

Figure 3.12. Opening clause of text, east side, stela C, Quirigua

place where the ancestors reside, and the portal that reaches to that sacred space is entered through the North Star.

Zero glyphs will appear frequently in Maya writing because the "zeroing out of time periods" is considered sacred, they being portals in time and therefore most likely to be commemorated in memorials of ritual events. Figure 3.12 is a rough sketch of the opening clause of a text on the eastern side of stela C at Quirigua. It begins elegantly and monumentally with an Initial Series Introductory Glyph (I.S.I.G.), which takes up four glyph block spaces in 1A and B and 2A and B. As usual with the Maya, time takes precedence over everything so the text begins with a date. The I.S.I.G. serves to announce to the reader that a date calculated in "big time" is forthcoming. The glyph itself represents a period of time known as the *alautun* and carries a value of 23,040,000,000 days or 63,312,328 *tun*, over sixty million years. It expresses the majesty of time. The mainsign in the glyph is the *tun* in 2A and B, the great base of all Maya time and chronology. Above it are fishbones, a reference to a mythological sharklike fish called *xoc*, probably the origin of the English word "shark." Here the Maya again make use of rebus writing to express abstract ideas, as *xoc* represents its homonym *xoc*, meaning "count" or "to count." The glyph itself signifies a grouping on the ninth level of counts beginning with individual days. When used as the I.S.I.G. in monumental texts it may be simply translated into English as "In the count of days. . . ."

A variable in the *alautun* glyph is

the god whose portrait appears in the center, the patron deity of the month arrived at in the *Haab*. This particular deity has not yet been identified, but we do know something about him. In another portrait, he bears the *be* or "road" sign, so at least we know that he is a portal enterer. We can be assured that this sign does not represent Venus as Venus is the patron of the tenth month, *Yax*. The day in the month arrived at is shown in 6A as Eight *Cumhu*. The month *Cumhu* is the eighteenth and last complete month in the *Haab*. Its glyph is built on the *kan* or "corn" daysign, but when written phonetically, its true meaning is revealed. The phonetic version is affixed with an *o* sign and suffixed with the *la* sign informing us that the *kan* sign here is to be read *ol*, meaning "portal."

The count begins in 3A with the count of the *Baktun*, the fifth level, a grouping of 144,000 days symbolized by the parrot. It tells us that thirteen *baktun* or 5200 calculating years of 360 days have been counted. This grand number in fact accounts for the total of all the days that need to be counted in the texts as the count of individual days on the first level in 5A has "zeroed out." Note the completion hand in the portrait of the parrot in 3B. Also see how all the numbers, which are considered sacred, appear in the left of the glyphs. Numbers may also appear at the top or east sector of a glyph but only in very rare instances will they appear below or behind in the inferior west and south sectors. All the gods depicted in the text face north to the sacred portal in the sky.

The count which we notate as 13.0.0.0.0. finally arrives at the date in the sacred calendar, Four *Ahau*, shown in 5B. In our calendar this would have been August 13, 3114 B.C., the starting point of Maya time reckoning in the present era and the so-called Creation Day. *Ahau*, Lord, is the final day in the twenty-day sequence. The daysign can also mean "flower" as it does in the Nahau calendar. Herein is hidden a wonderful mystery about the calendar. The lords are considered the flowers of the sacred ceiba tree. In one sense this tree represents the ancestral family tree that extends from the gods. In another sense it represents the cosmic World Tree at the center of the universe that traverses the three realms of existence. It has its roots in the first day One *Imix,* and it flowers on the final day Thirteen *Ahau*.

The tree as used by the shaman is the central portal to the spirit world. Conceiving of it in terms of the calendar, which represents time itself, we can ascertain the reason for the magnificent obsession of the Maya—the quest for the meaning of time. Time, which comes from the divinity and is part of its very being, permeates all and is limitless. In the penetrating mind of the Maya mystic it becomes a sacred portal.

After stating the date the text on stela C goes on to record the action that took place on that day, who did the action, and where it took place. In this version of the Creation, the emphasis is on the act of creation as the setting up of a portal allowing communion with the divine. The first verb (not shown) in figure 3.12/6B states *Halah y-ebal*, "It was manifested, the staircase." The

A   B   C   D   E

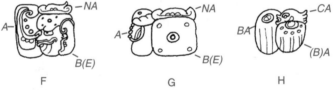

F   G   H

Figure 3.13 A-H. **The Nebaj Vase,** *rollout*

hand in this glyph provides the phonetic value *ye* besides serving to emphasize an act of making or manifesting. The *ba* sound is the waterlily of the *Imix* daysign. These symbols contain levels of meaning depending on the reader's depth of understanding. Both symbols carry the godsign of the sacred mirror, infusing them with divinity.

It is then described what the stairway—a portal—was. It says that three stones were set up. The first stone, a Jaguar Throne, was set up by the Paddler Twins, the Sky Creators, the gods of day and night who set time in motion. The jaguar, whose spots represent the starry night, is an allusion to the sky. In other words, in the first act of Creation the heavens were raised up and time was set in motion. This took place at *Na Ho-Chan,* "the place of first dawning sky," which I think is in the east.

The next stone was set up by an unidentified reptilian god at "earth center." This god bears a strong resemblance to the patron of the month. This stone was a serpent throne and, in contrast to the jaguar, a symbol of the Earth. The third stone was set up at

Cha'Chan, Lying-Down Sky, by the god *Itzamna*. It was a waterlily throne symbolizing the watery realms of the underworld. The text then states that all this was done under the aegis of the *Wakah Chan Ahau*, another name of the First Father, the Corn God who created everything. This title alludes to the *Wakah Chan*, the tree at the center of the world and the axis mundi, so in this version of the Creation it is viewed primarily as the setting up of a portal.

Let us turn our attention to some of the more mundane uses of the *mi*-hand in Maya art. This hand appears six times in what is generally recognized as one of the finest of all known Maya vase paintings—the seven-inch-high Nebaj Vase, which was excavated in 1904. It is diagramed in figure 3.13. The scene gives us an intimate view of the moment of an agreement concluding a successful trade transaction frozen in time. The meaning of the handsign, the shell, is the same as it appears in glyph form on the monuments. Here it means that the transaction has been completed as there are no fractional parts left over to be reckoned with or bargained. I suppose that one of the participants, who are *its'at*—artist-mathematicians who wear paintbrushes in their headdresses in the manner of Maya artists—actually painted this extraordinary vase.

The transaction was obviously a complicated one and it was important enough to be commemorated on a vase. The participants are nobles who acted as governors and administrators. Such lords were called *Sahalob*; these were known to have collected tribute so that technically the agreement concluded was likely to have been a payment of tribute.

The five glyph blocks apparently name and give the titles of the participants. The key figure at C wears the headdress of a fish nibbling on a waterlily which indicates that he is an *Ah Nab*, a title which literally means He of Water, but has deeper implications. Glyphs for this title are shown at F and G wherein the *be* sign indicates that those personages are enterers. The glyph at H is the title *Bacab*, "stood-up person," which is a related title. The artist has cleverly related the fish in the glyph that gives the *ca* sound to the fish in the headdress. A *Bacab* is a holy shaman in the sense of being "stood-up" between the three realms of the cosmos, an enterer who is capable of traversing these planes; therefore, whatever mundane functions these officials had, they were also regarded as priests and holy men. The *chi*-hand appears twice in the name block in B. The last glyph probably identifies this person as an *Ah-Kin*, He of the Sun, a priest of the sun cult. The apparel of the figure in A is covered with *be* or entering signs.

The ancient Maya were capable of performing extremely complex mathematical computations using the hands and toes. The figure at C is apparently bringing the toes into use and this would indicate large numbers having been enumerated. His assistant at D is making use of a codex box which probably contains mathematical tables, also indicating that large numbers had been calculated. [Author's Note: These boxes appear frequently in Maya art and are known to have contained manuscripts of all sorts including calendrical, astronomical, and mathematical tables and charts. The assistant is apparently manipulating objects on a mathematical table structured in such a way that various levels represent increasingly higher numerical orders or groupings much in the same way as a date in the calendar is written. This kind of format enabled the scribe to rapidly calculate solutions to complex mathematical problems involving very high numbers. The exact methodology that was employed is only beginning to be explored by researchers.] The main negotiators are at B and C. When complex transactions involving large numbers are carried out, seconders are used as assistants who monitor the calculations to avoid errors. The Sahalob at A and E are aiding the Sahal at B who signs back to A in a method that allows a number to be transmitted without the knowledge of the other party. Another advantage of using handsigns is that complex transactions can be accomplished without the parties necessarily knowing each other's spoken language.

The visiting dignitary sits to the left of the dais, its superior side. Here also is the merchandise involved, a pile of blankets and the objects in the woven basket on top of it. The assistant at D holds up a tubular jade pendant of a type being worn by the lord at C. The object that is obviously the concluding factor in the agreement is the spondylous shell offered by the Sahal at B. Another one of these is depicted on the floor beside him. These are jewel boxes; when excavated from burial sites they are often found to contain jade, a substance considered by the Maya to be even more

Figure 3.13 I,J,K,L

precious than gold.

The artist brilliantly captures the precise moment that the shell is offered. When this happens all the participants simultaneously sign "zero," meaning that the bargaining or tribute payment has been completed. The Sahal at E is caught in the act of transforming a number handsign into zero. The technique employed is one frequently used by Maya artists to solve the problem of depicting moving handsigns in a static medium. The figure is shown with two left hands, which was previously thought to have been an anatomical error. Actually it is a clever device frequently used to indicate that the hand is in motion.

We may safely assume that the vase was made to commemorate the agreement and that it was actually used as a drinking vessel by the very participants named on it, in rituals that celebrated the event. The P.S.S., shown in I, J, K, and L, would tend to support this conclusion. The artist has concisely contracted the P.S.S. into a block of four glyphs, which appears on the vase between E and A. The *a-ya* glyph (I) and the *Pauahtun* verb (J) infer that the vase is a holy object. An artist usually uses four glyphs to render *u-xubal*, but by a clever use of infixing, this master has contracted it into a single glyph block (K). Finally the artist ends the text with *y-uch'ab*, which includes the *be*, "road," sign surmounted by the *ch'a* wing (L). It is not improbable that these signs carry their full extended meanings, "to go (or fly in the manner of a shaman) on the road," "to open a path," and that to the Maya the vase as a ritual object was regarded as a holy grail, a portal to the spirit world ruled over by *Pauahtun*. So much for the more mundane uses of the *mi*-hand.

The *mi*-hand may be considered to be of paramount importance as it represents not only a number but also symbolizes a fundamental spiritual concept. Other handsigns derived from the system of enumerating on the hands appear in the art and, becoming associated with the gods of number, they thereby attain deeper spiritual significance as mudras representative of those gods. Besides this the origin of numerical notation in glyph formation is directly derived from the practice of handsigning numbers.

Some of the earliest dated writing in the Americas is Olmec in origin and is found carved on stone slabs from early Monte Alban, Oaxaca. From these a sequence of number glyphs is shown in

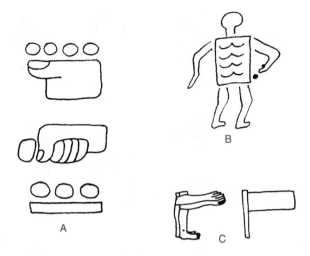

Figure 3.14. A. Olmec number glyphs, Monte Alban, Oaxaca; B. Plains Indian pictograph for "hunger;" C. The glyph "twenty" from Nahua codices

figure 3.14A. Dots are used to carry a value of one. The origin of this practice is extremely remote. In some of the earliest petroglyphs inscribed in the North American continent, the contraction of an extended finger to a dot is used to indicate "here" or "this is it." It is retained in the pictographic writing of the Plains Indians as shown in B. "Hunger" is written in a pictograph showing the protruding bones of the rib cage and a right hand signing "there is nothing." The left hand points to exactly where the hunger pangs are, which is emphasized by the dot. In number glyphs the dot symbols are abstractions that naturally evolve from the tips of the fingers being used for tallying.

A hand bundle in A indicates "five" in the number sequence shown, but in rendering "eight" the writer has apparently become tired of painstakingly en-

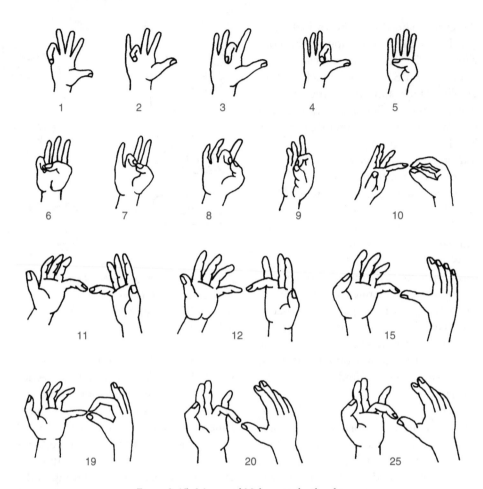

Figure 3.15. Maya and Nahua number handsigns

graving the symbol in stone and so the hand is contracted to a bar. Virtually all primitive peoples count on their hands, frequently assigning the number values "one" to the finger, "five" to the hand, "ten" to the hands. These quantities supply natural divisions and are always conveniently "on hand."

The origin of number words in many cultures can be traced to this process. In Nahuatl the word *ma-itl*, "hand," gives rise to the number words for "five" and "ten." The number twenty, *cempoalli*, means "one count"; it appears as a flag in Nahua codices and is thought to be a contraction of a pictograph depicting the hands and the feet, as shown in C. The use of a word meaning "man" to express the twenty grouping is practically universal. In Maya counting it is known as the *uinic*, "the person."

The Nahua and the Maya systems of counting on the hands are virtually

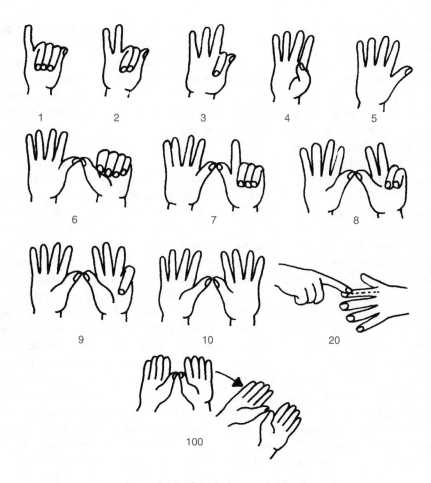

Figure 3.16. Plains Indian number handsigns

identical and are outlined in the chart in figure 3.15. It may be compared with the method generally employed by the Plains Indians, shown in figure 3.16. The most pertinent similarity is that they both start on the small finger of the right hand, a distinctive cultural imprint that strongly suggests that they are related. To sign "one" in the Maya system the finger is pressed into the palm of the hand, in the Plains Indian method the finger is raised. Some tribes, however, lowered the finger: The number word "one" in the language of the Dene-Dinje, a tribe of Indians living in the northwestern United States, means "the end (little finger) is bent." Conversely in Maya art there are examples of a raised finger used to indicate one.

The two most important developments in Maya mathematics were the use of zero and place value notation, both of which are inherent and arise from their method of numerating on the hands. The use of a "zero" hand is absent in the Plains Indian system. Another significant difference is that a Maya can enumerate all the numbers from one to ten on the fingers of one hand whereas the Plains Indian requires two hands. In either case all the fingers of the hand or hands are used.

It is practically a universal human trait that all the fingers being used up in expressing "ten" is referred to as the fingers being "dead," or as the Dene-Dinje number word "five" has it, "my hand is finished." The Maya take the idea to its full extension. *Cimi*, the ubiquitous God of Death, is the personification of the number ten.

To sign "ten" the Plains Indian will raise all the fingers of both hands. For "twenty" the fingers are opened and closed twice and subsequent groupings of tens are indicated in this way. A Maya can sign "ten" by pressing the fingers of one hand against the thumb but another method, which foreshadows the use of place value notation in the writing, is usually used. The left hand is used to

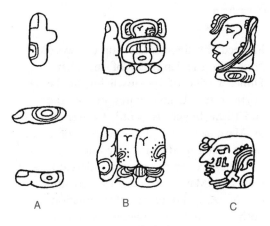

A   B   C

Figure 3.17. Maya glyphs for "one"

represent levels or gradations of the ten grouping. When "zero" is formed on the right hand and placed against the small finger of the left hand it expresses "ten" as "zero on the first level." Against the ring finger of the left hand it means "twenty" or "zero on the second level." This use of the *mi*-hand in counting as a way of entering into higher levels is an exact parallel to its symbolic meaning in Maya spirituality. There is a close association here between *Cimi* and the God of Zero and now we know why the Death God is referred to as "He who resides in the innermost twist of the conch shell."

A Plains Indian can also sign "twenty" by first signing "ten" and then drawing the index finger of the right hand along the index finger of the left as shown. Numbers up to fifty are indicated in this way and by reversing hands numbers from sixty to one hundred are enumerated. To sign in hundreds the "ten" sign is first swung in an arc and the same "twenty" sign now indicates 2000. In this way numbers up to 10,000 are easily signed. There can be little doubt that the Maya used similar strategies that radically changed the value of the basic numbers formed on the hands. Besides this the Maya commonly brought the toes into play in counting, thus utilizing a full gradation of twenty levels capable of expressing some of the vast numbers seen in their writing.

The process of ordering in a hierarchy is inherent in both the writing and handsigning of number. As mentioned the Maya consider the right hand as male and the left hand as female and the fingers are named as members of a family. The small finger of the right hand is known as the last born or fourth child. The ring finger is the third child, the middle finger is the second child, and the index finger is the first child and the grandfather. The thumb is called the "big finger" or the great-grandfather. The fingers of the left hand are named in the same pattern but refer to female members of the family, and the process is identical for the toes.

Since number is so intimately interwoven with the hand in the mind of the Maya, number is frequently expressed in the writing in terms of a hand or a finger. Samples of *hun*, "one," and some of its uses are shown in figure 3.17. In C it is written as the head glyph of the Lunar Goddess, the First Mother and the personification of the number one. The number gods, *Oxlahun Ti Ku*, Thirteen of God, reside in the thirteen levels of the heavens and aptly the Moon is in the first layer and intimately associated with the Earth. She is the patroness of the daysign *Caban*, "Earth," the first in an order of thirteen daysigns occurring within the twenty-day sequence, beginning with *Imix*, which embody or are emanations of the thirteen number gods. The most salient feature of her glyph and the *Caban* daysign in C is the extended lock of hair, derived from a universal handsign for "woman," the hand indicating the long hair or the

Figure 3.18. A. *The glyph* **Hun Hunahpu**; B. *The daysign* **One Ahau**

combing of the hair.

The name of the First Father, a personification of the Sun, is written as *Hun Hunahpu* in the glyphs shown in figure 3.18A. His son *Hunahpu*, a personification of Venus and firstborn of the Hero Twins, appears in the daysign One *Ahau* (B), the date of the great heliacal rising of the Morning Star in the Venus calendar. The dot and the finger both represent "one" in these glyphs. The use of the thumb in A and the index finger in B may connote familial relationships.

Following the daysign *Caban* is *Eznab*, "flint." The patroness of this day is the personification of the number two. She is a sacrificial deity who also functions as one of the *Bolon Ti Ku*, Nine of God, deities of the night who reside in the nine levels of the underworld. The main feature of her glyphs, shown in figure 3.19, is the hand held above the head. She personifies the flint or obsidian blade of sacrifice known as the Hand of God—"that which divides"

Figure 3.19. The glyph "two"

Figure 3.20. **Pauahtun Teaching His Students**, *cylindrical vase*

becoming an apt symbol for the number two. The actual blade need not be shown as usually a grasping hand is held above the head in a handsign that mimics the action of the sacrificer about to strike open the breast of the victim.

As the handsigning of number was a significant cultural trait of the ancient Maya, it is not surprising that numbers make their appearance in all forms of their art. The intention of the artist who painted the vase shown in figure 3.20 is to portray a humorous situation. In doing so, however, the artist inadvertently manages to incorporate in one painting the three main forms of number reckoning used by the Maya: counting on the hand, the written number, and calculating on the ground. In the scenes *Pauahtun* or an impersonator is teaching these arts to two students.

In the first scene *Pauahtun* demonstrates the method of calculating number on the ground. According to records from colonial sources this method was widely practiced by merchants and was a typical feature of the old Maya marketplace. The baffled novices clumsily grapple with forming the number on their hands. The artist skillfully captures their expressions of bewilderment as well as the scolding countenance of their teacher. One of the glyphs emanating from the speech scroll of *Pauahtun* has been interpreted as relating to *tataah ts'ib*, meaning "a sermon," especially in the sense of injurious or "hard" words, which is exactly what appears to be taking place. In the next scene *Pauahtun* introduces the initiates to the art of writing numbers while brandishing a brush before a jaguar-pelt–covered codex box used by scribes. The fledging students try to work out the numbers on their hands and the first one attempts a calculation on the ground to no avail. The painting is a comic treatment of the beginner's first confrontations with the complexities of an intricate and highly evolved art.

Seasoned practitioners are shown in the vase rollout in figure 3.21, which I call *The Number Signers* because the participants are depicted simply in the act of enumerating on the hand. There is no merchandise present, although

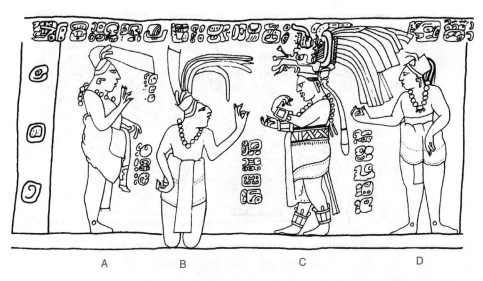

Figure 3.21. **The Number Signers**, *cylindrical vase*

they have adopted the standard format of trade negotiation with the intricate interaction of assistants (at A and D) and primaries who are at B and C. All are named in the four glyph blocks. The strikingly elaborate apparel of the figure at C suggests that he is an Ahau. The others, wearing the headdress that identifies them as members of their specific elite class, are *its'at*.

Again a vase painting provides us with an intimate view of daily life in the ancient Maya court. The group may be practicing numbers for their own intellectual amusement or more likely they are honing their skills prior to an important negotiation. The hands are in motion but time stands still in the very center of the composition where the hands of B and C conclude and correspondingly arrive at the number seven. The glyphs in the accompanying text are rather bizarre and remain obscure for the most part. Presently the commu-

nicative power of this painting relies primarily on the recognition of the number transmitted by these two handsigns.

The detail shown in figure 3.22 is from a vase painted by the same master who gave us the Nebaj Vase. This scene is likely to have been in the same place, and the merchandise is similar except here we see the addition of highly valued quetzal plumes in a woven basket similar to the one in the Nebaj Vase. The text is in a glyph block that forms an *ik*, "wind" or "spirit" sign. It begins with the *u-bah*, "he goes" or "he does," verb. Each glyph in it also appears in the Nebaj Vase. There the negotiations were shown at the moment of completion in the silent language of the hands, but here the participants are in the heat of bargaining orally while calculating the arithmetic on their hands.

The detail from a vase painting diagramed in figure 3.23 is indeed a curious one. The P.S.S. is reduced to a

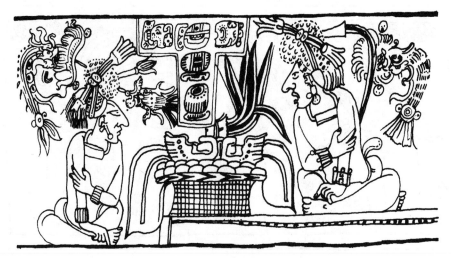

Figure 3.22. Cylindrical vase, detail

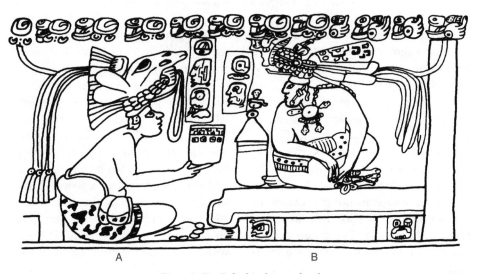

A   B

Figure 3.23. Cylindrical vase, detail

repetition of the introductory *a-ya* glyph, which changes only at the last four glyphs, the first of which is presumably a *tzuk*-hand. The *tzuk*, "it was presented," glyph frequently follows the *a-ya* glyph in the P.S.S. We may wonder if this somehow echoes the presentation or offering of the vase by the Sahal at A in the scene? Bargaining in the present-day marketplaces of Mesoamerica is somewhat of a ritual and evidently it was even more so in the ancient Maya court; the participants in this scene are richly attired in ceremonial apparel. We can be certain that whatever its significance, the Ahau seated on the dais responds to the offering by placing the right, "zero," hand on the small finger of the left hand, signing zero on the first level or "ten." As a class, the Sahal were known as "the feared ones" as it was they who collected tribute. The Ahau apparently was not in direct contact with the ordinary people and ultimately tribute was rendered to the Ahau by a Sahal in the abbreviated form of valuables.

As the basis of the economic system these cumulative transactions are frequently memorialized in the art as shown in figure 3.24. Interestingly the handsigns employed are illustrative of both of the handsigns used by the Plains Indians that mean "talk." The Sahal on the left who wears a jade pendant of the type shown in the basket, makes a handsign meaning "little talk." The index finger is repeatedly snapped against the thumb, expressing words that are "thrown out." To "speak at length" is signed by the Ahau on the right by holding his flat right hand out with the back down, in front of his mouth and repeatedly moving it outward. By utilizing handsigns the artist imbues the scene with energetic animation resulting in a slice-of-life portrait of realities in the ancient Maya court.

The fragmentary scene in figure 3.25 is similarly activated as the artist has focused on the movement of the hands to capture the dynamism of a transaction in progress. The main actor, assisted by a dwarf or possibly a youth, dramatically raises his hand in a number-signing position. The person holding the merchandise is apparently not yet

Figure 3.24. Ceramic art detail

satisfied by the quantity offered. The artist succeeds in capturing a moment in an age-old situation that is universal in human trade.

The Maya artist's acumen in using the handsign language in pictorial scenes is also reflected in glyph formation. Writing is the art of making thoughts visible and in this the *its'at* excels. The limestone lintel diagrammed in figure 3.26 at one-fourth its original size simply records a date but it does so with such grace and imagination that

Figure 3.25. Vase fragment

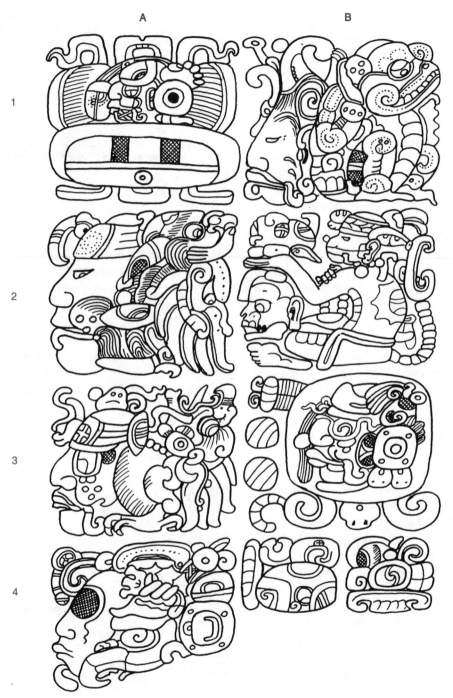

Figure 3.26. Limestone lintel, A.D. *February 12, 526*

each glyph in it becomes not merely a record of time but also a symbol or conglomeration of interacting signs meant for a deepening contemplation.

We would merely record this date as A.D. February 12, 526. It is a human trait to relate time to the divine, and our recording has religious connotations as it is counted from the birthday of Christ. This Maya correlation is counted from a creation day over three thousand years previous to that birth and the day here recorded depicts fifteen gods involved in what actually constitutes a single day.

The date in the *Haab* is not given in the text but it can be calculated as being the nineteenth day of the month *Pax*, a time period considered appropriate for sacrifice. The variable element in the I.S.I.G. in 1A is a portrait of the patron of this month. He is a sacrificial deity—above his jade earflare is the grasping Hand of God symbol. His forehead is a mirror god symbol, his eye is an *ik* sign, emblem of spiritual vision, his jaw is the crossbands of the Sun. Before his face is the phonetic *te*, which identifies him as a personification of the cosmic tree at the center of the cosmos. *Te* means tree, time, and also distance or space in Maya languages.

Nine *Baktun* are recorded in 2A. The god of the number nine is *Xbalanque*, second born of the Hero Twins, here paired with the parrot symbol of the *Baktun* with the characteristic hand covering the jaw. Within its wings is another bird head, which glares at the screaming eagle that symbolizes the *Katun* count in 3A and is paired with the Sun God, the personification of the

A   B   C

Figure 3.27. Jade plaque and variants of the glyph ku'-ch, *"vulture"*

number four.

Buluc Chabtan, another sacrificial deity, is the number eleven shown paired with the vulture, symbol of the *tun* in 4A. His eye is the *Caban* sign that means "Earth" and "the Moon Goddess" as well as "one," eleven being "one on the first level." The hand in the forehead of the vulture represents the *ch* sound in *ku'-ch*, one Maya word for vulture. (Variants of this glyph, each containing a *chi*-hand, are shown in figure 3.27. In C there is a purely phonetic rendering of the name of this bird. To the Maya time flies—all the larger groupings of days are represented by birds.)

Uo, the frog in 1B, is the ally of the Hero Twins and humankind and represents the *Uinal*, the count of twenty days. Beautifully rendered and paired with the Corn God who personifies the number eight, the frog cups a hand over an ear, as if anticipating the sound of the frogs that will announce the all-important coming of the rains, appropriate to this time of the year. Below the elbow is a *Cimi* death head that represents the seed that must die, then that is helped to germinate by the rains to produce corn.

Other actors in the drama of vegetation are shown in 2B, which is a highly elaborate way of writing "sixteen days" or *Kin*. The Sun in his creative aspect of the monkey-fashioner offers the head of the Wind God, *Ik*, the number six who is a close associate of the Rain God, *Chac*. In the eye of the offered head is the ax that breaks open the clay vessels in the heavens which contain the precious rains. The Sun God offers this

Figure 3.28. Jade earflare

head in a gesture indicating respect as he holds it aloft above the head of *Cimi*, personification of the number ten.

The total number of days counted may be written either 9.4.11.8.16., or 1,328,936 days, which would fall on the day *Ca Cib* or Two Vulture. This would have been, if correctly correlated to our calendar, A.D. February 12, 526. In Maya country this time of year is characterized by the coming of the light rains. *Pax* literally means "drum" and during this month *Chac* ceremonies using drums were held in honor of the rain gods. It is also the time in which

A

B

Figure 3.29. Gods from monumental inscriptions

the *Holcan Okot* or Dance of the Warriors was performed.

In 3B, the artist renders the vulture daysign, *Cib* in Yucatec, in its human form, which is very rare. The lord of the day shown has his hair bound in the manner of a sacrificial victim. In his earflare there is the *be,* "road," sign surmounted by the *och* shell sign meaning "to enter." In his eye is a shell sign meaning that this is a shaman who possesses the vision of one who can open or enter the road to the spirit world. In the upper left-hand corner of the glyph there is a phonetic *ta* sign that must refer to yet another name for a vulture in Maya languages. *Ta*, "excrement," refers specifically to *tahol*, the blackheaded vulture known literally as "excrement head."

The last two glyphs in this remarkable lintel tell us that the Fifth Lord of Night ruled or literally "wore the *Sak Hunal*," the white headband of rulership, which is shown in the last glyph. The Sak Hunal is the royal headband personified as a god so that in fact there are sixteen gods incorporated in this lintel to render a single day in the calendar. As the nine Lords of Night reside in the nine layers of the underworld arranged in an arc, the fifth layer is at the lowest level. In both Maya and Nahua cultures it is referred to variously as the place of the seven caves or the jaguar heart of the mountain, a portal to the underworld.

The symbols of the time periods were revered as gods themselves. The deification of time is evident in the two jade objects shown in figures 3.27 and 3.28. The jade plaque had its origins as

a fetish from an entirely different culture. When turned the other way, a head with two shallow grooves forming eyes and the arms and legs of a simple figural form reveals itself. This object had its origins in Costa Rica. Somehow the piece made its way into the Maya country around Campeche where it was turned upside down and reworked. The glyphs of the gods of the *tun* and the *uinal* were engraved and filled with red pigment. A hole was then drilled and the plaque was probably worn as a pendant on a ceremonial belt of a Maya ruler.

The jade earflare illustrated in figure 3.28 is a deification of the *Baktun* as the parrot. In the headdress is a bird who wears the Sak Hunal symbolizing rulership. In the hierarchy of birds the parrot reigns supreme. In Nahua culture the day was divided into thirteen "hours," each symbolized by a bird. The hummingbird, the swiftest and lightest, represented the first "hour" and the slower parrot presided over the thirteenth. The Maya no doubt maintained a similar system of symbolizing time.

The gods shown in figure 3.29 are from monumental inscriptions. They both form the numbers they personify on the fingers of the right hand. In A the portrait of the Corn God would suffice to indicate "eight" but here the artist provides the "eight" handsign, the thumb touching the middle finger. The left hand forms the sign of the Sun meaning by extension *kin* or "day." The glyph represents a count of eight days. The sole identifying feature of the god in B is the number nine formed on the right hand by the thumb touching the

Figure 3.30 A. Cylindrical vase detail; B. Death glyph or symbol; C. The handsign, "to die";
D. **Cimi** *glyph*

index finger, a particularly sacred sign and number at which the god intently gazes. The glyph may be read, "Nine *baktun* have been counted." The god is shown grasping a parrot in his left *chi*-hand by extension meaning "sun," or "days," and hence time itself.

That time was considered the most sacred of all things is evidenced by the fact that in monumental inscriptions the date as a rule precedes everything else. The same holds true in rare instances when a date appears in the P.S.S. in vase paintings. Illustrative of this is the detail

of the Altar De Sacrificios vase shown in figure 3.30. In A the day *Ahau* and the month *Zotz*, the Bat, (A.D. April 21, 754) are written prior to the introductory glyph *a-ya*, "it came into being."

The vase was one of fifteen found in the tomb of a nobleman. Some of the vases came from the middle Usumacinta area and were presumably brought as offerings by the famous ruler Bird Jaguar who is shown dancing in the scene. Others were brought from the central lowlands, probably by the noble from Tikal, who is shown floating in a

Figure 3.31. **The Death God and the Wind God,** *from a Nahua codex*

trance while offering a vase that is inscribed with an *Akbal,* "night," daysign. Such a vase is a powerful ritual object and will be discussed in detail in subsequent chapters.

The vessels found in the tomb were made expressly as mortuary offerings. This one vividly depicts the funerary rites of a noble. The accompanying text names the participants. The first two glyphs in the set on the left read *Nupul-Balam* and name the floating lord. The name is followed by the glyph *u-way* meaning "his animal spirit companion," referring to the *Balam* or jaguar part of his name. Through contacting his animal coessence he has entered the swoon

of a shamanistic trance in which he is seen to be floating. The last glyph describes him as a *Ch'ul Ahau,* a Holy Blood Lord of Tikal.

The first glyph in the set in the center names *Yax Balam,* Bird Jaguar. It is followed by a glyph that describes him as a *Ch'ul Ahau* from Yaxchilan. The third glyph immediately below his name is *u-way.* He is shown attired in the guise of his animal coessence spirit and he is engaged in a shamanistic dance that evokes his protector spirit. The rest of the glyphs in this set represent a mysterious and probably supernatural place that he has contacted, written as Four-Sky, Thirteen Gods.

Figure 3.32. **Coatlicue**, *Nahua statue*

Our main interest is in the seated actor who is in the bizarre process of decapitating himself. An implement similar to the blade he holds in his hand was found at the burial site so the scene probably depicts actual rituals that took place. He is named as *Ch'akba-Cimi* in the three glyphs in front of him. The ax in the first glyph is *Chak*, "to decapitate." Attached to it is the rodent head which gives the verbal expression *ba*. The glyph of the Death God, *Cimi*, which contains a sort of percentage sign symbol is shown in B. The sign is painted on the cheek of the victim. For a long time this symbol has been recognized as a "death" emblem but its origins have for many decades alluded epigraphers. A simple explanation for it may by found in the sign language as shown in C. The handsign "to die" means "to go under." The flat left hand is held in front of the body and the pointing right hand moves downward,

below it, and up. We have already seen how the hand becomes a bar and the extended finger is represented by a dot.

The right hand of the victim is closed in the fist of death, which may be compared to the *Cimi* glyph shown in D. We have seen how this hand is directly derived from the fingers being "used up" or "dying" in counting up to ten on the hand, becoming the symbol of the Death God. There are few instances in the development of human culture where we find such an intimate relationship between numerical and spiritual considerations. Another truly fascinating aspect of Maya culture is that, just as the writing retains its roots in handsigning, the religion, in spite of elaborate refinements, closely adheres to its origins in shamanism.

As a sacred symbol of the Death God, the closed fist appears frequently in Nahua art. Back-to-back portraits of *Mictlantecuhtli*, the Aztec god of death and the underworld, and *Quetzalcoatl* in his aspect as the god of the wind are shown in figure 3.31. The Wind God is a symbol of the spirit and by extension, life. These gods transform into one another as death and life are shown to be two sides of the same coin. Without death there can be no life and conversely, in the absence of life, death cannot exist. The Death God holds a rattle, which is surmounted by the closed fist symbol of death. Directly contrasting this the Wind God holds a planting stick, the symbol of growth and life.

Death generates life, so dangling from the ear of the Death God is a hand, the symbol of the "maker" or "doer." Both gods are shown pointing

Figure 3.33. **The Resurrection of the Corn God,** *cylindrical vase*

upward to the heavens in a gesture of prayer. *Quetzalcoatl* wears the shell, Wind Jewel of Life, as a pendant. On his knee the Death God is portrayed symbolizing the perception that within life there is some dying, within death there is the genesis of life. The artist here taps into some of the eternal truths of existence.

In the agricultural societies of Mesoamerica death is viewed as a generative power intimately connected with the germination of seeds, growth, and fertility. The Nahua statue illustrated in figure 3.32 shows *Coatlicue*, the female consort of the Death God, as a divine spirit, mother goddess of the Earth and fertility. She prominently displays the hands of death as a sacred mudra symbolic of the generative powers of life which she represents. The gods of death are deifications of forces in the cultiva-

tion process that produces life.

Exactly the same hand, carrying the same meaning, is seen displayed by *Cimi* in the vase painting illustrated in figure 3.33, another version of *The Resurrection of the Corn God*. In Nahua culture the twenty daysigns are associated with parts of the human body, the day of death being represented by the head, which symbolizes the seed. In Maya mythology the head of the First Father, the Sun God, is buried, then germinates into the corn plant personified by *Yum Caax*, the Corn God. The miracle of transformation is brought about by the magical action of the Hero Twins, but through the agency or under the auspices of *Cimi*, Lord of Death.

The painting is again strongly influenced by theatrical performances of events in the mythology. In it we first see the Hero Twins ritually dressing

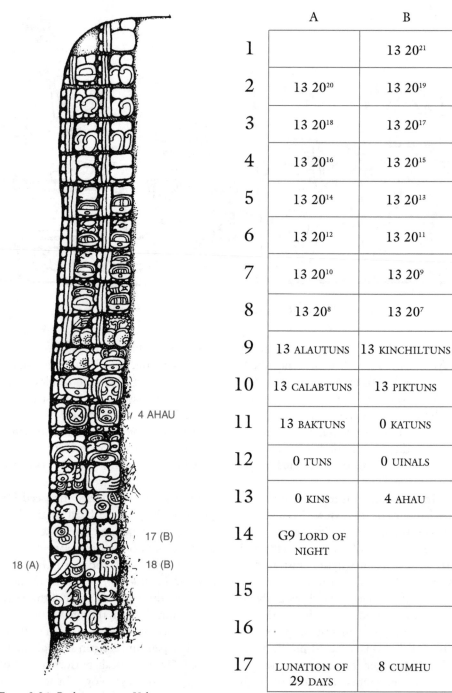

	A	B
1		$13 \cdot 20^{21}$
2	$13 \cdot 20^{20}$	$13 \cdot 20^{19}$
3	$13 \cdot 20^{18}$	$13 \cdot 20^{17}$
4	$13 \cdot 20^{16}$	$13 \cdot 20^{15}$
5	$13 \cdot 20^{14}$	$13 \cdot 20^{13}$
6	$13 \cdot 20^{12}$	$13 \cdot 20^{11}$
7	$13 \cdot 20^{10}$	$13 \cdot 20^{9}$
8	$13 \cdot 20^{8}$	$13 \cdot 20^{7}$
9	13 ALAUTUNS	13 KINCHILTUNS
10	13 CALABTUNS	13 PIKTUNS
11	13 BAKTUNS	0 KATUNS
12	0 TUNS	0 UINALS
13	0 KINS	4 AHAU
14	G9 LORD OF NIGHT	
15		
16		
17	LUNATION OF 29 DAYS	8 CUMHU

Figure 3.34. Rock inscription, Koba

their father for his rebirth. Then the triumphant Corn God is shown enthroned on his dais. *Cimi* kneels before him in an attitude of reverence and awe. The Corn God is clearly identifiable by his elongated head representing an ear of corn, with the hair bound up as its silk. The single dot on the cheek of *Cimi* is here an abbreviation of the death emblem. What is truly remarkable about this scene is the prominent display of the number handsigns "ten" and "eight" which actually become the sacred mudra of these gods; the number system manages to incorporate concepts inherent in the mythology. The Sun God, personification of the number four, has magically prolificated, doubling himself to become the Corn God, personification of the number eight.

From one kernel of corn come ten thousand. Such is the generative power inherent in nature and echoed by the Maya in their perception of the generative powers of number. The hands, the number ten, generate all the possible numbers in the universe and so *Pauahtun*, as Lord of Number, displays the hands of time as he emerges from his shell in figure 3.1. At Koba, Maya artists recorded the largest known number, written like kernels of corn on a cob, ever to be inscribed on stone. Analyzed in figure 3.34 is a number that represents 41,341,050,000,000,000,000,000,000,000 years of 365.2422 days, written in terms of the count of days, a truly cyclopean tower of numbers. The twenty group is the building block that forms all the

levels of rank.

Such an enormous number can in no way be tied to the practical life of the ordinary people or even to the use of very large numbers required in the calendrical computations of the elite. Here counting is used as a way to honor the sacred divinity of time. The inscription is a tower of numbers that explores the infinite progression of the number sequence: It builds up level upon level as it rises higher and higher above the world of mortals and on to superhuman heights in the realm of the gods. The act of climbing step-by-step ever closer to the gods is creating a ladder, another portal into the mystery of the divine world. There the initiated can no longer perceive numbers as quantities, the law of number mounting into purely spiritual levels of consciousness.

Our way of perceiving time is linear; it proceeds through infinity like an arrow in a straight line. Maya time is cyclical, consisting of eternal cycles within cycles. The Aztecs also conceived of cyclical time but to them it was finite. At one ending of a 52-year cycle the world was destined to come to an end. Time has also been considered finite throughout most of history in the West. The Judaic-Christian creation, having begun in 4004 B.C., was ultimately destined to end in destruction. To the Maya time reckoner that amount of time would be a mere flash in the pan. It was only in the last century that geologists began to conceive of "deep" time, whereas as evidenced at Koba, the Maya had for long been grappling with the concept of deep time and its cycles, written on an unimaginably large scale.

In perceiving time as unlimited and cyclical an inscription such as that at Koba not only probes into the distant past but also explores the future and the meaning of time itself as the unity of the past and the future in an eternal oneness. The inquisitive Maya mind always is on a quest to find the hidden unity in nature. The day arrived at is Four *Ahau*, in 13(B), and it fell on Eight *Cumhu* in 17(B), the beginning of our era, which was really the closing or "zeroing out" day of the previous era.

The closing date is a focus of attention in the monumental inscriptions as many rituals of the Maya shaman are ceremonial reenactments of the creation events through which a portal is opened to the realms of the spirit world. The date has significance as a key to the past and the future and it is the anchor date in reckoning time. The closing date of the present era will fall on 13.0.0.0.0 Four *Ahau,* Three *Kankin,* or A.D. December 23, 2012. It is not a mere coincidence that this date is in extremely close proximity to the winter solstice, the ending of the solar year. The calendar projects both forward and backward while remaining in harmony with the rhythm of astronomical cycles inherent in nature.

Many inscriptions contain dates of anniversaries of events projected thousands of years into the future. Recent research at Palenque has shown that historical events and dates current at the time they were inscribed are displayed along with dates and events that occurred far back in a distant mythological past sometime before the beginning of the present era. In these the contemporary events are presented as mirror images of actions that took place in the magical dreamtime of the gods. The patterns of the past are reflected symmetrically as mirror images in the present and future.

In 18(A) and 18(B), the Koba version of the Creation states *Holah K'o-bah,* "was made to appear, was made visible, the images," as if the Creation is an apparition manifested in the illusionary stage of time. The cyclical vision of time is a closed circle in which the past and the future meet and the present is conceived of as a unity. In a similar way, the Maya envision space or matter as a continuously transforming unity. Time and space are unified in the field of existence and the same gods who are deifications of time and personifications of number are also embodiments of the elements in a grandiose all-encompassing cosmovision of the intricately interwoven forces that make up Creation. In the Maya worldview the interplay of the primary elements, water and fire, plays a central role in the mystery of matter. Our exploration of these realms begins with the all-important Rain God, *Chac-Xib-Chac.*

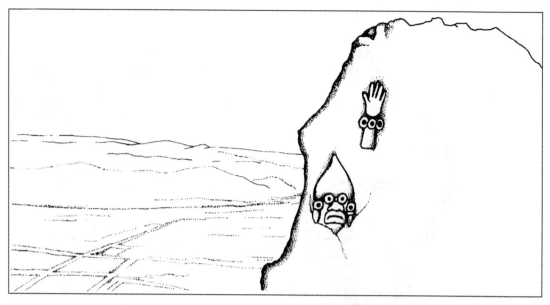

Figure 4.1. Rock inscription, pinnacle, Cerro de la Cantera Mountains, Chalcacingo, Mexico.

THE REAL GOD B

Drawing the immediate attention of the eye, the twin formation of the mountains of the Cerro de la Cantera conspicuously protrudes from the fertile fields of Chalcacingo, rising to a height of over one thousand feet. It is one of those holy places in Mexico which attracts the eye in such a way that one knows instinctively that this locale must have been regarded as sacred by the ancient inhabitants. A visit to the precipitous heights confirms these intuitions as on the north side of one of the mountains is an assembly of ancient designs, clustered in three stations on the cliffs, which reads like a veritable ancient Olmec manuscript. Known as the Sanctuary of the Reliefs, the inscriptions verify the existence of a rain deity in the Olmec pantheon and establish the characteristics of his attributes.

For our purposes the most intriguing iconography is the hand found at the very pinnacle of the sacred mountain as illustrated in figure 4.1. It represents another aspect of the cult of the hand, distinctly different from the sun-worshipping hand previously discussed. This hand does not face toward the Sun; it is a magic hand that

Figure 4.2. **Hunrakan**. *Taino ceramic figurine*

extends toward the clouds in a ritual of propitiation to the rain gods. The jade beads at the wrist are symbolic of the precious substance that was the lifeblood of the agricultural people who worshipped at the site. The hand faces northward to the great sacred volcano Popocatepetl or Smoking Rock, the legendary abode of the Rain God *Tlaloc* and his consort *Chac-hihuitlicue*, The Emerald Lady, whose children are the rain gods.

It is plausible to consider the goggle-eyed deity whose portrait accompanies the hand as a determinative, which further clarifies its meaning. Here we meet the likely forerunner of the Mesoamerican rain gods *Chac, Cosijo, Tajin,* and *Tlaloc*. The resemblance between this rain god and the Taino god *Hunrakan* shown in the ceramic figurine illustrated in figure 4.2 is astounding. The symbolic vocabulary used in

these images is virtually the same: The headdress is derived from a stylization of the rattles on the tail of the rattlesnake, a serpent whose activities are closely coordinated with the coming of the rains, and the "goggle-eyes" are representative of an affinity with four-legged reptiles who by tradition are the harbingers of the oncoming rains. The Maya also associated the rattles of the snake with *Tzab*, the Pleiades.

The now-extinct Taino were Arawakan Indians of the Caribbean islands and South America whose religious beliefs centered on a hierarchy of nature spirits and ancestors which closely paralleled the hierarchy of chiefs in their social structure. Theirs was the first language that the Spanish explorers of the New World came in contact with; consequently there were many word borrowings from the Arawak language including "canoe," "cigar," "cacique," "maize," "tobacco," and of course "hurricane." Herein lies a great curiosity as the semantic value of the word *Hunrakan* does not vary in Taino or Maya cultures and the same god in Nahua culture is known as *Hunrakan*.

In all these cultural cycles *Hunrakan* personified the tempest, rain, thunder, the lightning bolt, and the illumination produced by sheet lightning. In a classic example of how the demons of one culture can become the gods of another culture, the Taino largely relied on hunting and fishing so they had little use for rain and feared lightning and hurricanes. *Hunrakan* may have been revered but strictly as a powerful demon. The Maya and the Olmec, however, had worked out the basic techniques of intensive agriculture in the Formative Period from about 1500 B.C. to the beginning of the Christian era. In these societies *Hunrakan* was revered not only as a special deity but eventually as a god who was high up in the pantheon.

Hunrakan means One Foot in Maya languages; he is seen as the seven stars of the Big Dipper, hopping around the Polestar on one foot. All seven of the stars in this constellation are in ascendancy during the dry season from mid-October to mid-May but at these southerly latitudes they make a steep descent, disappearing below the horizon for half the night from mid-July to mid-October, the hurricane season. The origins of this god can therefore be traced back to this descent to the Earth in an ancient skylore. Yet we are now only beginning to realize why the hand crowning the Sanctuary of the Reliefs at Chalcacingo faces the north.

Why the hand is associated with the rain gods and the reason for its exalted position at the very top of the mountain is perhaps best explained by showing its use in Maya glyph formation. The titular glyph of *Chac*, the all-important God of Rain, is shown in figure 4.3A. Here it means "maker of life," as the hand, *kab* in Yucatec, is also a verb meaning "to do" or "to make something with one's hands." The rain gods are known as the Makers. A name of a specific divinity for example is *Kab Ul*, Powerful Hand. Among many other titles of the rain gods is *Ah Tzenulob*, the Nourishers or the Sustainers. The glyph carries the idea of germination and makers of life in general. The *ik*, "wind," sign forming the eye refers to the winds as allies of the rain gods but it also implies "life" and "spirit." It is the eye that perceives spiritual reality. The glyph has a reverential postfix indicating adoration.

In B the glyph is abbreviated and the mainsign is *Cauac*, the daysign of the rain and thunder deities. This daysign can carry the phonetic value *ku* and

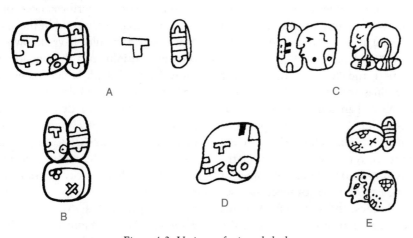

Figure 4.3. Variants of rain god glyphs

it can be simply read as *ku,* meaning god. When the Lunar Goddess is prefixed to this sign as in E we have *xku,* goddess.

A wise Huichol shaman once very simply and succinctly said, "We do not know how many gods there are." There are hundreds of rain gods or *Chacob* in the Maya pantheon. They are so numerous and so specialized that when they assemble a particular class known as *Xoc Tun Caan Chacob* (*Xoc* meaning "count") is required to keep account of them. The lesser *Chacob* reside in the forests or in caves when not engaged in rainmaking. The higher ranking *Chacob* reside in *Chun Caan,* "at the foot of the sky," in the east except when they take positions at the four cardinal directions during the rainy season. In the north is *Sac-Xib-Chac,* who is associated with the color white and the element air; in the west is *Ek-Xib-Chac,* black and water; to the south is *Kan-Xib-Chac,* yellow and earth. The supreme *Chac-Xib-Chac* takes his position at the top, in the superior eastern quadrant associated with the element fire. *Chac,* the first part of his name means "red" and "great" and it is he that came to be known as "God B."

Around the turn of the century Paul Schellhas analyzed the Maya deities and established an alphabetic nomenclature, assigning letters to the principal gods in the pantheon. His scheme proved to be very helpful but presently, since we now know the actual names of the gods, I think it has outlived its usefulness. Besides, the arrangement tends to give equal stature to all gods in the pantheon, whereas certain gods such as

"God B" fulfill uniquely important and central roles. Also, it is now known that some of the gods that are distinguished in the alphabetic listing are actually aspects of the same divine being.

Chac-Xib-Chac is specifically named in the glyphs shown in C. The first glyph combines *Chac,* "great" and "red," with *Xib* meaning "young man." In this I think that the deity incorporates another god, whom very little is known about in the Maya pantheon but who makes an appearance in the Aztec pantheon as *Telpochtli,* the Eternally Young Man. The second glyph is composed of the *Chac*-hand subfixed with the phonetic *c(i)* or *k(i),* which acts as a determinative. This is followed by a spiralic form that represents water and appears as a body mark or "god-sign" in his full-figure portraits.

It will become very apparent in this study that the god *Chac-Xib-Chac* transforms into human guise as *Hunahpu,* first born of the Hero Twins, and vice versa. The transformation of *Hunahpu* into *Chac-Xib-Chac* was a central theme in the theatrical performances of the *Popol Vuh* that every child in the ancient Maya world would have known. My own first insight into the phenomenon came from a glyph which names *Hunahpu* in a vase painting to be subsequently discussed in detail. Affixed to the head portrait of *Hunahpu* is the titular glyph of *Chac-Xib-Chac.* The artist has here "spilled the beans" and reveals to us the hidden identity of *Hunahpu.* It may be mentioned in passing that it is not a coincidence that the name *Hunahpu* bears a close resemblance to the name of the hidden god, *Hunab*

Ku, the all-present but invisible Giver of Movement and Measure.

An important but very poorly understood ichnographic attribute of *Chac-Xib-Chac* is the ax he wields. It was popularly known that the ax was used by the *Chacob* to break open the clay jars holding the precious waters in the heavens, causing thunder and releasing rainfall. The ax also carried a much deeper spiritual significance. We have seen how the hand in the "west" glyph can substitute for the snake-tail rattles carrying the phonetic value *och*. West is sometimes written *Och K'in*, Entrance of the Sun, being descriptive of the west as the portal through which the Sun daily enters the underworld in its journey through the Earth. A holy shaman also has the power to enter this portal along with the Sun. The ax in the *Batab* glyph is expressive of the shamanistic ability to break open portals into the spirit realms.

An actual early ceremonial axhead, illustrated in figure 4.4A, was found with other ritual objects in a tomb in Belize. The lord who was buried in the tomb probably entered the afterlife in the disguise of *Chac-Xib-Chac*, a not-uncommon practice. Remember that *Hunahpu* transformed himself into his guise of *Chac-Xib-Chac* in order to defeat the gods of death in the underworld. The mythological events are a reenactment of the nightly journey of the Sun.

The ax is greenstone, nearly nine inches in height, and the engravings are filled with a red pigment. Below the portrait head of *Chac-Xib-Chac* are four glyphs that represent a very early style

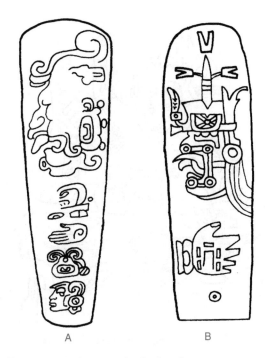

Figure 4.4. A. Ceremonial axhead, Belize; B. Olmec ceremonial axhead

but the second glyph can be recognized as the creative generative hand of the Rain God infixed with a water sign. Even earlier, and perhaps a forerunner of this axhead, is the Olmec ceremonial ax shown in B which bears a striking resemblance. Here the hand is infixed with an inverted u-shape design that signifies water. Below it is the circular bead symbol meaning "water," "jade," and "precious." The Rain God here displays bird characteristics and to explain these we must again revert to the great portal in the northern sky, the Polestar and the Big Dipper.

First, let's take a look at the sketch of an Olmec painting of a shaman rainmaker shown in figure 4.5 which was

Figure 4.5. Olmec cave painting

found in a cave. The imagery closely parallels that on the Olmec axhead. When they were not busy precipitating the rains, the *Chacob* were thought to reside in caves. Therefore if the expected rains were not forthcoming it was a common practice of the rainmakers to enter the caves to perform rainmaking ceremonies. Consequently many ritual objects related to *Tlaloc* are found in caves. In the painting the artist cleverly designs the waistband of the shaman in the form of an *ik*-sign. Two rain-hands also adorn his apparel. These echo the movement of the shaman's hands as they extend toward the waterbead in the sky and draw the life-generating substance to the Earth. The shaman sits on a sun-eyed jaguar throne. What is emphasized is the fanged, open mouth of

the roaring beast. This painting needs not only to be seen but it also should be heard. The roar of the jaguar is the rumbling thunder that will bring on the rains.

We see the shaman's face in an X-ray view through the mask of a macaw bird. The technique of using X-ray vision to see through masks was later to be a widely used convention in Maya art. The macaw, the principal bird deity in the Maya cosmos, is known as *Vucub Caquix*, "Seven Macaw," referring to the seven stars in the Big Dipper. His wife, *Chimalmat*, is the Little Dipper. The tail feathers of this long-tailed, brightly colored parrot are what we see as the handle of the Big Dipper.

Seven Macaw is also known as *Itzam Yeh*, "the Bringer of Magic," and as such he is considered to be the *way* of *Itzamna*, the first wizard of the Maya cosmos. Besides rain, *itz* can refer to the cosmic sap or blessed substance of the heavens that is universally sought by shamans through opening a portal in the sky. *Itz* can also apply to a variety of special essences and liquids including semen, morning dew, holy water, and it is compared to the nectar of flowers. In the glyphic representations of *Itzam Yeh*, the magical bird is paired with a *Cauac* sign. Below issues forth the sacred nectar of the gods. The *itz* of Seven Macaw pours forth from the portal in the Polestar around which he hovers in the sky.

In mythology, Seven Macaw was the "sun" of the former creation, not a true sun, but the antithesis of all behavior and values held dear by the Maya. He usurped the role of the Sun, stating,

"I am great. My place is now higher than that of the human work, the human design. I am their sun and I am their light and I am also their months." Eventually he had to confront *Hunahpu*, the synthesis of all those behaviors and values.

The origins of *Hunahpu* as a god extend far back to a remote era prior to the development of large-scale agricultural technologies that sustained the great Maya city-states. Apparently *Hunahpu* was a major god in a pantheon of earlier migrating hunting societies in which he was the God of the Woods. In Maya art he sometimes retains some of his earlier characteristics when he dons the apparel of a deer hunter. It is really quite amazing how Maya mythology reflects the transformation of migrating tribes into settled agricultural communities: The first successful humans, those of the present era, are created from corn by the gods. And we find the first evidence of domesticated corn around the time of the crucial calendrical date, August 13, 3114 B.C.

The name *Hunahpu* is composed of *hun*, "one," *ah*, which is occupational and means literally "he of," and *pu*, derived from the onomatopoetic *puh* meaning "blowgun." So the name can be translated One Blowgunner. It is with this instrument that the hero finally deals with Seven Macaw, who is usually depicted perched on top of the World Tree—the Milky Way—in the highest layer of the heavens. The fall of Seven Macaw is reflected in the night sky by the descent and disappearance of the Big Dipper beneath the horizon, a drama reenacted every year in synchronicity with the coming of the hurricane season. That is why the macaw is closely associated with the rains.

The residences of Mesoamerican deities are found in the stars. Rain gods are closely associated with the North Star, but they also have dwelling houses in the signs of the zodiac. In the Nahua system of daysigns, *Tlaloc* corresponds to *Cauac* and he resides alone in the constellation we know as Aquarius. His head portrait represents *Quiahuitl*, the Rain Day, as shown in figure 4.6A. The chief characteristics of the sign are the fanged jaws of the jaguar and the reptilian goggle-eye. Literally *Tlaloc* means

*Figure 4.6.A. Nahua glyph of **Tlaloc**; B. Nahua cylindrical stamp; C. The cedar tree glyph*

"path under the earth" or "long cave," an idea also contained in the *Cauac* glyph, which may be interpreted as a cave with water dripping from above into a pool below. As caves are regarded as sacred entrances into the realm of gods and spirits, the *Cauac* sign is sometimes used to signal the idea of a portal. *Cauac* or *caoc* is an onomatopoetic expression of lightning and thunder. It becomes descriptive of that extra body-soul called lightning, by which a shaman can access and communicate directly with both natural and spiritual worlds.

Daysigns as well as numbers and directions were revered as living gods. This was not only true of the ancient Maya, but is elegantly expressed in excerpts from the *Chuj Pantheon*, obtained in 1959 from Huehuetango, Guatemala:

> *There are twenty day gods who see us, take care of us each day. One day god sees us each day. . . . Those day gods have exactly the same power of the Sun, which is our god. . . . All those things are companions together, all are gods. The wood things, the crosses, they are really our gods, because that is where the day gods live. . . . Never let these things be lost, because they are alive. They are alive with the day gods and the day-night gods. . . . They are always united with the Sun, our god.*

The glyph *kuche*, the divine cedar tree, is shown in figure 4.6C. It means *ku*, "god," and *che*, "tree," and it alone was used in making wooden crosses, idols, and religious paraphernalia. The glyph is a cross with *Cauac* signs inset. Some of the ideas in the *Chuj Pantheon*

are also reflected graphically in the design from a cylindrical stamp illustrated in B which shows *Tlaloc* infused with an emblem of the Sun.

A *Tlaloc*, like a *Chac*, is thought to control one of the four kinds of water that can reach the Earth. Only one of these is beneficial, the gentle rain that relinquishes the sky to the Sun's rays, fathering the maize and fertilizing the Earth as symbolized in B. The creative and generative power of the Sun is emphasized by the extended and enlarged handsign of the Monkey God. As the human body is thought of as incorporating the twenty daysigns, the Day of the Monkey, *Ozomatli* in Nahuatl and *Chuen* or *Batz* in Maya languages, is associated with the left hand and represents the Sun as the Great Craftsman or Maker. The right hand corresponds to the daysign *Men*, the Eagle. In Maya writing both of these glyphs are used to designate artists, architects, and those in the craft professions.

In these cultures the Rain God and the Monkey God have a special relationship and both deities have an affinity with the Polestar: They represent primary creative forces and are initiators and enterers in the dynamics of the cosmology. As discussed, in one Maya version of the Creation, written in the *Chumayel*, the cosmogenesis commences on the day *Hun Chuen*: "On One Monkey he raised himself to his divinity, after he made heaven and Earth." On Two *Eb*, "He made his first stairway. It descended from the midst of the heavens, in the midst of the water, where there was neither earth, rocks, nor trees." On Three *Ben*, "He made all things. . . ." *Ben* in Yucatec (or *Ah* in Quiche) is the day of the lord who fosters the growth of the maize stalk. It symbolizes the growth and development of humanity. On Four Jaguar, "sky and earth were tilted." I take this to mean that the ancient Maya were well aware of the tilt in the Earth's axis. On Five *Men*, "He made everything. . . . "

Another creation event from Maya cosmogenesis texts states that "he (the first father) began to turn the north axis." He raised the sky above the Earth before setting it in motion by establishing the *Wakah-Chan*, Six-Sky, Raised-Up-Sky, or the Tree at the Center of the World. The idea is paralleled in the Nahua calendar, which began in the early spring with the planting of the maize. By the fourth month, *Hueytozoztli*, the Great Vigil, all the plants had sprouted and the rains were anxiously awaited. In front of the temples of *Tlaloc*, trees were set up marking the four cardinal directions. In the center was a large tree called *Tota*, Our Father, symbolizing the center of the cosmos and establishing communication with the divinity in the Heart of Heaven.

In figure 4.7 are three Maya glyphs meaning "north." In A a head portrait of the Monkey God is affixed by the phonetic *na* or *nal* meaning "place." Curiously this glyph reads *xaman* and is pronounced like the English word "shaman." In B a substitute for it bears the emblematic markings of the Vision Serpent, the medium of communication with the ancestors and the spirit world. The glyph in C shows where contact with the ancestor takes place. The mainsign *chan*, "sky," is altered, showing the

Figure 4.7. *Maya glyphs meaning north*

flared opening of the portal at the top of the sky. In Nahau culture the abode of the ancestors, *Mictlan*, the Land of the Dead, is situated in the north.

Glyphs shown in figure 4.8 are related in that they refer to a fundamental principle of Maya cosmology that is deeply rooted in shamanistic traditions. The glyph in A reads *Wakah-Chan* and is imbued with layers of meanings. The god of the number six, *Wak*, prefixed to the mainsign sky (*chan* in Cholan, *kan* in Yucatec) means "Six-Sky" or the four cardinal directions and the nadir and zenith. The ax-eye of the Rain God indicates that he possesses the inner vision that penetrates reality and breaks open portals to the spirit world. The sound *wak* combined with the phonetic *ah* (a double *Ben* daysign) renders the word *wakah*, or "raised up"; and the *Wakah-Chan* can refer to the Milky Way raised up on its north-south axis. This creates the tree at the center of the world, the path to the spirit world traversed by the dead and through which shamans gain access to the realms of the unknown.

The glyph in B is *tzuk-te*, which refers directly to the World Tree that extends into the Otherworld through the portal of the Polestar represented by the Monkey God. In pictorial compositions the World Tree will usually contain a head portrait of the Monkey God, here suffixed by a *te* sign meaning "tree." In C is the glyph of the number thirteen personified as *Chac-Xib-Chac*. As the number thirteen, he wears the headdress of the daysign *Chuen*, the Day of the Monkey. Since all the stars in the night sky appear to revolve around the Polestar, it is called the Heart of Heaven. The thirteen layers of the heavens are presided over by the *Oxlahun Ti Ku*, the Thirteen of God, the number gods who are the main actors in the drama of time. When the layers are

spread in a giant arc across the sky, the highest level will be in the center or the seventh layer. Viewed this way the Heart of Heaven is the god seven, the Jaguar of the Night Sky and the daysign *Akbal* or Darkness. The levels are alternatively envisioned as being mounted vertically in an ascending order, reaching the Polestar at the highest level. In this arrangement the counterpart of the Jaguar of the Night Sky, *Chac-Xib-Chac*, occupies the portal of the Polestar so as the god of the number thirteen he sometimes dons the headdress of the Monkey God. The daysign of thirteen is *Muluc* or Water.

The glyphs shown in D are *Xaman* as the First Lord of Night. The hand represents the presentation of the Sun to one of the twenty day gods at dawn. The Monkey God is shown imbibing *itz ka'an*, the blessed substance of the sky. At night the nine levels of the underworld revolve into the sky. Paradoxically

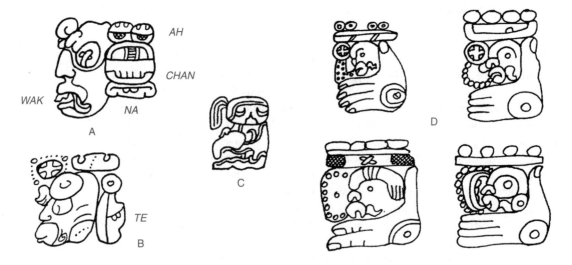

Figure 4.8. Related Maya glyphs

 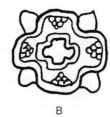 

A   B   C

Figure 4.9. Maya symbols of the portal

the glyph of the First Lord of Night is affixed by the number nine. The reference is not to the number sequence but to the highest and most sacred place in the heavens which must be the First Lord of Night. On the first created day of our era *Xaman* was the Lord of the Night. In the Nahua system it is *Tlaloc* who reigns as the ninth or highest of the *Yohualteuctin*, the Gods of the Night.

We have seen that to the Maya the setting up of an altar is a sacred ceremony that "opens up the road" to the spirit world. The glyph shown in figure 4.9A is taken from stela 9 at Copan. In the center is the *be*, "road," symbol reached by steps or ladders and surrounded by the time-space cosmogram which provides the transcending access that communicates between the material and spiritual worlds. Glyphs in B and C are excerpted from altars at Copan. The *Ik* and *Cauac* markings have meanings that extend far beyond "wind" and "rain." *Ik* here means "spirit," and the *Cauac* signs are indicative of *Ku*, God, and the spirits of the ancestors residing beyond the great portal in the sky.

A Huichol shaman once said that "Everything is alive; there is nothing dead in the world. The people say the dead are dead; but they are very much

alive." Maya glyphs come to life when it is realized that, in the hidden underlying framework based on the orientation of the principal time-space cosmogram, the gods are by convention all depicted facing north, gazing through the portal into the sacred realm of the ancestors and *Hunab Ku*. The One God is unseen but in this unique device manifests a permeating presence throughout practically the whole corpus of the art, magnetizing and uniting all the other gods in the orientation of the eternal in time and the all-in-one in space. There is nothing more hidden than that which is so blatantly obvious and pervasive that it is inconspicuously veiled as in a shroud of invisibility.

Maya art cannot be understood by merely looking; it must be seen and experienced within the context of the cosmological principles from which it springs forth. Viewed in reference to the spiritual traditions it embodies, the art itself becomes a portal through which we peer into the very consciousness of ancient shaman-artists. They not only used their art to give order and meaning to their lives but used it as a tool to penetrate into the mysteries of human existence. The communicatively powerful art and writing they left behind are tes-

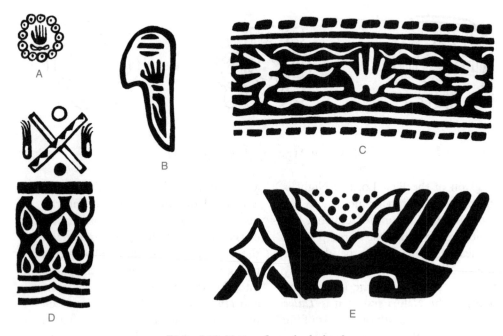

Figure 4.10. Various flat and cylindrical stamps

timony to that quest. The matter of Maya art not being generally accepted even today as true art, but regarded as the product of mere tribal conventions and traditions, will be dealt with in subsequent chapters. Here it is beginning to dawn on us that we are dealing with one of the most uniquely formidable and artistically adept schools of art and script in all the annals of art history.

Some of the art that actually *is* tribal is nevertheless revealing. It is safe to assume that the vocabulary of symbols previously discussed was utilized by an elite class of rulers, priests, priestesses, and highly skilled professional castes of artists. However, the designs shown in figure 4.10 were mass-produced by ordinary people to fulfill the nonindividualistic immediate material needs of

agricultural communities. They show us that the typical *tlalmaitl*, a "hand of the earth" who worked the land but did not own it, was probably conversant with much of the symbolic language of the elite and at the very least had a knowledge of the basic tenets of the belief systems. As these motifs originate from widely distant parts of Mesoamerica, and similar ones are found in the Maya country, they also indicate that the belief systems were remarkably coherent and unified. The designs are from stamps that were created for the mass production of art used in ceremonies concerned with rain god propitiation. They were probably used as body markings but could also have been used to imprint clothing and other objects.

In A, the hand shown is certainly

that of the Makers as it is surrounded by a circle of thirteen jade or water beads. In B, the hand is extended toward a water sign and inset within the ax of the Rain God. In all likelihood the seven stars of the Big Dipper were yet another image; as the constellation was seen to plunge down below the horizon, signaling the hurricane season, it would be hard not to see in it the descending ax of the Rain God.

The hands in C are moving amidst wavy lines indicating water. The hands in D are sometimes referred to as "jaguar" claws but they bear little resemblance to an actual feline claw. Rather they have much more in common with the elongated digits of reptiles, closely associated with the coming of the rains. Above the sky crossbands, the Sun is appropriately positioned in the east and the Moon is in the west. Below this a net pattern describes a cloud saturated with water, each mesh containing a drop of the precious rain. The water produced is represented as the three wavy lines. The Olmec design in E has a hand that bears a close resemblance to a handsign still currently used in Maya country. It means "the moon that retains water." The hand is inset with a cave or earth symbol and the water held is in the form of a cloud saturated with rain, symbolized by the thirteen drops it contains.

The creative, manifesting hand is the central motif in the great metropolis of Teotihuacan. The placename means "the place where humans become gods" or "Place of Deification." Numerous legends and traditions attest that this was the site of the Creation. Archae-ological excavations beneath one of its great pyramids revealed that it was built over seven caves. Nahua myth asserts that human beings emerged from seven caves:

> *When there was night,*
> *When there was no day,*
> *When there was no light,*
> *There was a reunion.*
> *There was a convocation of the gods,*
> *Down there in Teotihuacan.*

The position of the front of the Pyramid of the Sun, 15°30' east of astronomical north, is such that the Sun sets exactly in alignment with it on the day it reaches its zenith, that is, when there is no shadow at noon. It is interesting to compare the Pyramid of the Sun—one of the greatest archaeological monuments of America, built around the year 100 B.C.—with the Cheops Pyramid, the largest in Egypt, built in the year 2650 B.C. The base of the Cheops Pyramid measures 247.33 yards on each side, whereas the Pyramid of the Sun measures 246.66, the difference being two-thirds of a yard!

Some of the hands in Teotihuacan art manifest watery substance such as that shown in figure 4.11A. In C, the hand of a priest, or god impersonator, generates water as he sows the seeds of creation while praising the gods in flowery scrolls indicative of poetry and song. A Nahua saying "In *xochitl* (flower), in *cuicatl* (song)" is an expression meaning "poetry," the only earthly truth. The murals are a celebration of the gods and the poetry of their paradises and earthly creations. The bird, butterfly, and flower form of *Xochipilli*,

Figure 4.11. A. *Teotihuacan mural, detail*; B. **Xilonen, Princess of Unripe Maize**, *Nahua statue;*
C. *Teotihuacan mural, detail*; D. *Teotihuacan, vase painting detail*

the personification of the soul shown in D, is taken from a vase painting depicting him as "he who has the power of giving spiritual flowers."

The generative power of the hands shown in the murals is reflected in the Nahua statue of a rain goddess *Xilonen*, Princess of Unripe Maize, illustrated in B. In the fourth month of their calendar, young bare-breasted girls in the guise of the rain goddess made a procession to the cornfields in ceremonies that invoked the expected and by then

sorely needed rains. Even if the rains had already arrived the procession was performed to insure the continuation of the downpours. The goddess is shown manifesting the rains as she extends her upheld hands in a universal gesture: The rainy season has arrived. This was a crucial period in the agricultural cycle. If the proper type of rain did not arrive at the right time, the tender green sprouting corn would be withered by the devastating rays of the Sun. An entire crop could be destroyed causing thousands

Figure 4.12. Art from Teotihuacan murals

to starve, so intensive ceremonies were performed to induce the sympathy of the rain gods.

It is little wonder that the demon of the early hunting societies made a rapid advance to the very pinnacle of the pantheon in agricultural communities. In the City of the Gods, *Tlaloc* reigned supreme. In a mural illustrated in figure 4.12A, he is shown in his watery paradise, *Tlalocan*, surrounded by flowing fountains of the precious substance he generates from his hands, which display open seashells. The waters are alive with turtles and waterlilies. A Maya resident or visitor to the sacred metropolis would have been charmed and delighted by the instantly recognizable symbolism of this imagery; and indeed many were as the *Tlaloc* cult eventually made its way southward deep into the Maya heartland.

Water is shown emanating from the hands of two priests who offer poetic praises to the Rain God. The artist fur-

ther infuses their hands with symbolic meaning as each holds an incense burner known as a *Tlemaitl*, the Hand of Fire. (In Nahua culture, the incense burner was revered as a ritual implement central to the fire ceremony and referred to as the Hand of Fire. The butterfly, because of the flickering movement of its wings, was a symbol of fire besides being an emblem of the soul. The wonderful flat stamp from Tula, Mexico, shown in figure 4.13, is actually a personification of the Hand of Fire.) The image represents a deification of the elements fire and water in which it is the function of human shaman-priests to balance these primary forces in nature. This balanced and harmonious pictorial composition includes the fire element in a symmetry that exists in the aquatic paradise but that can also be achieved on the earthly plane of existence.

While the water element is the more obvious, the mural expresses the union of opposites. Immediately below the macaw headdress, the rhomboid eyes of the mask are characteristic of the Fire God. Above the headdress is a halo, the symbol of the *papalotl*, the butterfly, personifying fire. In the order of the thirteen hours of the day, the butterfly represents the seventh hour, the Heart of the Sky or noon, when the Sun reaches its highest point in the sky. This time of day is ruled by *Xochipilli* who is shown in the guise of a butterfly in D. Rhomboid forms with sun symbols adorning the necklace of *Tlaloc* in B represent very ancient symbols of the Fire God. Here *Tlaloc* appears in Jaguar-Bird-Serpent aspect, a deity creating the world of forms as he unites opposing

Figure 4.13. A cylindrical stamp from Nahua culture depicts a butterfly symbolizing fire with a human hand meaning a Tlemaitl, the "Hand of Fire" or an "incense burner"

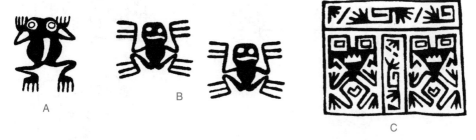

Figure 4.14. A & B. Flat stamps, Teotihuacan; C. Flat stamp, Guerrero

cosmic forces and reintegrates the three planes of existence.

In C *Tlaloc* holds luminous arrows of consciousness representing the interior lightning that reveals a state of holiness. From his right hand, gloved in a jaguar paw, emanate eyes representing the interior vision that sees beyond external illusions and perceives the unity of matter in reality. The cosmic union of fire and water is masterfully expressed in the image of *Xochipilli* in the vase rollout shown in D. Referring to the doctrine that matter "buds and flowers" because of the power that unites opposing forces in nature, symbols of water and fire gods are fused in a single icon. Exuding creative spirit and energy the arms are extended to form a cross in which the figure echoes the *ik* sign, forming the mouth and symbolizing the breath of life. On the breast of the deity, the crossed bands of the hieroglyph *Ollin*, Movement, which corresponds to the Maya daysign *Caban* or Earth, appear directly above the heart, the place of unity.

In both Maya and Nahua cultures, frogs are the associates and allies of the rain gods. The croaking of frogs announces the coming of the rains; and if the downpours are not forthcoming, young boys perform ceremonies of sympathetic magic in which they squat while imitating the croaking sounds to invoke the rains. Designs from flat stamps found in Teotihuacan, shown in figures 4.14A and B, and one from Guerrero in C, were probably used to tattoo their bodies in preparation for such ceremonies. The pronounced use of the hands in these designs, especially in C, shows that the appeal was made to the rain gods as "the Makers," "the causers of germination."

The Maya word *uo*, "frog," is the specific name of a black frog with a bright orange line down its back. It is also the name of the second month in the calendar. Since the Maya word *u* means "moon" and "month," the frog becomes closely associated with the Moon and is a symbol of the *uinal* in the count of days. The Moon Goddess, *Xau*, is the patroness of the rains, floods, and cloudbursts gushing water, and is known as Lady Rainbow and Lady Sea among many other names. In the time-space quadrant her position is below in the female quadrant in the west, representing the element water, opposed to the male quadrant at the top

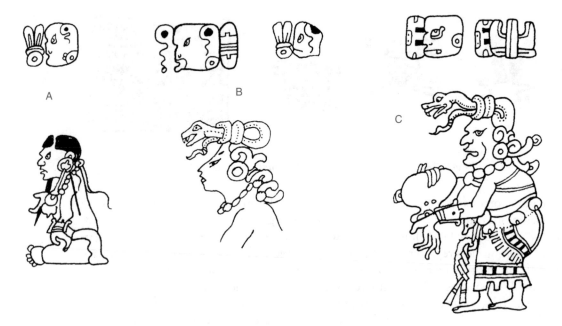

Figure 4.15. Glyphs and portraits of the Moon Goddess from the codices

representing fire and her husband, the Sun. She is sometimes associated with the north and the color white. Her name glyph in the codices can be prefixed by *Sac* or white as shown in figure 4.15A, or by *Chac* as shown in C, so as a rain goddess she has much in common with *Chac-Xib-Chac*. Her special attribute is the rain-bearing clay jar she holds as a sky goddess, which also figures in some of her name glyphs. Her transformations as an old goddess or a young goddess are reflections of the age of the Moon.

Her most characteristic handsign, "moon" in American Indian Sign Language, is made by curving the thumb and the index finger of the hand to form a segment or quarter moon. In the sign language the gesture resembles the sign for "sun." A Plains Indian will sometimes sign "night" first and then "sun" meaning "night sun" to refer to the Moon. In Maya art the sign "moon" is usually quite distinct, the arc formed being much wider than the more circular "sun" sign. Note the handsign shown in C.

The sacred mudra of the Moon Goddess is emphasized in one of her dramatic appearances in the art as illustrated in the vase in figure 4.16. Her handsign echoes the glyphic rendition of the lunar crescent in which she is enthroned astride the back of a feathered Vision Serpent. She holds a rabbit, a fertility symbol that is mythologically associated by the Maya with the full Moon and whose physical features are thought to appear therein. Three gods appear in the encoiled loops of the serpent. On the left the Monkey God appears with an *Akbal* or "darkness" sign. The two other gods appear to be be *Chac-Xib-Chac.* In the lower right corner of the illustration is a stepped portal that begins with the head of a personified *Akbal* sign. *Akbal* is associated with the west, the mouth of the underworld, the cave entrance into Xibalba, the land of the dead into which the Sun enters each night. It seems likely that this vase was used in funerary rituals calling forth and materializing the gods of the night to aid and guide the soul of the departed in its perilous journey, metaphorically compared to that of the Sun.

It is most extraordinary that the contemporary Maya handsigns carrying the same meanings for various aspects of the Moon can be seen in the ancient art. In figure 4.17A, a handsign in use today meaning "the young moon is rising" is shown.

In figure 4.17B is a handsign that refers to the dry season, meaning "the moon retains water." The *Chac* in figure 4.18A clearly makes this sign as the water flowing from his jug, which is decorated with the emblem of the four corners of the world, flows upward and does not reach the Earth. The handsign in figure 4.17A also refers to the rainy season and means "the moon lets water escape." In figure 4.18B, a *Chac* is shown releasing one of the four kinds of rain that can reach the Earth. This is the most beneficial, the gentle rain that relinquishes the sky to sunshine. Here the *Chac* forms the *K'in*-hand, which is juxtapositioned to the emblem of the Sun directly beneath it.

The real God B then is the supreme Rain God, *Chac-Xib-Chac,* a deification

Figure 4.16. Cylindrical vase featuring the Moon Goddess

Figure 4.17. Contemporary Maya handsigns

of the element water who can transform into his avatar, or human aspect, the Hero Twin *Hunahpu.* As firstborn of the Twins he precedes the rising Sun as the Morning Star in the eastern sky. He makes his residence in the highest level of the heavens when not busy making rain. His position in the pantheon of gods is paramount and central; consequently he appears with great frequency in the codices and in monumental in-

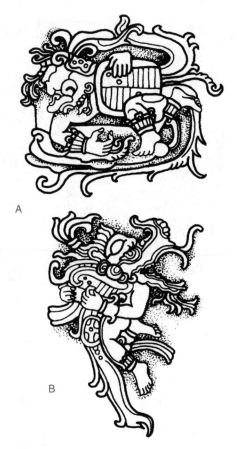

A

B

Figure 4.18. Architectural portraits of **Chac-Xib-Chac** *in stone; from Copan*

est level of the night sky. The number *bolon* or *Yax* has numerous connotations in Maya languages including "fresh," "new," "immeasurable," and "infinite." The other illustrations are taken from the codices wherein there are consistent aquatic associations (except in F). In B, he presides with his ax over a *cenote* or water hole, another kind of portal. In C, he transforms into a water serpent. D shows him immersed in his element complete with sand and shell symbols from which he harvests a flower, the blossom of true life with its origins in the primordial waters. In E he sits in the sky-band throne of the thirteenth heaven, holding the *Wakah-Chan*, the Serpent of the Milky Way.

In F he is depicted as a god who possesses the unifying vision that sees the reality behind the world of illusion. Shown is the Maya equivalent of the "third eye," the *chakra* of mystics of the East that, when opened, reveals penetrating knowledge. In H he appears in reptilian form grasping a catfish from the waters. In the *Popol Vuh* the Hero Twins transform into catfish for the initial stage of their resurrection. Maya nobles are frequently depicted wearing elaborate headdresses in which a catfish nibbles on a waterlily, which I think is a reference to this episode. A catfish barbel appears on his cheek in his most frequently used name glyph shown in A.

Chac-Xib-Chac can be regarded as the most intriguing and vibrantly dynamic image ever created by the human imagination. He was the product of the fertile minds of a people who independently developed true writing, an advanced system of mathematics, and one

scriptions, some of which are shown in figure 4.19.

In A there is a variant of his name glyph as it appears in monumental inscriptions. The number three is a reference to the daysign *Cauac*, third in the number sequence that starts with *Caban*. It may also refer to the three realms of the Maya cosmos through which, as a supreme shaman, he can ascend and descend at will. The "nine" here probably refers to a place, the high-

Figure 4.19. Various portraits of **Chac-Xib-Chac** *from the codices*

of the most fascinating and most accurate calendars in the world. As a divine being he personifies an element, a number, and a cardinal direction. He is a divinity that embodies animal characteristics and yet becomes incarnated in human form as a hero-trickster who triumphs over the gods of death in the underworld. As a sky divinity he reigns in the highest heavens, totally benevolent toward humankind in producing the rains. In certain individual traits he may be compared to some of the gods or heroes of other religions and mythologies, but in his totality, as a composite creation, he is unique and incomparable throughout all the annals of human history, with one exception. Ultimately his personality and feats are matched by his counterpart, *Kauil*, the personification of fire.

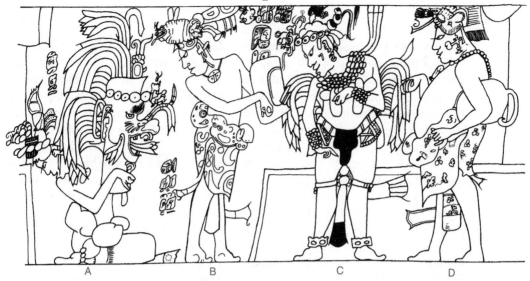

A   B   C   D

Figure 5.1. **The Apparition of Kauil, 1,** *cylindrical vase*

THE SMOKING MIRROR

By the time I had come to comprehend the precise nature of the ceremony depicted in figure 5.1, I had already ascertained a number of pertinent facts about it. The mask held by the courtier in A represents an image of the god *Kauil*, the Smoking Mirror. Above the crest of the forehead is a mirror emanating two plumes of smoke, the logographic emblem of *Kauil*. The ornament projecting from the headband of the mask is a head portrait of the god which also appears on the headband worn by the lord in C. Aspiration toward the divine is reflected in masks and feathered ornaments representing degrees of spiritual consciousness through which the body is converted into a hieroglyphic mystical formula. The lord in B displays the sacred mirror while the participant in D holds an enema bag containing hallucinogenic substances. The scene portrayed contains all the necessary ingredients of a sacred rite in progress in which the performers seek to attain a superhuman state of transcendence by invoking the divine presence of *Kauil*.

The glyph in E (at the top) serves to confirm this initial impression. *Ahk'ot* is literally translated "to dance," but by extension it means "to perform ceremonies that manifest divine beings." In Mesoamerican cultures, dancing was a primary way of contacting the spirit world and gaining sustenance from the gods. Even now communal dancing in the Huichol country is the primary activity in religious gatherings performed to materialize the gods and establish contact with the spirit world. Such dancing can extend continuously throughout the night, even go on for days. It is regarded as the work or effort necessary to pay the gods for letting the rains fall and allowing corn and squash to grow. When the glyph *Ti ahk'ot*, "He or she went or goes dancing," appears in Maya texts it does not necessarily mean that the person physically performs a dance, although this is implied and sometimes depicted. The glyph actually refers to the performance of any ceremony that contacts or manifests a divine presence.

Directly below this glyph, and in the geometric center of the composition, is the sacred mirror displayed by the lord in B as he signs the mudra of *Kauil* with his right hand. This handsign contains within it two of the god's most fundamental characteristics: *Kauil* as the avatar of the Sun, which is the sign being formed on the hand; and *Kauil* transformed into *Xbalanque*, the second born of the Hero Twins, associated with the Sun, and the personification of the number nine.

Nine, as we have seen, is expressed in the handsign language by pressing together the index finger and the thumb. It is not a mere coincidence that this is also the sign of the Sun; rather it demonstrates an intricate system of symbols interlinking gods, number, and handsigns. The same sign is displayed by the lords in A, C, and D. The mutual display of this sign signals the manifestation of the god: We are looking in on a climactic moment of a rite that materializes the divine presence of *Kauil*, the founder of Maya culture, the serpent of the east, the creator of humanity and organic life, and the sacred being who is the embodiment of spiritual force in the material world.

The main actor in this drama is the lord in C who is probably named as the dancer in the text. His attire is indeed that of a dancer, the feathers likening his shamanistic "dance" to the flight of birds. His left hand reverently displays the sacred mudra of *Kauil* while his right hand points downward in a gesture that, as we shall see later, is cognate with the glyph *yalhiya*, meaning "he spoke it, he manifested it." In fact, both of these handsigns make their appearance in the writing as manographs. They describe precisely and succinctly what the performer is doing, that is, enacting a form of the ancient and widespread Mesoamerican rite known as "bringing down the sun."

While the handsigns, the glyph, and the imagery provided insights into the meaning of this intriguing vase painting, there was a fundamental element in the composition that completely eluded me and created quite a dilemma for a long time. The actors in A, B, and C are engaged in a very specific activity: They simultaneously gaze intently at something the artist does not depict in the painting. Obviously this is an essential element in the ritual depicted which cried out for an explanation and I was not "getting it." I found this disturbing and eventually I taped the rollout diagram of the vase painting to the wall immediately above my desk.

The Aztec counterpart of *Kauil* is *Tezcatlipoca*, "the mirror that sees all the world in its reflection." The name is derived from the Nahua words *tezcatl*, "obsidian mirror," and *popoca*, "smoking." Late one night I was at my desk reading some post-Conquest ethnographic accounts concerning *Tezcatlipoca* that were originally written in Nahuatl and Spanish by a Franciscan priest who arrived in Mexico in 1529. In his *Historia general de las cosas de nueva España*, Bernardino de Sahagun describes ceremonies held during *Teotleco*, the twelfth month of the calendar (September 20-October 9), marking the return of the gods. *Teo* means "god" and *tleco* means "return." During this month *Tezcatlipoca* leads a procession of gods or god impersonators in a return to the Earth from a sojourn in the skies. The priest writes:

At midnight they ground a little maize flour and made a good thick mass of it; they made this mass of flour round like cheese, upon a rush mat. By this means they perceived when all the gods had arrived, because a small footprint appeared in the flour; then they understood that the gods had come. A priest . . . remained waiting all night when this sign of the arrival of the gods was to appear, and he came and went many times an hour, to look at the mat and when he saw the footprint in the flour, then that priest said: "His majesty has come." (p. 204)

I raised my eyes from the book and looked at the diagram immediately before me on the wall. Suddenly it became animated as a slice of Maya spiritual life frozen in time. The climactic moment in the drama of an ancient ritual is depicted as the priests stare in awe and wonder at the appearance of the footprint! The most important element in the painting is that which is unseen, the appearance of the divine presence of *Kauil* in his aspect of the Invisible God. Although the hidden deity is not physically rendered, the scene is imbued with his presence and saturated with his titular symbols. The interwoven elements of the mask, the mirror, the apparition, and the accompanying handsigns are intricately orchestrated in the painting, itself like a mirror image of the event. Through it we can intimately perceive a reflection of an invocation of *Kauil*, transporting us to the innermost sanctuary of an ancient Maya court.

Sahagun goes on to record that after the pronouncement "His majesty has come" is made, the other priests and ministers of the idols ". . . rose and played their conches and trumpets in every temple, in every district and in every village . . ." (p. 204)

A second version of *The Apparition of Kauil*, shown in figure 5.2, is from a cylindrical vessel that had its origins in the Maya lowlands during the Late Classic period (A.D. 600-800). This painting, though far removed from Sahagun's world in space and time, nevertheless serves as an apt and vivid illustration of the ceremony he describes. A lord, who the text states is from a polity now known as Motul de San José,

A   B   C   D   E

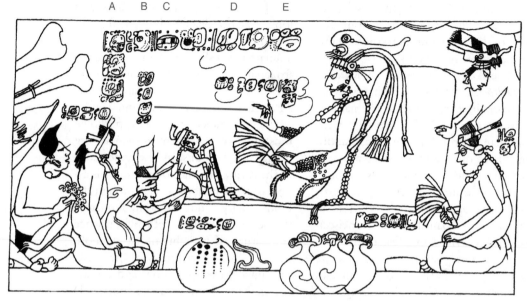

Figure 5.2. **The Apparition of Kauil, 2**, *cylindrical vase*

peers into a mirror manipulated by a dwarf. Reflected in the mirror is the handsign of an attendant who is positioned behind the pillow upon which the lord leans back. Without our understanding of the nature of the ritual being portrayed, this attendant presents a very mysterious image. We now become aware that he studies the ground in anticipation of the telltale footprint signaling the sacred apparition. The scene portrays the precise moment of recognition. The attendant signals the arrival through his handsign, which is perceived in the mirror by the lord. The lord is apparently making a vocal pronouncement, indicated by glyphs surrounded in speech scrolls, but the hidden divine presence is primarily proclaimed by the display of the *chi*-hand, exaggerated in size and placed in the geometric center of the composition.

With the raising of the right hand in this mudra, a trio of musicians raises a salute—the tips of two wooden trumpets and a conch shell are seen protruding from the palace wall on the left. Again, what the artist portrays is the critical climax of the ceremony. In this moment in time another dwarf is shown kneeling below the dais and imbibing liquid from a large ceramic vessel. We may safely surmise that the contents of this vessel are the same as those in the large clay pot directly before him and adjacent to an enema bag followed by three enema pots. Further on we will come to know why these substances are part and parcel of the ceremony described in the painting.

Behind the dwarf a hunchback raises his left hand in the sign of the Sun. The small finger of his right hand, which is associated with the number one and the Earth, is extended downward, as is the small finger of a third seated participant who raises a bouquet of flowers. This gesture signifies the descent of the god to Earth from the heavens. These shamans are engaged in the activity known as "bringing down the sun." In the opposite corner of this formalized and delicately balanced composition another lord, on the extreme right, displays the same elegant gesture as he raises a staff of feather plumes.

Mesoamerican shamans performing religious rites and ceremonies are rarely seen without one or more such plumes in hand. The plumes are considered to enable the shaman to see and hear everything above and below the Earth. With their assistance the shaman performs magical feats such as transforming the dead and curing the sick as well as "calling down the sun." When a shaman wishes to bring the supernatural forces of the plumes into action, the baton is given a slight trembling motion, as the power of the hanging feathers emanates from the tips. In vase paintings such as these, the artist clearly and vividly documents these activities.

The text written on this remarkable vase is not yet fully understood; however, the meaning of a number of key glyphs in the writing can now be deciphered. The main text refers to the enthroned lord depicted who is obviously the owner of the vase. It begins in A with the general verb *u-bah* meaning "he goes," "he went," or "he did," followed in B by a variant of the Smoking Mirror glyph, which exactly describes the activity depicted. Variants of this glyph are shown in figures 5.3A and B and may be

compared to the glyph that appears directly above the headdress of the lord who holds the bouquet of flowers.

The glyphs in figure 5.2C, D, and E are titles and in fact we can safely assume that the entire text succinctly describes the activity and names the owner of the vase. The glyph in C can be read as *Ah Caan*, He the Sky Lord. The *hel* glyph, in D, always refers to a change of some sort. In this context it refers to the lord's position in a ruling dynasty and states that he is the eighth successor from the dynasty's founder. The glyph in E states exactly where that dynasty is located, declaring that he is a *K'ul Ahau* or Holy Lord of the polity we now identify as Motul de San José.

The mirror carries a wide range of symbolic inferences in Maya culture. In lowland Maya languages the word *nen* has a triple meaning expressing "mirror," "ruler," and "to contemplate." An *Ahau Nen*, Mirror Lord, was viewed as both the reflection of the populace and a seer of the truth. Rulers were seen as "mirrors of the people."

There is an alignment of related glyphs and handsigns that lie horizontally around the cylindrical vessel. I have drawn a red line extending from the central handsign to a glyph in the alignment to which it is closely associated. It appears as part of the title, *K'inich Chilam Ok*, Sun-eyed Priest, shown in figure 5.3C. Glyphs spelling *chilam*, "priest," are shown in D as a *chi*-hand and an inverted *ahau* sign. The title in E and F, *K'inich*, refers to the *Ah Kinob*, "those of the sun and time." An *Ah K'in* is a priest of the sun cult. In E, the *chi*-hand is infixed in the head portrait

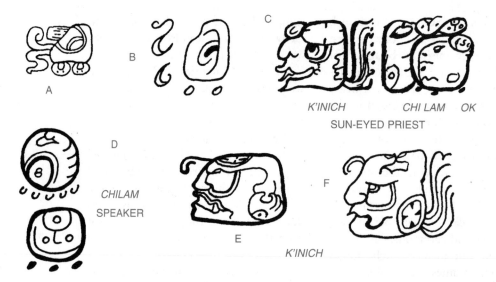

Figure 5.3. The glyphs of the **Smoking Mirror** *and* **K'inich Chilam**

of the Sun God. In F, the hand becomes the personification of the Sun God, and in the poetic symbolism of the Maya it implies all the associations connected with the hand, especially as a verb meaning "to make." *K'in*, the Sun, is the maker of days, the day itself, and time, all of which are considered divine. Time is not considered an abstract entity: It is a reality, a divine being, the origin of the cycles that govern all existence.

The square eye in the hieroglyphs in E and F connects the Sun God with the Old God, the god of time who rules over the cardinal points. It is a profound image that symbolizes the vision that sees into the four corners of the cosmos. The mirror eye in F is symbolic of the mirror vision that perceives that the world of forms is but a reflection of a hidden reality. The material world is a reflection of the spiritual world.

These hieroglyphs are the titular emblems of the members of the sun cult and it should not be surprising that they appear on vase paintings that depict ceremonies invoking the Smoking Mirror, who is the patron of wizards. The glyphs in E and F demonstrate conclusively that the *chi*-hand is the handsign for "sun." It is important to note that the hand shown in these glyphs is specifically a right hand. As a left hand it carries the phonetic value *hu*.

It has been explained that the *chi*-hand can also carry the numerical value of nine. *Kauil,* who was born in the present creation, is the mirror image of the Sun God, his father, who was born in the previous creation, according to texts at Palenque. The emblem of a special aspect of *Kauil* is shown in figure 5.4. It features the number nine along with footprints indicating the *Bolon Mayel,* divine presence of *Kauil.* The image is taken from a vessel that was used in funerary rites. Such pots were called *ol*, a word meaning "portal," "in the center of," and "the heart of something." The vase itself is a holy grail and is regarded as a portal to the spirit world. (The ancient artist could not have anticipated that these creations would become portals in another sense. Vase paintings have become our portals into the past, providing us with spectacular and intricate vistas into ceremonies which would otherwise be forgotten and unknown.)

Bolon, the number nine, is a personified form of *Kauil*—the Hero Twin *Xbalanque*, the Jaguar of the Night Sky. The latter represents the night celestial sun or the Sun in its journey through the underworld, which is equated with death and therefore frequently appears in funerary imagery. In Nahua culture the jaguar is the *naqual* or "animal disguise" of the creator god *Tezcatlipoca*. The Fire Serpent is an aspect of the Sun on its diurnal journey across the sky.

The image in figure 5.4 is compacted with information in the form of symbols. The number nine is juxtapositioned with a *nik*, "flower," emblem, a variant of the *ahau* sign, which can be read as *may* or "twenty," symbolizing all of the twenty daysigns. In this context the "nine" refers to the *Bolon Ti Ku*, the Nine of God who are the Lords of Night, and together the two symbols express all possible days and nights and therefore the totality of time. The earflare is a *be* or "road" sign and carries associations with the god of the center and the number five, which abolishes all opposites. "To enter the road" is a metaphor for death.

BOLON MAYEL FLOATING IN CH'ULEL

TAN
CENTER

XAMAN - NORTH

Figure 5.4. The **Bolon Mayel** emblem

In Maya cosmology the number nine refers to a supernatural location in the Otherworld. The *Oxlahun Ti Ku*, the Thirteen of God, who are deified personifications of number, are all assigned to directions and arranged according to an intricate ordering pattern.

```
                 EAST
                  13
                 [ 9 ]
                  5
                  1
NORTH  10  6  2   4  8  12  SOUTH
                  3
                  7
                  11
                 WEST
```

Nine is above in the east, which is associated with dawn, red, and the element fire that rises. The number three, a rain god, is below in the west, which represents the element water and the color black. Ten, the Death God, is positioned in the north, the land of the ancestors whose color is white, and is associated with the element air. Yellow is the color of the south and contains four, the Sun God and eight, the Corn God, and the element earth. It is curious that green is the color of the center; in the color spectrum of light discovered in comparatively recent times, green is at the center.

When the twenty daysigns are arranged according to their associated directions, the same pattern is generated, forming a cross. The cross symbolizes the World Tree in the center of the cosmos, a central portal into the realms of the spirit world. The sacred calendar of the Maya does not merely record time; it is known as The Great Idea because it is a mandala that unites time and space, spirit and matter, in an all-encompassing cosmovision. It is also conceived of as a divine tree that has its beginnings or roots in the east with *Imix* and comes to fruition as *Ahau* flowering in the south. In the center of this wonderful tree is *Chuen*, the Day of the Monkey, the eleventh daysign, which is presided over by *Xamen Ek*, the Monkey God of the North Star, center of the night sky. Now we know why, when a Maya artist depicts the World Tree, the Monkey God will appear inside.

In the center of the image of *Bolon Mayel* and forming its eye is the hieroglyph *tan*, "center," which is shown in figure 5.4B. In the image the glyph has cross-hatching, suggesting the obsidian mirror that sees through everything. The divine being portrayed possesses the vision of the center that sees through the world of illusions and views the changes of external phenomena from the inner, eternal, and unchanging center. The marvelous emblem is surrounded by beads of *ch'ulel*, the life force or soul stuff that is conjured from the spirit world by shamans. As a ritual object in a funerary rite, the image serves as an appropriate reminder of the Nahua dictum, "Only a moment here on Earth. It is untrue that we have come to live here on Earth."

Christian missionaries among the Aztecs of course viewed *Tezcatlipoca* as the devil. Italian text in the Codex Rios has this to say about him: "This was the figure of *Tezcatlipoca*, which is to say 'Mirror which sends forth Smoke,' who is the Devil. They paint him in this way, but on the other hand, when the devil

Figure 5.5. **The Emblem of the Divine Presence,** Teotihuacan

becomes visible to them, they cannot see all of him, but only the foot of an eagle or fowl." The eagle and the turkey are symbols of different aspects of the Sun in Nahua culture. The image in figure 5.4 is a feathered god. The claw is a substitute for the hand or foot. An image from Teotihuacan expressing the divine presence is shown in figure 5.5 wherein both the hand and footprints are used as indications of the presence of the Invisible God.

In some of the most ancient Chinese writing, the divine presence of the Ancestor is symbolized by the right hand, usually shown in the act of making an offering. In the inscriptions in figure 5.6A, the hand extends to the temple of the deceased Ancestor, a sacred niche from which transcendent influence emanates. Remarkably, this same sacred cartouche design is the cosmogram affording access to the realm of the ancient Maya ancestors. In B, a footprint also appears in the designs. In his book, *Chinese Characters*, written at the turn of the century, Dr. L. Wieger, S.J., made this observation regarding this symbol: "Sometimes the offering is made to a footprint, or to footprints of the deceased Ancestor. Now-a-days, as of old, the Chinese try to discern the footprints of the departed on planks strewn with sand or ashes." It is also very curious that the object common to all shamans in Central Asia is a mirror in which the shaman can see the souls of the dead.

Among the most beautiful objects manufactured by the Olmec were concave mirrors of iron that could throw pictures on a flat surface and start fires

Figure 5.6 A & B. Ancient Chinese inscriptions

on tinder. Rulers used these to impress the populace with their seemingly supernatural powers. In a third and highly schematized version of *The Apparition of Kauil* shown in figure 5.7, the main actor in 3 signals the arrival of the divine presence with his handsign as he peers intently into an obsidian mirror held by an attendant. His right hand forms the number seven, and it is in diagonal alignment with the mirror, the right *chi*-hand of the lady in 2, and curiously, the

Figure 5.7. **The Apparition of Kauil, 3**, *cylindrical vase*

glyph in U, the mainsign of which is also a *chi*-hand.

Simultaneously his raised left hand forms the *chi*-hand in another alignment with the mirror, the *chi*-hand presented on the left hand of the lady in 2, and the mask held by the lady in 1 who also displays a *chi*-hand. The attendant in 5 is apparently manipulating the mirror to reflect these channels of communication through which the participants enter into a discourse with the gods in the realms of the spirit world through the medium of handsigns. The ancient Maya prayed with their hands.

An important part of the ceremony that manifests the divine presence of *Kauil* is vividly portrayed here: The lord in 4 is depicted in the process of administering a peyote enema. The glyph, *ch'ok*, in Z describes him as a lineage member of the royal family. The glyph

in Y has not yet been fully deciphered, but it is prefixed with the phonetic *ah*, "he of" and contains *tok*, "flint." The *to* superfix shows smoke plumes and fire sparks. The same elements are contained in the glyph of the God of the New Fire. The emblem that appears on his apparel is, by extension, the ancient symbol of fire—the three stones of the traditional Maya hearth.

There is a discernable link among Mesoamerican cultures associating fire and peyote. Sahagun's description of the Smoking Mirror ceremony places it in the twelfth month of the Aztec calendar which corresponds to October. The patron of the twelfth month of the Maya calendar, *Ceh*, "deer," is the God of the New Fire. The connection between fire and peyote can perhaps best be understood through the ceremonies of the present-day Huichol who still perform the ancient pilgrimage, a vision quest to the peyote country, each year during the month of October.

The Huichol, whose name means Doctors or Healers, have preserved many of their ancient traditions and have much in common with the Maya. Although they presently live in the state of Nayarit in Mexico, their traditions hold that they originally came from somewhere in the south. Like the Maya, their gods are natural phenomena personified, the principal gods representing the four elements, fire and air being male, water and earth being female. The greatest of their gods, Fire, is known as Grandfather because he existed before the Sun, who is referred to as Father.

The journey to the peyote country passes through an area in western Mexico where I was living and consequently I was often able to witness groups of Huichol traveling on their annual quest. It is wonderful to see a solemn procession of Huichol pilgrims adorned in ceremonial attire as they walk single file on their sacred mission. The principal leader carries in his pouch the fire-making implements and he alone is allowed to strike fire while on the road. He represents Grandfather Fire and is called so by that name. The gathering of peyote, or *hikuli*, "the drinking gourd of the God of Fire," as they call it, brings health, luck, and life to all the members of the tribe. However, this powerful hallucinogenic substance has some adverse side effects. Consumption will result in euphoric states of consciousness, but if taken orally it initially induces sickness and vomiting. The Maya cleverly avoided these unpleasant experiences by injecting the substance anally so it was directly absorbed in the intestinal tract.

Enema bags appear frequently in scenes depicting *Kauil* invocations but I know of no other instance wherein the utensil is actually shown in use as it is here. This painting therefore stands as a unique and important documentation. The text, although largely consisting of the P.S.S., is also revealing. It can now for the most part be reread, and it is directly pertinent to the religious rite portrayed.

As if emerging from an image projecting from the crest of the main actor's headdress, the text in figure 5.7 begins in A with a purely phonetic rendering of *a-ya*, "it came into being." The usual mirror mainsign of this glyph has been suppressed, possibly in order to focus attention on the mirror in the pictorial matter. The *chi*-hand in B is the mainsign of *y-ich*, "the painting or writing surface," which is a noun. The *na-ha* glyph in C qualifies it by transforming it into a past-tense verb; thus we have "it was painted or written." The *hoy-i*, "it was blessed," glyph in D normally directly follows the *a-ya* introductory glyph, but one wonders if the artist has not been playful in positioning the head portrait of *Pauahtun* on the crest of the headdress of the attendant holding the mirror. The headdress is the net-bag of the *its'at* and the titular emblem of *Pauahtun*. Many members of the Maya court were artists. Note that the lady in 2 wears two brushes thrust into her headdress in the manner of the ancient Maya artist.

In E is the *y-uch'ab* glyph meaning

"his drinking vessel." It identifies the object and states that it is owned. The next four glyphs tell us what it is used for. In F, *ta y-utal* means "for his sustenance." In G is the head portrait of the Lunar Goddess of the Number One, here read as "first" and by extension *tsih,* "fresh." H is the head portrait of *Yahuate,* the Lord of the Tree. Although they are head portraits of deities, together the glyphs in G and H may be translated as the adjective "tree-fresh" describing the next glyph in I, *cacao,* who is also a god. Cacao is a liquor derived from the tropical evergreen plant *Theobrama cacao,* used as both the primary ceremonial drink and an aphrodisiac. In Nahuatl it is known as *xocoatl,* "bitter water," the probable origin of the English word chocolate. The Maya added corn, vanilla, and various spices to produce a milder flavor. Throughout Mesoamerica cacao beans were regarded so highly that they became the main medium of exchange.

The next three glyphs title and name the owner of the vase who is the main actor in 3. In J, *ch'ok,* "lineage member," literally means "sprout" and refers to members of the royal lineage as being sprouts of the ancestral tree. The participants in 1, 2, and 4 also possess this title; it is likely that they are of the same lineage and are engaged in a family tradition that invokes the ancestor. A fundamental function of *Kauil* is that of a lineage deity.

The mainsign of the glyph in J is a gray squirrel, usually emblazoned with the emblem of the Sun. I cannot help but think of the squirrel as a dweller in the ancestral tree. We do not know the

reason for the sun symbol from Maya sources, but here again Huichol traditions offer a probable explanation.

To the Huichol, there is very little distinction between animals, spirits, and the ancestors. When the Sun first rose in the darkness of the beginning of time, the nocturnal creatures—the jaguars, mountain lions, wolves, coyotes, gray foxes, and the serpents—were angered as the light of the Sun hurt their eyes, but the gray squirrel guided the Sun on its first journey across the sky and defended him, leading him to the portal in the west and placing an altar there so he could safely pass.

The wolf and the jaguar killed the squirrel, but to this day the Huichol offer sacrifices to this hero god. In the Huichol conception the diurnal habits of the squirrel show that this animal is the Sun's companion and delights in his company. It is thought that the squirrel knows more than other animals as is shown by the hiding of nuts and being able to find them again. A similar myth must have been known in the Maya country where it seems apparent that the squirrel earned the right to wear the sacred emblem of the Sun. I would further suggest that the glyph implies that a *ch'ok* is one who has this entitlement and it distinguishes him or her from other stratas of Maya society.

The glyphs in K and L flow into the elegant headdress of the main character and in all probability represent his name. The mainsigns in these glyphs are daysigns, but in fact daysigns frequently appear in Maya names. This has its roots in the Mesoamerican tradition of naming a person after the sign of the day on which he or she was born. Also, in Maya art the headdress will frequently represent the name of the person portrayed; note that the glyph in L is featured in the headdress.

In the P.S.S. the nominal will invariably follow the *ch'ok* glyph as it does here and this will be followed by a placename or placenames if they are present. Normally it is here that the statement ends, but in this text something very unusual happens. It goes on to describe the pictorial content of the painting. After naming the main actor it describes exactly what he is doing. The message continues in M with the general verb *u-bah*, "he goes," "he went," or "he does." This glyph should not be confused with the *ch'ok* glyph, which will always contain a *ch'o* or *ko* phonetic sign to distinguish it. *U* means "he" or "she" and *bah* is the verb and also the Maya word for "gopher."

I am almost certain that the glyph in N is One *Ahau*, among the most revered days in the sacred calendar, and the day on which *Kauil* was born. It was a ritual day for the heliacal rising of Venus after the inferior conjunction and it became a collective title for Venus gods. It is known as an Ancestor's Day by the contemporary Maya; present daykeepers make offerings at shrines before the ancestors. A person born on this day may become an *ajnawal mesa,* a medium for voices of the deceased.

In the verb in O, *ahk'ot,* "dancing" or "to dance," is the mainsign. The glyph in P is a vulture's head that carries the phonetic value of *ti,* a general preposition meaning "to," "in," "on," or "from," prefixed by a phonetic *ti*

sign. [Note: *Ti* very frequently follows *ahk'ot* in Maya writing. This is definitely *not* an exception to the consistent practice. Maya writing is sacred, but also artistic and sometimes playful; besides, the Maya artist is depicting gods of sound. A Maya reader would immediately recognize the glyph as the general preposition. Therefore, the artist can play, giving us a picture of the vulture god of the sound *ti* prefixed with the sacred symbol of the sound. The artist playfully and artistically juxtaposes two aspects of a single sound.]

Inevitably this glyph will be followed by glyphs that state the exact nature of the dance, as is the case here. The glyph in Q is *yilah,* "to see," "to observe." The mainsign is a head with an enormous *yi*-eye prefixed with the *la* phonetic and an *h(i)* superfix. In R, the hieroglyph of *Kauil* tells us what he saw. Concluding the section is the title in S, *u-lats,* "he of the generations," which often appears in the P.S.S. referring to an owner of a vase. The entire passage can thus be translated: "He goes on the day One *Ahau,* dancing (performing ceremonies), to see *Kauil,* the Smoking Mirror, he of the generations."

The subtext in T, U, and V is similar in format to passages in M through S, but it is greatly abbreviated. It refers to the courtier in 1 and begins with *u-bah,* "she goes," and ends with the title *ch'ok* in V. The verb in U succinctly describes her activity. It is simply the *chi*-hand prefixed by an *o* phonetic sign rendering *och,* "to enter." In this context, entering is establishing contact with the spirit world—in which the ancestor resides—through the portal of the sacred mirror and the accompanying rites surrounding the cult. In the accompanying portrait she raises a mask that is probably the flayed face of an actual deceased relative! Her role is that of a *chilam*, the priestess "speaker" who provides the voice of the manifested ancestor, now fully animated by the appearance of *Kauil*.

The subtext in W and X is even further contracted as the implied *u-bah* verb is dropped but in X the necessary *ch'ok* title is retained. These glyphs refer to the lady in 2. The glyph in W is not fully translated, but the mainsign appears to be *tan*, "to center." This would be consistent with the designs on her dress, which are for the most part symbols of the center just as the shell designs on the apparel of the lady in 1 are consistent with the Maya concept of zero as entering into a higher plane of existence.

It is extraordinary that the essential Maya altar, both in the past and the present, consists of setting up the four cardinal directions, or alternatively the extreme positions of the Sun on the horizon, and establishing the center as an entrance, road, or portal to the Otherworld. The same quincuncial symbols on the dress of this shamaness are still used by women in the Maya country today, and carry the same fundamental meanings.

In a fourth and very curious variant of the Smoking Mirror ceremony, shown in figure 5.8, the participants are three priestesses and two rabbits. In keeping with the Maya preoccupation with time, the artist focused on depicting the precise moment of the arrival of the divine presence, shown on the right of the diagram. The priestess in 3 extends an open left hand as she peers into an obsidian mirror in anticipation of an image. The instant is symbolized as she is shown raising the same left hand while closing the thumb and the index finger to form the *chi*-hand, the sacred sign of *Kauil*. Great plumes of smoke emerge from the mirror and a rabbit adorned in ceremonial attire suddenly leaps from her lap while emitting speech scrolls.

On the left, two priestesses are unaware of the arrival event as they gesture vigorously toward the heavens in anticipation of the descent of the god. As if in preparation for signing the number nine, the priestess in 1 displays an eight hand while the one in 2 extends her raised hand in the same preliminary gesture that was employed by the priestess in 3. Although it is rather clumsily drawn, the artist has captured the communicative power of the moving hands of the Maya.

The setting in which this scene takes place is likely to be the inner sanctuary of the perpetual fire, as it is known that official ancestral state fires were maintained in Maya kingdoms, and attended by virgins who were considered to be wives of the Fire God. The priestess in 1 is enthroned on a dais adorned with two emblems of the Smoking Mirror.

No depiction of the sacred fire is known to exist in Maya art, but it seems to me that such a fire is hidden in the vessel directly behind the priestess on the dais. The container emits a large plume of smoke, and "where there is

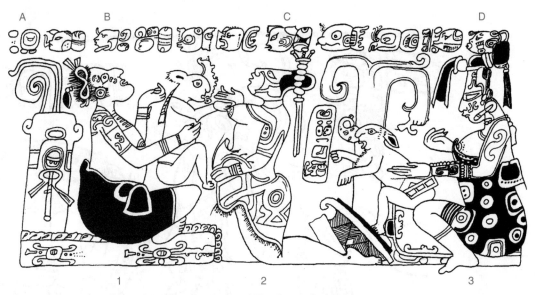

*Figure 5.8. **The Apparition of Kauil, 4**, cylindrical vase*

smoke there is fire." Only the most sacred of fires would be enthroned above an emblem of the Smoking Mirror. We cannot tell if these priestesses are virgins, but the bare breasts and shorn hair would not be typical of a noble Maya married woman. There are no human males around, but the rabbits wear specifically male attire. We do not know if the priestesses are married to the Fire God, but it is hard to conceive of an image with more phallic characteristics than the vessel containing the fire.

There is something else very curious about this painting. The glyphs are as unique as the scene itself. Only the daysign *Ca Ik*, Two Wind, in A and the title *ch'ok* in C and lunar goddesses in B and D can be recognized; beyond this we are lost in unknown and bewildering territory. The only explanation I can presently offer for the appearance of these strange glyphs is that in Maya languages women sometimes use words and terms completely different from those employed by men. This text may be the glyphic equivalent of this phenomenon, representing a special esoteric form of writing developed and used exclusively by female priestesses of the fire cult.

These priestesses apparently administered fertility rites that cured barrenness in women by invoking the intercession of *Kauil*. The priestess in 2 is lifting her dress as she exposes herself to the rabbit who is fondling her breast. Fire, the element personified by *Kauil*, despite its destructive potential has—like its opposite, water—numerous creative and generative aspects. In Maya agriculture fire clears the fields and creates the fertilizing ash that promotes growth. In manufacturing artifacts it is fire that transforms porous clay and dirt into useful vessels that have the capacity to contain liquids. In Nahua mythology, before there was land, the Earth Mon-

Figure 5.9. **He Manifested It**, *cylindrical vase*

ster hid beneath the great waters. *Tezcatlipoca*, Fire, tempted her to the surface with his foot, which he lost in the process; but he succeeded in creating the Earth and its fertile soil. He was rewarded with the superior foot of a serpent.

Kauil makes a vividly dramatic visible appearance in a childbirth scene diagrammed in figure 5.9. The vase painting essentially commemorates the birth of a child, but no other nativity scene in all the annals of the history of art compares to it in shamanistic scope, fantastic imagery, and intense spiritual vision. This painting was undoubtedly deeply appreciated and admired in its social milieu. It was probably calmly and matter-of-factly viewed by contempo-

raries of the artist as a realistic depiction of an event that was not particularly extraordinary. It would have been totally in keeping with accepted traditional conventions and the canons of the art that were seen as beautifully but accurately recording the event for the purpose of its ritual celebration. What startles us, overwhelming us with awe and wonder, is the magnitude of its imaginative power.

Undulating through the scene is the sinuous serpentine right foot of *Kauil,* transformed into a gigantic Vision Serpent. It encircles the woman giving birth and rears up, opening its gaping jaws to emit *Pauahtun* who in delivering the infant, beckons it forth into the world. With a commanding

YALHIYA
(*YA-AL-HI-YA*)

HE SAID IT,
HE SPOKE IT,
HE MANIFESTED IT

A

U TZAK   *CH'U*
SHE CONJURED   GOD

shout and the insistent motion of his handsign, *Kauil* instigates the action. The emphatic gesture he employs is universally and naturally used and understood even by those who are not versed in a handsign language. It conveys a command, demanding "do it and do it now." It is used to "make something happen" or "to bring something down." Its glyphic equivalent shown in A is the manograph *yalhiya*, "he said it, he manifested it." In a more subtle gesture the woman places her hand to the ground, alluding to the Maya metaphor for birth, "he touched the earth."

The "earth-touching" gesture is directly below the beginning of the text and in this slice of the painting we read the initial statement, "On the day

Thirteen *Muluc*, in the seventeenth day of the month *Pax*, he touched the earth." The third glyph is *sih*, "birth," followed by four titles: the first mainsign, *ch'ul*, is "holy"; the second, *chak ch'ok*, is "great lineage member"; the third is the vulture head variant of *ahau*; and finally *Ah Cuauc* or *Ac* is "Turtle," identifying the child as a member of a ruling clan of that name.

The text continues in the upper left with the probable name of the person born. It contains *Balam*, "jaguar," and an *Ik*, "wind" or "spirit." Following are two more titles, the first mainsign the *chi*-hand and the next reading *Ahau Tun*, literally, "Lord of the Year." As the *Ah* prefix is used in reference to males, these titles must be those of the person born. Then comes *yal*, "the child of the mother" or literally, "her manifestation." In the same way, the glyph *u nik* for "the child of the father" literally means "his flower." Here again the artist interplays handsign with glyph as the *yal* sign appears to emanate from the mouth of *Kauil* so that what he says and what he signs mean the same thing.

Below this the text reads *Na-tzak ch'ok chan na-way*, "She conjured the lineage member, the Vision Serpent, her animal spirit companion." This declares that the birth was accomplished by a magical act in which the mother transformed into her spirit counterpart, the Vision Serpent, who is known to also be the *way* or the animal spirit companion of *Kauil*, the Lord of Lineages. The birth is thus described as not being ordinary but accomplished through the intercession of gods, thereby linking the birth on the human plane with a lineage directly connected to the divinities.

Whoever commissioned this work, undoubtedly a family member, had a hidden agenda. The underlying message conveyed is that the infant, Jaguar Spirit, has the right to rule, as his birth had been preordained and initiated by the gods. In imagery borrowed from the P.S.S., *Pauahtun* is shown ready to deliver the child, a direct reference to the *hoy-i* glyph, intimating, "it was made proper," "it was blessed." Ceremonies celebrating the birth of the child, in which this vase was a central ritual implement, were therefore carefully orchestrated. The participants were being primed through the art, which sought to convey, in not very subtle terms, that

the newly born infant is the heir designate and has the legitimate right to rule.

This extraordinary painting was produced in the environment of the intricate intrigues of a Maya court and its continual power plays of asserting and legitimizing rulership. In the documentation of this birth, the artist was not only recording an event in the immediate past. He or she was projecting into predictable situations that would unfold in the future, carefully preparing the audience for the time when this infant would fulfill his destiny by proclaiming his right to rule, and hopefully do so unchallenged. As a final comment on this painting, it should be noted that the birth takes place on the day *Muluc* or Water. The artist takes advantage of this by alluding to the fact that *Kauil* as the God of Fire is the patron of this day, and by extension an avatar of those born on this day.

One product of the advancements in the decipherment of Maya writing is the realization that many public monuments were state propaganda works that affirmed the legitimacy of the current ruler. Invoking *Kauil*, the bringer of fire and the creator of humanity and all organic life, was a primary strategy in asserting rulership. As King of Kings, *Kauil* rules over the institution of kingship. A prime example of this legitimization is the portrait of *Na Kak-Be*, Lady Fire Road, from a lintel illustrated in figure 5.10. She is shown performing a ritual in which she conjures *Kauil* on the day *Ca Oc*, Two Dog, or A.D. February 17, 795. *Oc* days are still known today as days favored by sorcerers, and she is depicted in the climax of a ritual in

Figure 5.10. **Portrait of Lady Fire Road**, lintel

which she has accomplished an extraordinary magical feat. She has not manifested an image or the presence of an invisible god. She has conjured the actual physical presence of *Kauil*! Anyone who can do this certainly has a right to the throne, so we know that she is either a ruler in her own right or the wife of a king.

Her mode of operation, as is clearly illustrated, is through the magical power of sacred handsigning. The portrait is surrounded by text, and in the diagram I have extricated three glyphs as they appear in position. On the left is *hom*, "ends," "completes," "passes," a manograph coupled with a moon sign and indicating the end of a lunar period. On the right the glyph of the Smoking Mirror is part of a phrase describing the ceremony performed. Inside the mirror is the emblem of the Sun. The noble

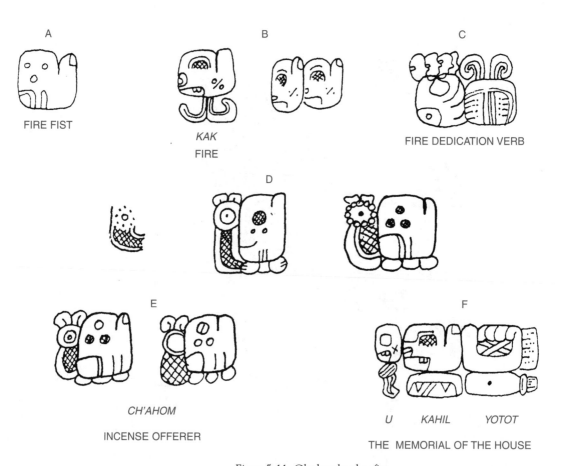

A

FIRE FIST

B

KAK

FIRE

C

FIRE DEDICATION VERB

D

E

CH'AHOM

INCENSE OFFERER

F

U   KAHIL   YOTOT

THE MEMORIAL OF THE HOUSE

Figure 5.11. Glyphs related to fire

lady signs the mudra of the Sun and lowers her left hand "to bring down the sun," a gesture that manifests *Kauil*, the avatar of the Sun, on her right hand. *Kauil* mirrors the gesture with his left hand and focuses attention on it by pointing with his right. The subject of the lintel is not only a portrait of *Na Kak-Be*; it also pays tribute and is a homage to the power of a specific sacred handsign, exalting it and conferring the right of the lady to display it. In doing so she proclaims publicly with an outward and visible sign that she is of

the *Ah K'in*, "those of the sun and time," and therefore is legitimately entitled to rule.

Below the hieroglyph of the Smoking Mirror the lady is named. The glyph is prefixed by the title *Na* or Lady, a portrait of the Lunar Goddess. Above the mainsign is *Kak*, Fire (which is also shown in figure 5.11 along with personified variants in B). Below the *kak* sign is *Be* or "road". These are valid literal translations, but I am sure that in ancient times the name was pronounced differently. When these signs are combined they have deeper ritualistic con-notations than when they are considered individually. The quincunx emblem that forms *Be* is the familiar symbol of setting up the center or making a road to the spirit world. Glyphs referring to fire rituals often contain the verb "to enter." (See the fire dedication verb in C. A stack of flammable offerings emits smoke plumes. The smoke rattles, *och*, are a rebus for "to enter," which is qualified by the *chi*-hand.) The nominal phrase was probably a title that described the lady as an "enterer," a shamanness or sorceress, exactly her capacity as depicted in her portrait.

The fire-fist in 5.11 forms the main-sign of the honorary title *Ch'ahom*, Incense Offerer, examples of which are shown in E. The three dots represent the *yax-ux-tunal*, the "first-three-stone place" in the constellation Orion, a triangle formed by the stars Alnitak, Saiph, and Rigel, in the center of which the Great Nebula of M42 represents the flame. In Maya mythology, as we have seen, these stones were set up at the beginning of Creation. The fist contains elements of the glyph *tan*, "center." From it smoke emerges and sometimes a circle of dots representing sparks appears. In F, the glyphs *u kahil yotot* represent "the memorial of a temple or house" and indicate a ceremonial dedication of a temple. The fire-fist is personified and the phonetic *yo*-hand here does much more than simply represent a sound. The "sun-in-hand" motif is of course indicative of a ritual observance.

The fist of fire and the hand of water are symbolic of the entire universe envisioned in terms of active and pas-sive, positive and negative, masculine and feminine forces. We have examined these hands separately. In the next chapter we will explore the way they interact. Just as the concept of yin and yang permeates Chinese culture, the dynamic interaction of these two prime elements is the hidden underlying force that generates an entire range of symbols, forming the fundamental basis and essence of Maya culture in general. The Two Paddlers, Night and Day, Venus and the Sun, the Moon Goddess and the Sun God, the First Mother and the First Father, *Chac-Xib-Chac* (water) and *Kauil* (fire), and the Hero Twins, *Hunahpu* and *Xbalanque*, are all symbolic outward forms of an inner unity that orders and gives meaning to the Maya cosmic vision.

*Figure 6.1. The hieroglyph of **Burning Water***

THE ROAD TO XIBALBA

The image illustrated in figure 6.1 goes a long way toward completely summing up the whole doctrine of the native Mesoamerican concept of existence and reality. It consists of a skull, the symbol of death. Out of the top of the skull springs forth the Smoking Mirror emblem of *Tezcatlipoca*, the creator of life. The Maya refer to the corn seed as a skull because it is only through the death of the seed that the plant can sprout. Out of the mouth of the skull, water adorned with a water-bead symbol and two shells plunges downward. Arising upward from the mouth is a flaming fire emblem. This is the hieroglyph of Burning Water, symbolizing the unity of all existence.

Fire is in the east and represents energy; water, below in the west, is representative of time. The skull here is an earth symbol representing matter in the south. At the apex of the dome of the skull is the north where *Tezcatlipoca*, as the constellation we know of as the Big Dipper, is seen to hop around the Polestar. The sky is associated with air, wind, and spirit, and represents space. Thus the artist manages to

A-YA	TZUKAH	Y-ICH	Y-UCH'AB	TA TSIH
IT CAME INTO BEING	WAS PRESENTED	ITS SURFACE	THEIR DRINKING VASE	FOR FRESH

Figure 6.2. **The Hero Twins Meet Itzamna in the Underworld,** *cylindrical vase*

express the four cardinal directions, the four prime elements, and the four roots of all things—energy, time, matter, and space—synthesized in a unified logographic composition.

Paradoxically as *Teoatl-Tlachinolli,* "water and fire," the glyph is used in Nahua culture as a metaphorical expression for "war." On the plane of earthly existence the original unity of all things becomes diversified; time fragments into past, present, and future; space splits into the various directions in a grandiose struggle of opposing forces. Maya art, religion, calendar making, ritual, mythology—as well as the *Popol*

Vuh, the central legend that permeates practically all of the culture—all strive to achieve the vision of a whole unified ordered cosmos that lies hidden behind the veil of a seemingly diverse, random, and disordered universe. The journey of the Hero Twins to Xibalba, in the *Popol Vuh,* is really a metaphor of the human being's mystic search to acquire the unified vision and achieve supreme liberation. In illustrating episodes from the great epic, the story of heroic human triumph over both the spirit world and the world of matter and the duality of life and death, Maya artists created some of the most profound and beautiful

TE'EL	KAKAW	YAX-BALAM	HUN-AHUA	O-	K'U
FROM THE TREE	CACAO	THE HERO	TWINS	PORTAL	GODS

paintings the world has ever seen.

One of these, diagramed in figure 6.2, describes the first confrontation of the twins *Xbalanque* and *Hunahpu* with *Itzamna* in Xibalba, The Place of Awe. At night the underworld revolves up from below and appears as the starry nocturnal sky. *Itzamna* is seen at the left enthroned on a two-headed celestial sky band that represents the ecliptic. The entire scene takes place on a skyband, so we are situated in the dark world of night, the realm of death ruled over by *Itzamna*. (The Nahua equivalent of *Itzamna* is the old *Ometecuhtli* who has as his counterpart *Mictlantecuhtli*, the

skeletal Lord of the Land of the Dead.)

The special emblematic sign of *Itzamna* is *Akbal*, Night or Darkness, the third in the series of twenty daysigns. It is curious that the Nahua equivalent of this daysign is *Calli*, House, which is a pictograph of a temple. The Maya word *na* means "house," "first," and "to know," especially through dreaming. An *Itzam* is "one who does *itz*," the precious blessed magical liquid substance of the sky which is universally sought after by shamans through portals opened in the sky.

Two principal kinds of the cosmic

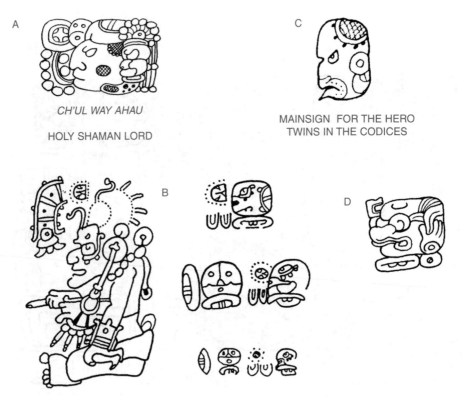

Figure 6.2. Maya glyphs: A, Shaman; B, **Itzamna**; C, The Hero; D, Twins

sap appear in Maya art. One emanates from the day sky out of the portal of the Sun as can be seen in the glyph *Ch'ul Way Ahau*, Holy Shaman Lord, shown in A. The shaman imbibes the special essences as droplets of *ch'ul* falling from the emblem of the Sun. A *Ch'ul Ahau* is a Lord of the Life Forces, *ch'ul* or *k'ul* being the basic "soul-force" of the universe. *Ch'* in Cholan languages corresponds to Yucatec *k'* and in writing the symbol means "holy," "spiritual" and "divine." *Ch'ul* is practically synonymous with *itz*; in fact, the glyph contains an *itz* postfix, a beaded flower from which the blessed nectar of the gods flows down.

The other kind of *itz* emanates from portals opened by the shaman in the night sky. It is seen emanating from the *Akbal* sign in the forehead of *Itzamna*, from the codices and in his nominal glyphs shown in B as well as in the painting itself. The portraits feature a ladder development and a flower emblem, the special blossom out of which *itz* nectar flows. *Akbal* is the number seven, known as the Heart of Heaven because it is numerically at the very center of the thirteen levels of the heavens. These symbols are sacred to *Itzamna*, the first shaman and one of the gods who drew the constellations in the night sky at the Creation. I take this to mean that the alternating revolutions of day and night, the flow of time itself, were set in motion and fueled through the infusion of the divine *itz*.

The Hero Twins represent the pairing of the opposite primary elements, water and fire, as well as being personifications of Venus and the Sun. Usually *Hunahpu*, as the Morning Star announcing the rising Sun, appears in front in seating arrangements of the Twins. In figure 6.2 the order is reversed and *Xbalanque* is in the forefront as is his nominal glyph above in the P.S.S. The nominal glyphs of the Twins are followed by another interesting pairing. The Twins have entered Xibalba through the door at the right of the diagram. Directly above this entrance in the P.S.S. is the *Moan* or Screech Owl glyph, the nominal of *Ah Coo Akab*, the Mad One of the Night. He is a harbinger of death and a portal god of the underworld, and it is he who has summoned the Twins to an audience with the Lords of Death in Xibalba. His glyph is coupled with that of *Xaman Ek* whom we know as the portal god of the celestial realm of the Maya cosmos, the Monkey God of the North Star.

The Twins are seated with their arms folded in the traditional posture of reverence as *Itzamna* extends his hand in an invitational gesture, as if stating, "Welcome to my den"—as the spider said to the fly. The artist brilliantly portrays the skeptical facial expression of *Xbalanque*, who knows that the Lords of the Underworld had killed his father, the Sun God, on his visit to the underworld.

Hidden from the view of the Twins is the skull of their father mounted on top of a huge *olla*, "water jar." *Ol* means "portal" and this is a very special kind of portal indeed. It contains, enfolded in the darkness of its interior an *ik* sign, the glyphic emblem of spirit and life, now covered over in cloth wrappings. It is the sacred mission of the Hero Twins to uncover and release this vital force and to infuse it into the skull of their father in order to resurrect him as the Corn God, consequently giving birth to Maya civilization itself.

The accompanying text is a glyphic elaboration of the idea portrayed in the pictorial content of the vase painting. It begins immediately in front of the Twins with the nominal glyph of *Itzamna* followed by *Chac Hunahpu*, a curious and interesting variant of the name of the first twin. The *cauac* "rain" sign is superfixed above a hand referring to *Hunahpu* as the avatar of *Chac-Xib-Chac*, the personification of water. Another rather fanciful variant of the *Hunahpu* nominal glyph appears in the P.S.S. We can identify it as his nominal glyph since it immediately follows that of *Yax Balam*, First Jaguar, the classical name of *Xbalanque*. Furthermore in order to clarify this, the artist actually attaches the glyph to his headband with a cord.

The nominal glyph of the Hero Twins as it appears in the codices is shown in C. It is a combination of symbols of the snake and the jaguar, the *wayob* of the Twins and two of the most powerful "animal spirit companions" in the Maya shaman's repertoire. The Lords of Death may have killed the Sun God and they will succeed in killing the

Twins in their human form. But ultimately the Twins will triumph over the perils of Xibalba because they are dynamic magicians who can transform themselves as the supernatural *Chac-Xib-Chac* and *Kauil*, water and fire, unifying all opposing principles in nature and emerging invincible in all conflicts.

The mainsign of the third glyph in the text is the skull of the First Father which is prefixed by a *sac* sign meaning "white" and by extension "pure." It is postfixed with an *ahau* variant, an enclosed earplug in the traditional form of a flower of the sacred ceiba tree. Maya lords were considered as the flowers of the cosmic tree. The fourth glyph beginning the next column is also a nominal glyph of the Sun God, but a transformation has taken place.

A portrait head of the First Father frequently substitutes for the mirror mainsign of the *ay-a*, "it came into being," glyph of the P.S.S., as it does on this vase painting. As a symbol of brightness and light the mirror naturally becomes an emblem of the Sun. The skull "comes into being" and shines forth in the light of life in the image of a mirror. The mainsign is prefixed with an *imix*, "waterlily," sign but it is infixed with an *ahau* sign, which changes it into the phonetic *ma* or "great" in ancient Maya titles. Flowing down from this glyph is *itz*, the precious fluid of life.

In the two concluding glyphs, through a clever manipulation of the symbolic language of hieroglyphs, the artist tells us how the marvelous transformation took place. The *Chac Hunahpu* nominal glyph is repeated for a specific purpose. The head portrait of

Hunahpu in the first nominal glyph has the characteristic ceiba flower earplug but here it has been transformed into the ax of *Chac-Xib-Chac*, directly and playfully alluding to the well-known honorific title *Chakte*, Ax-Wielder. The ax shown is that of the rain gods, who crack open the jars in the sky to allow rain to fall, and also the shaman's ax that breaks open portals in the heavens. The ax *Hunahpu* wields breaks open the container that is the mainsign of the final glyph in order to liberate the spirit of life within it, directly referring to the *ik*-sign in the pictorial imagery. The prefix shows *itz* gushing forth from the container and cascading down from the heavens. The *ik*-sign itself is a pairing of opposites: In two simple lines the artist symbolizes creation by crossing the horizontal and the vertical—time and space, heaven and Earth, energy and matter, male and female—the intrinsic formula for the generation of life. The power of symbol lies in its ability to succinctly and concisely express a visual representation of reality in an all-encompassing logograph containing conceptions that reach far beyond the communicative capacity of words.

The *its'at* who painted this vase was a refined and fully competent manipulator of the traditional Maya language of symbol, a scholarly individual well-versed in the cosmology, mythology, religion, and philosophy of the culture. He or she was, as well, a highly accomplished artist who masterfully combined painting and calligraphy. In creating a ceremonial implement to be used in funerary rites the artist cunningly compared the jar in the subject matter with

*Figure 6.3. **The Hero Twins Meet Lord One Death in the Underworld***

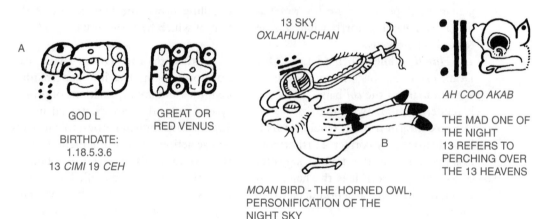

A

GOD L

BIRTHDATE:
1.18.5.3.6
13 *CIMI* 19 *CEH*

GREAT OR
RED VENUS

13 SKY
OXLAHUN-CHAN

B

MOAN BIRD - THE HORNED OWL,
PERSONIFICATION OF THE
NIGHT SKY

AH COO AKAB

THE MAD ONE OF
THE NIGHT
13 REFERS TO
PERCHING OVER
THE 13 HEAVENS

the vase itself, and the releasing of *itz* with the ritual imbibing of fermented cacao. Inventing a strange and unique symbol containing droplets of liquid, the artist directly linked the glyph *y-uch'ab*, "their drinking vessel," to the image of the jar in the painting. The glyph contains all the allusions that have been previously discussed but here the artist pushed the symbolic vocabulary even further, personifying the glyph as representative of a *living* holy object that commemorates the triumph of life over death. By penetrating into the hid-

den meaning of hieroglyphic writing the communicative power of the media speaks to us today just as it spoke in the past when the *y-ich* or "writing surface" was not yet dry.

As we have seen, the theme of the Twins' descent into the underworld was a favored subject featured on numerous vases; the one diagramed in figure 6.3 is of particular interest. Here Lord One Death takes the place of *Itzamna* in representing the lords of Xibalba. We met him in chapter two in *The Vase of the Seven Gods* where he was seen presiding over the creation of this era. Like *Itzamna,* Lord One Death's nominal glyph, shown in A, reveals that he too is "one who does *itz.*" The second glyph in his nominal is *Chak Ek,* Great Star or Venus, implying that he is a harbinger of the Sun. His *way* is the *moan,* the horned screech owl shown in B, that is crowned with the glyph *Oxlahun-Chan,* Thirteen Sky, referring to the mythological bird that perches above the thirteen heavens. His other *way* is the jaguar or the night sun. In the painting he is portrayed as a magician, a "wearer of the jaguar skin," performing a fire ritual as he raises a flaming torch while gazing toward the heavens.

Hunahpu kneels behind Lord One Death extending his arm and gesturing with a variant of the *chi*-hand. The hand is rendered about twice the size necessary to conform to what would normally be anatomically correct. Furthermore it is positioned in the geometric center of the composition; it is the hand that generates the magical action depicted in the scene.

Juxtaposed to the *chi*-hand is a snake emanating from the headdress of Lord One Death and spouting plumes of vital life force energy from its mouth. Curiously, this essence, called prana in Sanskrit, is also symbolized by the snake in yogic iconography and it is coincidentally called chi by the Chinese. It is fundamental not only to the practice of yoga in Asia but also to the martial arts, magic, and various forms of oriental culture, particularly painting. The Maya equivalent is *itz,* cosmic sap or *ch'ul,* the "soul-stuff" thought to reside in human blood. In the painting its presence permeates the entire composition with an invisible but perceptible vital life force.

It is from the hand of *Hunahpu* that the magical energy is generated, manifesting a marvelous metamorphosis. *Xbalanque* kneels behind *Hunahpu,* swooning as if enraptured in the ecstasy of a mystic vision as he gazes into the heavens. He is shown not in his human form but transformed into his supernatural divine counterpart, *Kauil.* His right hand is raised displaying a mudra, also the *chi*-hand, his titular handsign. *Kauil* elegantly sweeps his torch downward as if calling down the fiery forces of the Sun of which he is the avatar.

Although the Hero Twins can transform themselves into supernatural divinities and are incarnations of primary elements, they are portrayed in the *Popol Vuh* as human heroes, role models whose actions express the highest ideals that Maya culture aspires to. Fundamentally they are identified with and represent humanity. In Christian, Hebrew, and Islamic art, the divinity is worshiped and adored; human beings are doomed sinners who must seek salvation through God. The Maya worldview is quite the opposite. Gods are revered and respected and their actions are often beneficial to humanity—for instance, Lord One Death and *Itzamna* take part in the Creation and *Pauahtun* holds up the Earth above the underworld. But the gods cannot be totally relied upon; sometimes they can get out of hand, and there are earthquakes. The *Popol Vuh* does not focus on the Sun God, whose excesses can cause droughts, but rather on his human sons

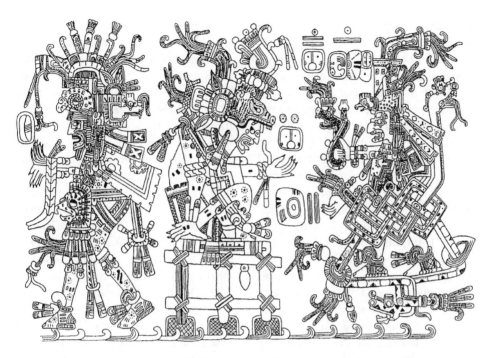

Figure 6.4. **Lord One Death and the Hero Twins**, *mural, Santa Rita, Belize*

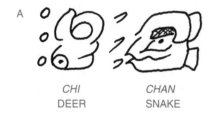

A

CHI   CHAN
DEER   SNAKE

B

who represent balance in nature. The Death God *Cimi* may assist in bringing forth the flower of life but a rampant *Cimi* will bring on plagues. Pestilence, famines, hurricanes, and sickness are all considered excesses of the gods in the Maya scenario.

It is the duty and destiny of humanity to sometimes intervene and establish order and harmony in the universe when the gods get out of control and come into conflict with Maya ideals, which are essentially human. The Ahau of an ancient Maya kingdom was empowered and expected to wield influence over the gods. The gods were seen to rely on their sustenance from human ritual just as much as the humans sought the benevolent favor of the gods. The *Popul Vuh* is a life-and-death struggle between the Hero Twins representing humanity, truth, and light and the world represented by wily gods who cunningly scheme in the realms of mystery and darkness in the underworld.

As we have seen, the *Popul Vuh* was continuously performed throughout the generations in ancient Maya times; was still being performed at the time of the Conquest; and probably will be staged as long as the Maya exist on the planet. Another version of *Lord One Death and the Hero Twins*, shown diagramed in figure 6.4, could have been painted as late as A.D. 1500, demonstrating a continuity of firmly established traditions throughout centuries of time. While retaining essentially Maya characteristics, it is painted in a style derived from southern central Mexico and some of its symbolic elements are derived from the Mixtec-Pueblo region, the source of the Codex Nuttall.

The mural was found painted on the walls of a buried building at Santa Rita, Belize, in 1896. The site was probably the ancient capital of Chetumal, a small Late Postclassic polity in the northern lowlands. The scene takes place in the primordial waters of the underworld and once again the focus is on the *chi*-hand displayed by *Hunahpu*, which he is deeply contemplating. In the center of the composition the right hand is raised in an anatomically impossible configuration; therefore the artist is showing a ritual gesture indicating that a ceremony is in progress. Around the hand there is a conglomeration of glyphs, symbols, and images that interact, representing the type of ritual performed. Here we are witness to a complex alliance between humans and gods, ancestors and animal spirits.

When they appear together in Maya art, the deer, *chi*, and the snake, *chan*, are indicative of the rite of the Vision Serpent whose glyphs are shown in A, where the *chi*-hand substitutes for deer. In the mural the artist plays on this relationship by positioning the hand of *Hunahpu* in close proximity to the deer effigy in his headdress and to the snake held by Lord One Death. Another focal point in the composition is the glyph *nen*, "mirror," which appears at the far left. The eyes of *Xbalanque* and Lord One Death are in alignment with the mirror in which they stare fixedly. Lord One Death's left hand is positioned downward and is more or less closed. By way of contrast the hand of *Xbalanque* is raised and fully opened. These hands too are meant to be viewed as being in motion, describing the climax of a Smoking Mirror ritual. The raised foot of *Xbalanque* indicates dancing but it is also a step, *och* or *oc*, also meaning "to enter." The artist makes a further play on this word in the headdress of *Hunahpu* wherein a circular *o* phonetic sign is juxtaposed to the deer head to render *och*.

The other glyphs in the mural are probably half-*katun* ending dates (ten-year intervals), entry points in time reserved for the performance of such rituals. The date above is *Buluc Ahau Uac Yaxkin*. As we have seen the patron of the month *Yaxkin*, New Sun, is the Sun God. The *yax*, "new" or "fresh," sign is clearly in the center of the compound, but for the usual sun symbol the artist has substituted a personified *chi*-hand.

It is more than likely that both *Itzamna* and Lord One Death were in

*Figure 6.5. **The Hero Twins Dance with Death**, cylindrical vase*

the remote past worshiped as sun gods. They are classic examples of how the deities of a previous era can become the demons of a subsequent era. As *Kinich Ahau*, *Itzamna* was worshiped as the son or solar manifestation of the supreme and only god, *Hunab Ku*. He was also known as *Itzamna Kabul*, "the maker with his hands."

The snake held by Lord One Death is *Quetzalcoatl*, the Feathered Serpent, a borrowing from early Mexican culture and another symbol of the union of opposites. Lord One Death soars above the waters of the underworld on two intertwined snakes, also symbols of the unity of opposites and an allusion to the two-headed snake symbol of the ecliptic, the path taken by the Sun in its journey through the sky. (On his portrait in the Codex Nuttall, shown in B, *Tonatiuh*, the Sun God or an impersonator of the sun god, is performing a "bringing down the sun" ceremony on the day Eleven Grass, which as a working hy-

pothesis I place in the year A.D. 1047. He displays the *chi*-hand as he points to the sky. Above him are the glyphs for One Death, the titular name of the Sun God in the codex.)

In their sojourn in the underworld, the Hero Twins are compelled to play ball with the Lords of Death during the days and they are subjected to a series of ordeals during the nights. On the first night they are placed in the Dark House and given a torch and two cigars, which they are commanded to light and yet, impossibly, return intact in the morning. The Twins outwit the lords by placing fireflies at the tips of their cigars and passing a macaw's tail as the flame of the torch. A firefly ally of the Twins, with *Akbal* markings, is portrayed brandishing a torch in the upper right of the vase rollout shown in figure 6.5.

Although the Twins cunningly manage to survive all their various trials in the Dark House, the Cold House, the Jaguar House, the House of Fire, and the House of the Bats, they are at last invited to a game of jumping over a huge stone fire pit in which the Xibalbans are brewing an alcoholic beverage. Resigning themselves to their inevitable fate, the Twins join hands and willingly plunge into the fires of the pit. They have however taken precautions that will ultimately result in their resurrection. Knowing that the Lords of Death will ask the advice of the wizards, *Xulu* and *Pacam*, for disposal of their remains, the Twins plot with the seers to instruct the lords to grind their bones and cast the powder into a river. After being immersed in the waters for five days, the Twins miraculously come back to life as catfish.

Transforming into human form again, the Twins return to Xibalba disguised as vagabond magicians who perform great feats of wizardry to the amazement of the inhabitants. They sacrifice dogs and bring them back to life. One of these resurrected dogs can be seen grinning contentedly in the lower right-hand corner of figure 6.5. When the lords hear of these superb magical skills, these itinerant wonder workers are invited to court, especially to enact one of their most impressive performances: One Twin decapitates and dismembers the other, and then brings him back to life.

In the illustration, *Hunahpu* appears on the left in the guise of *Chac-Xib-Chac*. Wielding an ax he raises a flat oval disc bearing the image of *Xaman Ek*, which as a phonetic sign functions as the syllable *K'u* or God, marking an object as a "holy thing." From a death collar decorated with detached eyes symbolizing inner spiritual vision hangs an inverted *Akbal* vase out of which a snake emerges, indicating the flow of *ch'ul* or *itz*, the elixir of life. The shamanic ability to produce this holy substance allows the supernatural feat of transforming death into life to take place.

Raising a cloud of dust in an energetic sacrificial dance *Chac-Xib-Chac* is about to dispatch *Xbalanque* who appears in his form as the Sun God, Baby Jaguar. Gesturing ecstatically, the Jaguar God waves his paws vigorously; his hair is bound in the manner of a sacrificial victim. He reclines on an altar that is the huge head of a personified *cauac* sign; it

Figure 6.6. **The Hero Twins in the Court of Lord One Death,** *cylindrical vase*

also can function phonetically as *cu* or *K'u*, God. Out of the stone the skeletal form of *Cimi* emerges to join in the bizarre performance of the sacrificial dance.

The text seems to emerge from the waving hands of the enthralled God of Death. It begins by recording a day in the sacred calendar and the day of the month it fell on. The glyphs following—*yal* and *Kauil*—refer to a specific ceremony and mean "to manifest or display the Smoking Mirror." The glyphs in the second line are names and titles of the owner of the vase, the last glyph being *Chahtan Uinic,* the Person of the Dark Place, a title that applies only to the dead. We can be reasonably certain

that the vase had a function in funerary rituals commemorating the named owner. These rites, including the not shown but clearly stated manifestation of the Smoking Mirror, were in all probability meant to assist the deceased in the perilous journey through the underworld and to insure—by invoking the exploits of the Hero Twins—a successful rebirth in the land of the ancestors.

The Lords of Death are unaware, of course, that the marvelous magicians are none other than the reborn Twins. In one of the most beautiful and theatrical of all known Maya painted ceramics, illustrated in figure 6.6, the Twins are in the court of Lord One

Death decapitating a supernatural victim, whose body bears *Akbal*-God markings. The true identity of the Twins is hidden behind their masks. Because he appears first and wears a *chac* effigy and a deer ear in his headband, the twin on the left is undoubtedly *Hunahpu*. The victim closes his fists in the handsign of death, a gesture commonly displayed by captives who are about to be sacrificed in court scenes. *Xbalanque* extends his hand in the universal gesture of presenting the performance.

Lord One Death, played by an old man, is distracted from the event as he nonchalantly ties a bracelet on the wrist of the Goddess of the Number Two, whose role is performed by a beautiful young lady. She is a sacrificial deity, the seventh of the nine "lords" of night and a personification of the flint blade of sacrifice. The mainsign of her glyph, written directly behind her, is a hand that menacingly holds the blade poised above her head. A second Goddess of the Number Two is also named and she elegantly touches the foot of the first goddess to alert her attention to the decapitation. Yet a third Goddess of the Number Two leans upon Lord One Death's couch, curling her left hand to express death as she holds her right hand over her mouth, a known American Indian handsign that denotes astonishment and awe.

The two unnamed goddesses in the scene may represent Goddesses of the Number One, other inhabitants of the night sky, the artist cleverly alluding to the lunar deities who pour rain down to Earth from celestial water jars. I would hazard a guess that the rabbit scribe seen painting in the pelt-covered codex box in the forefront of the scene represents the signature of the artist, Rabbit and Flint, represented by the *etz'-nab* sign in his ear, fairly common nominals in the ancient Maya courts. The rim text is an abbreviated P.S.S. followed by the expected names and titles of the owner of the vase.

Four glyphs below the P.S.S. begin with the day *Uaxac Caban*, Eight Earth, beginning a chain reaction of interrelated symbols that could not be entirely coincidental. They contain allusions that would certainly be recognized by astute and learned members of the court. The *Caban* daysign is a personification of the Moon Goddess, and all *Caban* days are under her patronage. Maya astronomers recognized that the Moon, in which they saw the configuration of rabbit much as we see a man-in-the-moon, is relatively very close to the Earth. It becomes the first of the thirteen layers of the heavens and the Moon Goddess therefore personifies the number one.

The following glyph, *Ho Yax*, states that the date fell on the fifth day of the month *Yax*, a *cauac* mainsign prefixed with what is clearly a *yax*-sign meaning "green" or "fresh." The patron of this month is Venus. Anciently it was a period reserved for renovation ceremonies with *Chac-Xib-Chac*, strongly reinforcing the fundamental axiom underlying the principles of Maya art in general: *Hunahpu* represents water, Venus, the snake, and *Chac-Xib-Chac* while *Xbalanque* is a personification of fire, the Sun, the jaguar, and *Kauil*. It is a yin and yang type of relationship that expresses the unity of opposing forces in

A-YA	HOY-I	Y-UCH'AB	TSIH TE'EL	KAKAW	AHAU CHAN	XUL	SAK-CHUEN
CAME INTO BEING	WAS BLESSED	HIS DRINKING VASE	TREE-FRESH	CACAO	SKY-LORD	NAME?	PURE ARTISAN

Figure 6.7. **The Dance of the Hero Twins**, *cylindrical vase*

nature. The two glyphs following the date represent the event that occurred on that day. I think that the Goddess of the Number Two glyphs are a further elaboration of the definition of a specific day in the calendar, and the artist is indicating that it was that goddess who ruled the night following that day. That day was carefully chosen for the pre-planned ritual reenactment of the episode from the *Popol Vuh* recorded for posterity in the vase painting.

By sacrificing one of the inhabitants of Xibalba and bringing him back to life the Hero Twins alleviate any fears or suspicions the Lords of Death may have held regarding their miraculous skills. The lords then want to undergo the experience themselves, an action that ultimately seals their doom. They insist on a command performance in which they will be subjects of the sacrifice, the precise moment being the theme of the vase painting illustrated in figure 6.7.

The scene is again highly theatrical as Baby Jaguar, played by a dwarf, obliges the demands of Lord One Death and raises a spear aimed at his heart. The action reiterates much of the imagery already discussed in reference to figure 6.5; however, now the victim of the sacrificial dance is a Lord of Death rather than one of the Hero Twins. Here the Twins will overcome the lords in Xibalba by *not* resurrecting them.

In the rim text the artist substitutes the usual mirror mainsign in the introductory glyph of the P.S.S. with the ceiba tree earplug symbol synonymous with *Ahau*, "lord" and by extension "mirror." *Pauahtun* is shown generating and imbibing *itz* or *ch'ul* in the *hoy-i* glyph. A footprint is substituted for the *be*-sign in the *y-uch'ab* glyph. The Moon Goddess head portrait stands for first, and by extension "fresh" and "tree" are represented by *Yahaute*, the Lord of the Tree. The cacao glyph is the usual fish god followed by the expected name and titles of the owner of the vase. He is called *Ahau Chan*, Sky Lord, and described as a *Sak Chuen*, Pure Artisan, the mainsign being that of the Creator Monkey God. That Maya hieroglyphs were considered sacred writing is clearly evident from the number of gods who are incorporated and interplay in a short passage describing and tagging the vase. The raven or crow in the lower right-hand corner that gazes up at the introductory glyph is probably the *way* of the artist and represents a signature.

A focal point of the composition in figure 6.7 is the handsign thrust forward by Lord One Death which commands the performance. This gesture is

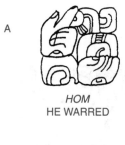

HOM
HE WARRED

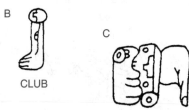

CLUB

*Figure 6.8. **Hom** glyphs*

widely used in Aztec, Mixtec, and Maya art wherein it retains the same fundamental meaning. We have previously discussed it in relationship to the *yalhiya* glyph. It is a very close relative and variant of the handsign that appears in the *hom* glyphs shown in figure 6.8. *Hom* in Cholan and Yucatec means "to end up or finish" and its homophone means "to knock down or demolish buildings or hills." The glyphs, which usually contain two hands, invariably indicate warfare. The *te'* sign shown in C, and appearing in B, represents an ax. When referring to time the *hom*-hand indicates the end or finishing of a time period.

In the Codex Nuttall, Mixtec artists used the war handsign repeatedly. The detail shown in figure 6.9 depicts the same Eight Wind that we met in chapter two, in the act of declaring a great historic war. At the top the date is given as the day One Rain in the year Four

FOUR HOUSE
ONE RAIN

EIGHT
WIND

NINE
HOUSE

THREE EAGLE

Figure 6.9. Codex Nuttall, detail

House, which I estimate fell sometime in or around A.D. 977. It would have been on the seventeenth day of the fifteenth month, which in the Aztec calendar was known as *Panquetlaliztli*, The Lifting Up of Banners, a month that honored the god of war and completed the circuit of festivals of war gods.

Next the subject, the Jeweled or Holy War, is expressed by the emblematic glyph showing the war-hand emanating from a jewel. The event occurs in a place called the Monkey Hill. Eight Wind's proclamation is the result of a conference held with family members that included his wife and allies. Two female participants in the war council are shown in the detail—Nine House, who

Figure 6.10. Panel from the Codex Becker

confirms the declaration of war with her handsign, and Three Eagle, who raises an eagle claw baton while grasping an incense bag. War was a sacred affair in ancient Mesoamerica. Eight Wind sits in a temple with thirteen steps representing the thirteen levels of the heavens. With an angry, menacing facial expression and speech scrolls issuing from his mouth, he decisively displays the handsign that commences a holy war.

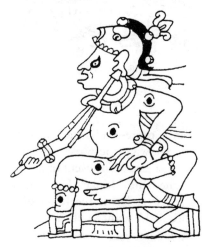

Figure 6.11. Portrayal of the **Morning Star**, from the Dresden Codex

Painting hundreds of years later Nahua artists used the same visual sign language to express war during the time of the Conquest. In a panel from the Codex Becker shown in figure 6.10, the artist depicts a war conference of the type that took place among the noblemen and leaders of various Mexican tribes held in subservience by the Aztecs as Cortez and his followers progressed inland. After meeting the Spaniards in battle, one tribe, the Tlaxcalans, decided to join them as bearers and warriors. In the scene the lord on the right raises the hand of war as the lord on the left extends his open hand in a gesture indicating submission to the declaration.

The leaders of the various tribes spoke different languages and naturally communicated through the mutually understood sign language as shown in the panel. Incidently, traveling with Cortez and acting as his interpreter was *Ce Malinalli*, One Grass, known to the Spaniards as Doña Marina. When she was born, Aztec priests interpreted special signs in the sky, accurately predicting that she would throughout her life be opposed to the war god of her Aztec people. In order to protect her life her mother presented a false daughter to the priests, one that had been born dead to a slave she owned. One Grass was sent to the Maya people in the Yucatan where she mastered the sign language she undoubtedly used to communicate with them.

Brother Diego de Landa recorded that the Maya used to hide in their houses when Venus first appeared as the Morning Star. Having just emerged after his voyage through the realms of darkness, the god was considered vengeful and angry. In the Dresden Codex the first rays of the "star" are usually symbolized by spears. In the portrayal of the Morning Star from the Venus tables of the codex shown in figure 6.11, the star is named and personified as *Hunahpu*. He thrusts forward his right hand in the war handsign, which the artist has substituted for the usual spear. Venus was called *Noh Ek*, the Great Star and the Day-bringer, as harbinger of the Sun. The left hand of *Hunahpu* in the portrait is greatly exaggerated in size and forms a *chi*-hand, a sign which as we have seen can be qualified by the flicking of fingers to mean star in the American Indian Sign Language.

As the Morning Star, Venus was also known as *Ah Ahzah Cab*, the Awakener, and associated with dawn—the best time for hunting—and with the god *Xulab*, the patron of hunting. *Hunahpu* as depicted in Maya art is often depicted wearing the traditional hat of the deerhunter. In this codex portrait he wears a skull headdress and a death-eye collar and bracelets as he glares menacingly while displaying his threatening handsign.

The Dresden Codex contains a five-page Venus table along with other tables devised by Maya astronomers to keep accurate track of the Moon, and apparently Jupiter, Mars, and Mercury. The eclipse pages give a synodic month of 29.52592 days, which is only seven minutes away from the modern value. The synodic period of Venus was calculated to be 584 days (the modern value is 583.920 days), divided into Morning

Figure 6.12. The Venus cycle episode in the Codex Nuttall

A

Star (236 days), Superior Conjunction (90 days of invisibility), Evening Star (250 days) and Inferior Conjunction (8 days of invisibility). Inscriptions show that the Venus calendar already existed in the Classic period, and it is now abundantly clear that the apparent movements of Venus were the determining factors for the dates of important battles fought between the ancient Maya city-states. I was amazed to discover hidden in the sinuous pages of the Codex Nuttall the identical recognition of a 584-day Venus cycle and the same associations of Venus with warfare.

The episode relating to the Venus cycle is illustrated in figure 6.12, which begins on page three of the codex. The heroine in the events is Nine Monkey who plays a variety of roles in the codex. Here she is a warrior chieftain; as a shamaness on page four she takes part in a magical ritual that includes the primordial shaman Two Dog, and resurrects two fallen warriors, while on page ten she sits on the jaguar throne as a ruler of her people.

The narrative starts in the lower right-hand corner with a placesign showing a stony hill and a cave entrance out of which a human face is peering at another placesign, *Tlaloc* Hill or the Hill of the Rain God, which is in the territory of the Mixtecs. The two placesigns are placed in opposition to each other, symbolizing a war between the Mixtecs and a strange people whom we know very little about except that they originate from the Cave Hill. Their striped body markings and knobby curlicues indicate "stone" and they are therefore known as "the Stony Men." In the scene above

the placenames they are seen to have invaded Mixtec territory and captured Nine Monkey who raises her right hand in a gesture of acquiescence.

The next event is shown immediately below the warriors, beginning with a date and an extremely concise description of where and what happened on that day. In my tentative correlation, I place the day Six Dog in the year Three Reed, around the year A.D. 963. It would have occurred in the month *Teotleco*, the Return of the Gods, or about October. The place is Jewel Flower Hill and its sign contains a *huehuetl*, a drum that is indicative of high military rank. Surmounting the hill is a frieze, representing an edifice, a temple or a town. Within it is a portal or a cave out of which protrudes the disappearing feet of Nine Monkey as she escapes from the confinement of her enemies.

That she has successfully escaped is made clear in the next panel which is centered on the yearsign Five House (A.D. 965). Above it is the daysign Six Eagle, placing the event in the fifth month, *Toxcatl*, the warrior new year roughly corresponding to May. Preceding this another daysign, Seven Snake, appears inside the Jewel Flower Hill placesign. It occurs in the first month of the year, *Atlcoulco*, in which was celebrated the feast of the Warriors of the Sun, the two competing orders of the knights of the *Cuatli*, Eagle or day sun, and the *Ocelotl*, Jaguar, the night sun. The day Seven Snake, Five House is repeated on page ten where we again encounter Nine Monkey. It opens a scene portraying *Tonatiuh*, the Sun God, holding in the palms of his upraised hands two opposing warriors, one wearing an eagle helmet and a feathered costume and the other in the guise of a jaguar.

Page three depicts the Six Eagle event in which a triumphant Nine Monkey treads on top of the Jewel Flower Hill in full battle regalia including an *atlatl* (wooden sheath used to throw light lances or darts) and *tecpactl* (arrows with pointed flints). She brandishes a *tezozapo chimalli* (shield with two cords) above which waves the war banner of a chieftain. At the foot of the hill her *nagual*, the *Uicictl* or Hummingbird, whose quick movements symbolize the warrior, attacks the Stony Men. Ferociously swooping down from the heavens above is her ally *Chicomecoatl*, Seven Snake, wielding a *macana* (war club).

The image shares a number of characteristics with a portrait of Venus personified by a serpentine warrior in the Venus calendar of the Dresden Codex. (p. 49) Both have the iconographic symbol of the snake emerging from their mouths. That Seven Snake represents an alliance between Nine Monkey and the powerful spirit forces of war generated by Venus is further evidenced in the relationship of the time periods elapsing between the three dates given in the episode.

The days between Six Dog, Three Reed, and Six Eagle, Five House number 584, a Venus cycle. That this is not merely coincidental is strongly suggested by the fact that the days between Seven Snake, Five House, and Six Eagle, Five House number 90, the period of Superior Conjunction and invisibility within the Venus cycle. It would seem that the artists have intentionally equated the triumphant return and reemergence of Nine Monkey with the first appearance of the Evening Star after the disappearance of Venus in the underworld.

A final confirmation of the correlation is given on page ten of the codex and shown in A wherein Nine Monkey is literally named or given a title as a personification of Venus. Her portrait has much in common with that of *Hunahpu* as the Morning Star (figure 6.11), including the skull headdress and the death spot on her cheek. She is shown officiating at a war council held at Zacatepec on the day Seven Snake, Five House. This means not only that the attack on the Stony Men was timed to coordinate with the Venus cycle, but also the meeting that planned the attack and formalized the alliances necessary to successfully carry it out was ritually synchronized to Venus appearances in the sky. Attending the meeting is the prominent warrior-priest Five Flower; this initially may be confusing to a reader of the codex as on page two he seems to be portrayed as one of the Stony Men. An examination of the details on this page reveals that he is really being depicted as an old enemy of the Stony Men, being attired in the flayed skin of a captive, not as one of them.

Directly below Nine Monkey's portrait is the emblem that closely associates her with Venus. It consists of a sky-band segment with circles representing stars. In the center a skull represents the Great Star, a dot placed firmly in the cheek. The design device sur-

rounding the skull is identical to the Maya emblem of Venus as *Xux Ek*, the Wasp Star.

The two other nominal or titular glyphs are of interest. One combines two elements, a hummingbird and a spindle, cleverly symbolizing Nine Monkey's dual role as both warrior and shamanness. The hummingbird is a symbol of the warrior. The spindle identifies her as a priestess of the cult of *Tlazoteotl*, the Goddess of Love who consumes the sins of humanity. Rites of confession are practiced in the presence of her priests and she unravels the fabric of evil the penitents have woven. She is known as Great Spinner of the Thread and Weaver of the Fabric of Life, spinning and weaving representing life, death, and rebirth in a continuing cycle

Figure 6.13. **Bird Jaguar the Great and Lady Six-Sky** Ahau, *lintel 41, Yaxchilan; presently in the British Museum, London.*

characterizing the essential nature of the Mother Goddess. A third glyph names Nine Monkey as Jeweled Skull.

Curiously this glyph appears in Maya art as the nominative of a male warrior documented as being captured on A.D. May 9, 755, and here again we find the same preoccupation with the apparent motions of Venus and war.

The capture of Jeweled Skull was both referred to in texts and depicted as monumental art in the Maya city-state of Yaxchilan in southern Mexico. The most famous of these, lintel 41 illustrated in figure 6.13, shows Bird Jaguar the Great, the renowned high king of Yaxchilan with one of his wives, Lady Six-Sky Ahau, completing the prebattle ritual of arming and donning full warrior regalia in the early hours of May 9. Bird Jaguar grasps a flint-bladed lance while finalizing and sealing the rite with a display of the *hom*-hand. We can be certain that the activity takes place at dawn or in the early morning because lintel 8, also dated May 9, shows Bird Jaguar dressed in the same outfit and wielding the lance as he reduces Jeweled Skull into submission.

The text begins in the upper left-hand corner with the day Seven *Imix*, the eighteenth day of the month *Tzec*. The second line in the panel begins with the war glyph, a Venus sign over a shell symbol, followed by a glyph containing flint and fire mainsigns. This must qualify the war glyph in some way, either naming the battle or the ritual preceding it, as portrayed below. The verb, *chukah*, "he captured," made up of the phonetic elements *chu*, *ka*, and *ah* begins the center panel and is followed by Jeweled Skull's nominal glyph. The third glyph is read phonetically as *u bak*, literally "his bone" but practically

meaning "his captive." Next is Bird Jaguar's pictographic nominal glyph followed by his title.

The panel in the lower right contains three more of Bird Jaguar's title glyphs beginning with *Ah Kal Bakob*, He of the Twenty Captives. The artist has actually linked these two panels with the verb *hom*, "he warred," expressed not glyphically but as Bird Jaguar's handsign. The transitional phrase therefore would be translated, ". . . Bird Jaguar, title, *hom*, he warred, He of the Twenty Captives . . . ," which makes much more sense than merely listing a series of titles. Moreover, in doing this the artist has succeeded in integrating the handsign language in the pictorial matter with the written language in the text. This technique represents a unique achievement, unsurpassed in the history of writing, unknown in any other writing systems, and an astonishing development in the utilization of possibilities inherent in the art of visual communication.

In the remaining titles in the lower panel is the glyph *Ux Katun Ahau*, Three *Katun* Lord. At the time of the event Bird Jaguar was 46 years old and therefore had entered his third twenty-year period, an age that was by no means considered too old to be going on the warpath. His father is recorded as still leading troops in military campaigns while he was in his eighties, after entering his fourth *katun*. The last glyph is the vulture variant of the Ahau title and reads, *Ch'ul Ahau*, Holy Lord.

The name and titles of *Na Uac Chan Ahau*, Lady Six-Sky, appear in the panel above her portrait. In the first glyph the number six is prefixed by a female variant of the *Chak te'* or *Batab* glyph. The mainsign in the second glyph is *Chan*, Sky, modified by an *Ahau* prefix. The third glyph informs us that she is a Lady Ahau of the Ik polity (San José de Motul in the Peten). Bird Jaguar perhaps married this noblewoman for a number of reasons including her spiritual powers but certainly to implement the complex political strategies he engaged in throughout his life. Forming and cementing alliances within and outside of his own city-state through marriage played a highly significant role. The last title reads *Na Bacab*.

Although a large part of the lintel has been destroyed by erosion, the remaining imagery conveys a great deal of information regarding the war preparation ceremony and the role of the female in it. Here the *nawah*, or "dressing" ceremony, is totally integrated with bloodletting rites, which invoke the protection and power of spirit forces in order to insure victory on the battlefield. Although essential, it is obvious that bloodletting would seriously weaken a warrior faced with the mission of not merely killing, but the far more difficult task of capturing his opponent. His female counterpart therefore performs the actual bloodletting on herself and in this way actually participates in warfare. In similar scenes depicting war preparation rites females are sometimes shown in earlier stages of the ritual and evidence of bloodletting on their part is still visible. Here the ceremony is already finished and the artist has captured the dramatic moment when the

Ahau takes leave of his palace to lead his warriors on their sacred mission.

Lady Six-Sky's blood has long since been sprinkled in jaguar spot patterns onto the paper strips that form Bird Jaguar's cape and that have been wrapped into his headdress during the *nawah* ceremony. The sacred bloodletting instrument she used has been returned to its jaguar-pelt sheath. It now appears inserted through a section of cut spondylous shell worn in her warrior-style headdress. The outcome of the confrontation will depend at least as much, and probably more, on the efficacy of the rituals to invoke unseen spirit powers than it will on any physical forces. Whatever military prowess Bird Jaguar can bring to the field will fail if the hidden forces of war gods are not on his side.

The *Tlaloc*-Jaguar costume of the Yaxchilan warrior-kings worn by Bird Jaguar transforms him into a walking hieroglyph symbolizing and embodying those powers. In the center of the pectoral over his heart is enthroned the Jaguar Protector. A mask of *Tlaloc* the Thunder God is tied around his headdress. In the field of battle Bird Jaguar will strike like lightning and fight with the invincible ferocity of the jaguar. The eye of the mask is the star in the circle, a symbol generated by the calendrical union of eight solar years and five Venus cycles, whose powerful destructive forces will also be channeled and unleashed against the enemy. Meanwhile we can be assured that Lady Six-Sky will not be standing by idly admiring the beauty of the temple grounds. In acts of sympathetic magic she will be burning the remaining strips of blood-stained paper, not in the usual rites invoking the Vision Serpent, but raising up the *Waxaklahun Ubah Kan*, the supernatural serpent who influences war. War was a cosmic affair, a sacred struggle taking place on interacting human and spiritual planes, the victor being determined on battlefields both on the Earth and in the skies.

Engraved on the walls of Maya temples and painted on Maya ceramics are recorded the activities of some of the most remarkable and extraordinary people ever documented in all of human history—the Maya Ahau. Their ideal of a well-rounded individual surpassed even the Western concept of the Renaissance Man. Besides being the chief shaman, the leading warrior, and the ruler of the people, the Ahau was known to excel at once as an artist, astronomer, and architect, a calligrapher, mathematician, and city planner. As well the Ahau was traditionally expected to demonstrate prowess as an athlete in the ball game.

At Yaxchilan, Bird Jaguar, his father, and his grandfather are all portrayed in one place or another dressed in elaborate costumes and performing feats of skill in the ball court, an architectural feature of every Maya city-state known. Playing ball was not merely a game; it was often a life-and-death struggle and the Maya brought to it all the interactions of cosmic and supernatural forces that they carried into warfare. In fact very often the end result of a war event is staged in a ball court so that sacrifice at the ball court is really an extension of ritual warfare.

The concluding rite of the *nawah* ceremony initially performed by Bird Jaguar on A.D. May 9, 755 took place at a much later date with the sacrifice of Jeweled Skull at a ball court. A portrayal of the specific event was not made— or has not been found—but the events can easily be reconstructed as Bird Jaguar's mode of operation was traditional and its various stages are well documented in the art.

The final sacrificial rituals were pub-

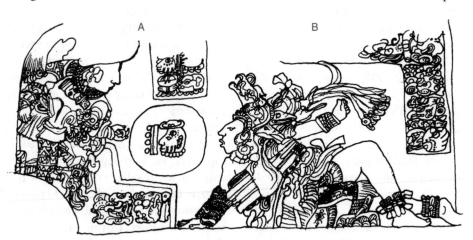

*Figure 6.14. **The Defeat of Four White Jaguar of Calakmul***

lic, or at least well-attended, celebrations of victory, a repayment in blood for the cooperation of the war gods—probably timed to the movements of the planets—and finally a state propaganda spectacular reinforcing the king's right to rule. Inevitably the preliminaries included *nawah* ceremonies just as in combat. The main event was the one-on-one ball-game match between Bird Jaguar and Jeweled Skull.

Ball playing is a central theme of the *Popol Vuh*. It is the annoying noise of the Twins' game that causes the lords of the underworld to summon them to Xibalba in the first place. Just as reenactments of episodes from the epic were performed on stage, impersonators of the Hero Twins and the Lords of Death played ball in ritual pageants that re-created mythological events. These are well documented in the art. In them we see the Twins playing together, *Hunahpu* contending with the God of Zero, and *Xbalanque* against Lord One Death. The combination of religion and mythology with sporting events must have been a great delight to the audiences. Bird Jaguar undoubtedly participated in such ritual reenactments; he is portrayed as a ballplayer in numerous panels, and all ball games to some degree or another re-create the games in the *Popul Vuh*. In other rituals Bird Jaguar appears both in the guise of *Chac-Xib-Chac* and of *Kauil*.

The kind of game played between Bird Jaguar and Jeweled Skull would have closely resembled the one-on-one match illustrated in figure 6.14. It has been fairly well established by scholars that the players are Ahauob, based on

the remaining glyphs, and that the one in A is the victor, based on the iconography. He wears a jaguar balloon headdress, and B's headdress has bird motifs. It is known that when this imagery is juxtaposed the bird is always the loser. Furthermore, the punched holes in the garments of strips of cloth worn by B mark him as a captive, however elegantly dressed otherwise.

This observation would be confirmed by a reading of the handsigns. The loser touches his right hand to the Earth in a gesture of acquiescence and respect. Resigning himself to his fate he raises his left hand in the death sign. He stares intently at the hand of sacrifice displayed by the victor which reveals his immediate destiny. His apron is embellished with zero signs. In the panel above him he is named as *Chan Ti Balam*, Four White Jaguar. The last glyph in the panel is the toponym *Ox-Nab Tunich,* which is in the kingdom of Calakmul.

The most obvious indications of the winner are that B is sprawled out on the ground and A hovers over him. Also, the hidden spatial grid in which east is at the top is always in effect unless special circumstances allow for exceptions. Adhering to this scheme, ball-court scenes will generally place the winner in the superior northern or left segment of the grid.

In lintel 8, where Jeweled Skull is captured, he is stripped of his armor and warrior regalia. For the ritual this apparel is returned with the addition of ball-game equipment, and certain alterations are added. In this panel besides the alterations the loser is wearing what

Figure 6.15. **The Ballplayers**, *cylindrical vase*

appears to be the scarf of a sacrificial victim; by contrast A wears both the death-god pendant frequently worn by an Ahau in battle and a huge *Tlaloc-Death God* pendant. It seems therefore that the outcome of these games was predetermined. We don't know to what degree fair play was involved. With the minor exception of talons embedded in A's forearm padding, the panel does not reveal any handicaps imposed on the captive but we cannot expect it to; it was created as a propaganda piece to honor the victor. We do know that in every instance recorded the captive is the loser.

Sometimes a captive is blatantly disadvantaged, being given mock weapons and set against a number of opponents with real weapons. There is a story of one captive who managed to emerge victorious from such an encounter. He was given his liberty but demanded to be sacrificed as his right and privilege.

As a grand finale to the Jeweled Skull episode, he was taken to a temple with a long staircase. Similar sacrificial rituals performed by Bird Jaguar suggest that this would have been the pyramid, structure 33, known as the Hieroglyphic Stairs. Here he was bound into the form of a ball and cast down the stairway.

Like ghosts or phantoms, three strangely attired ballplayers, wearing the scarves of sacrificial victims, boldly dance out onto the ball field in figure 6.15. They wear slotted helmets that protect their heads from the hard rubber ball that speeds rapidly and menacingly as it rebounds around the court. The game they play is unknown. In the classic contest touching the ball with the hands was forbidden but their hands are prepared to come into direct contact with the ball: In their right hands they grasp a shell-like implement that could

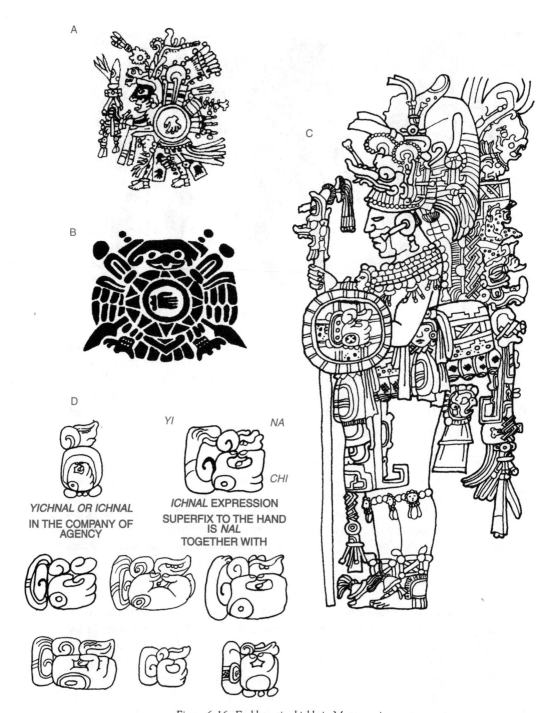

A

B

C

D

YI   NA

YICHNAL OR ICHNAL

IN THE COMPANY OF
AGENCY

CHI

ICHNAL EXPRESSION
SUPERFIX TO THE HAND
IS NAL
TOGETHER WITH

Figure 6.16. Emblematic shields in Mesoamerican art

have been used to pierce and cast the rubber ball in offensive plays. Their left hands, wrapped in cloth padding, are obviously used in defensive maneuvers. Their bodies are covered in a thick hide or perhaps a rubber suit, so their outfits are designed to provide maximum protection.

The hand emblems on the arms and legs of the players are symbolic expressions of protection. The concept is derived from that most basic ritualistic use of the hands in prayer—the exposing of the palms at dawn in an appeal for the Sun's protective powers. For this same reason the hand appears as an emblem on shields in Mesoamerica and also on the plains of North America, retaining here the same fundamental meaning. Examples of Mesoamerican shields are shown in figure 6.16. Besides a distinctive hand emblem in the shield brandished by the warrior in A, the protective emblem is imprinted on cloth strips hanging from his belt. Other symbols packed into this image are overtly aggressive. The facial war paint is the awesome hand over the jaw, a Maya device symbolizing the ultimate sacrifice— the removal of the jaw. The warrior grasps a flaming flint spear and sprouting about him are symbols of the blossoming war. In B the protecting hand in the shield is surrounded by symbols of aggression—crossed arrows and the owl, harbinger of death.

We can always rely on refinements and subtleties from the Maya and so the shield in C, displayed by the Ahau, Flint Sky *Kauil*, contains a highly elaborate extension of the basic protective hand motif. In the center of his shield is a hieroglyph, samples of which are shown in D, composed of a *yi* prefix, a *na* superfix, the *chi*-hand mainsign, and sometimes an *l(a)* subfix rendering the word *yichnal*, meaning "in the company of," "together with," or "in the agency of." The glyph appears together with a solar cross that contains jaguar-pelt markings, the symbol of the Jaguar Protector God. As the reader has probably long ago surmised, Maya glyphs contain metaphors, allusions, and symbolic ramifications that go far beyond the meanings supplied in simple English translations. This is a perfectly ideal case in point.

The *chi*-hand supplies the *chi* sound of the word and it can be read simply as that, but symbolically it has further implications as the emblematic seal of the Sun and simultaneously as the number nine. The personification of the number nine is *Xbalanque*, whose *way* is the jaguar and who is the human incarnation of *Kauil*, whose image surmounts the staff held by the ruler, forming part of his name. Get it? A Native American not at all versed in the intricacies of Maya hieroglyphs would recognize the hand and its fundamental meaning. For a literate Maya the ramifications of the signs run deep, cycling and overlapping into various layers of hidden meanings, overtures, and relationships. It is no wonder that the Nahau word for artist is *tlacuilo*, the "putter down of thoughts" about whom it has been written in poetry,

The good painter;
Toltec artist of the black and red ink,
Creator of things with the black
    water . . .

Figure 6.17. **The Umpire**, *figurine from the Peten area*

The good painter;
Understanding God in his heart,
Deifies things with his heart,
Dialogues with his own heart.

It is quite impossible to pass by the portrait of this magnificent Ahau, a walking hieroglyph, without relating a few terse remarks. I think that the front of the image portrays the physical presence of the ruler and the backrack represents his *way* or soul. In dance these sacred objects augment and amplify the swirling motions of the performer. In the headdress of the Ahau is a mask of *Chac-Xib-Chac* complementing the image of *Kauil* on his staff. Above the mask are the beaded signs for *tok*, "flint," another allusion to his name. From head to foot there are numerous signs referring to his other nominal *Chan*, "sky." Below his belt hang shells with *nen* signs designating him as a mirror of the people and in his apron is an image of *Xaman Ek* who appears in the trunk of the World Tree and is at the center of the night sky. This implies that the Ahau is the embodiment of the *axis mundi* or the central axis of the kingdom.

The backrack contains an entire cosmology and is in fact the cosmic tree surmounted by the celestial bird. Below this a roaring Baby Jaguar rears up, leaping out of the headdress of an image of *Kauil*. Trailing off the backrack is another image of *Xaman Ek* with a mirror sign in his forehead. The backrack is a reflection of the physical image of the king presented in front of it and it is representative of the World Tree as the central portal to the spirit world, of which this material world is but a fleeting mirror image.

One of the most haunting and forbidding images ever to come out of the Maya ball court is the figurine illustrated in figure 6.17. I have titled this remarkable statue *The Umpire* for a number of reasons: That he is not actively engaged in playing is evident simply because he is seated. Before him lies a flat stone, an implement used for the essential task of suspending the ball above the ground. It is here that the game both commences and comes to an end and the ball must never, under any circumstances, come in contact with the earth. The ball is a sacred thing; it is given a name; it is representative of the moving planets. Tucked into the figure's waistband is a measuring rod or ruler that was probably used to make determinations of some kind on the playing field.

Most revealing, however, are the handsigns dramatically displayed. They represent opposite values, the closed right hand being the hand of death while the open left hand is the protective hand of life. The right handsign means "out" and the left handsign means "safe." It is an extremely amusing and truly amazing coincidence that these are the very same handsigns utilized by umpires in modern baseball.

The slot in the protective helmet is cut out in an *ik*, "life" or "spirit," sign. The ball game is above all a sacred ritual; just as actors on the stage represent the fabled contest between gods and heroes so do the players on the field. Not all ancient cultures developed a ball game but among those that did the Maya game was probably the most advanced partly because they had the advantage of a ball made of rubber whose recoiling buoyancy was unsurpassed.

The Indians of the southwestern United States had a ball game similar to the Maya game, while northern tribes developed lacrosse, a variation of which became modern hockey. The Celts were avid ball players who centuries ago played handball and hurling, which survive intact to this day. The athletic-minded Greeks, who gave us the Olympics, must have had some sort of ball game whereas the Romans were much too preoccupied with gladiatorial combat in their coliseums—a ball game would have been considered a triviality. I do not know of an ancient Egyptian ball game, but that does not mean that one did not exist. For the practical-minded Chinese the idea of a ball game simply was unthinkable; all athletics were funneled into the more useful mar-

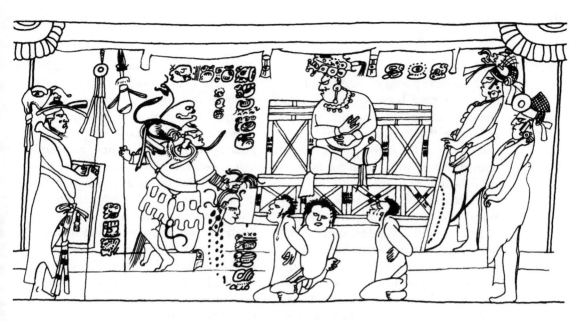

Figure 7.1. **On the Holy Day Eighteen Zak**, *cylindrical vase*

THE QUEST FOR THE VISION SPIRIT AND RITES OF SACRIFICE

While doing research on megalithic structures in Ireland, I became interested in the question of why many of these monuments were associated with the practice of human sacrifice. I found that this notion stemmed from an association of the sites with Druids. But where did the involvement of Druids with this practice derive from? There is no archaeological evidence to support the claim and, although Druids appear frequently in ancient Irish literature, I could find no reference to them engaging in human sacrifice.

Eventually I was able to trace the entire fallacy back to a single source. Julius Caesar in his book, *The Conquest of Gaul*, had described the Druids as performing elaborate mass human sacrifices. This allegation, although probably hearsay, was to become a major belief regarding the character of the Druids until this day. It can be dangerous to place too much confidence in descriptions of vanquished cultures that have been written by their conquerors. And of course Caesar, in describing these atrocities, never compares them to the barbaric mass executions that were actually taking place in the coliseums of Rome.

Likewise, the colonialists in "New Spain" who gave us detailed descriptions of human sacrifices in Mesoamerica did not see any comparisons with the ceremonial executions of heretics during the Inquisition, concurrently being performed back home in Madrid. (Ironically enough, exaggerations by Spanish writers in America were paralleled by Protestant writers who placed the number of heretics executed during the Catholic Inquisition way out of proportion in order to arouse revulsion and horror in Europe. Actually the number of those condemned for heresy was never very large, and in fact many Roman Catholics in Spain were vehemently opposed to the introduction of the Inquisition.)

Similarly a distorted view arose of the practice of human sacrifice in America, unfortunately to the extent that the pre-Columbian cultures have become closely associated with ritual killing. For example, as we have seen in a Maya codex, *Quetzalcoatl* is depicted apparently performing acts of ritual human sacrifice but the reverse appears to be true. Legends attest that *Quetzalcoatl* was in fact responsible for the complete banning of such practices.

Undoubtedly many of the human sacrifice scenes that appear in Maya art can be taken quite literally. However,

they often function on a cosmological level: A real human sacrifice does not actually occur; it is performed on a metaphoric level or, as we have seen in a vase painting, the sacrifice is part of a mystery play, a reenactment of a mythological event. It is necessary to place the entire practice of ritual human sacrifice in Maya culture in a proper perspective.

Human sacrifice does not occur solely in the domains of the ancient Maya. Ritual killing is an observable mode of human behavior exhibited by practically all known societies at one time or another. Sigmund Freud maintained in his last major work, *Moses and Monotheism*, that the origin of ritual and religion is to be found in sacrifice. In general, sacrifice is motivated by the desire for communion between members of a social group and their gods.

In the Aztec religion the performance of self-sacrifice in the form of bloodletting was heavily emphasized; this pattern of worship reached its climax in the rituals of human sacrifice performed in central Mexico where allegedly they became excessive. It is only in the Postclassic period of the Maya that this practice appears to occur with any frequency. Evidence of human sacrifice in Classic times includes an incised drawing at Tikal, two Piedras Negras stelae, and various painted ceramic vessels. The last recorded case occurred in Chiapas in 1868 among the Chamula but here again whether this was part of a staged performance of a play or an actual event is not known.

Of course, not all captives met their end on the ball court. Lesser ranking captives were ceremoniously sacrificed in the courts as shown in the vase painting in figure 7.1. Above the Sahal who holds the severed head of a victim the text begins, *Ta hoy Uaxac-lahun Zac,* "On the holy day Eighteen *Zak* . . ." The two glyphs following this are sacrifice glyphs describing the event that happened. The first has a heart as its mainsign and the other shows a dismembered jaw. These glyphs complement the handsign, the sacred mudra of sacrifice, made by the enthroned Ahau. A bound captive seated below him also makes this sign. The result is that the pictorial subject matter, the glyphs, and the handsigns are in perfect agreement.

Another captive displays the *chi*-hand as captives frequently do in similar scenes in Maya art. In this context the *chi*-hand is an appeal to the Sun for protection. On the far right an *its'at*, probably the painter of this vase, gestures in a salute to his Ahau by placing the *chi*-hand on his shoulder, signifying that he recognizes the Ahau as the living embodiment of the Sun. Glyphs that appear in groups of three in the painting name the participants; those directly in front of the severed head probably name the victim. Anciently any bloodshed in the month of *Sak* was considered an abomination except human sacrifice. *Sak*, "white," is a homonym for "terror." The vase records the gruesome event for posterity and was used by the participants and their descendants to celebrate it.

It is easy to be judgmental regarding the barbaric nature of these human sacrifices. My only comment is that in our modern "civilized" society, states regularly and systematically execute prisoners although the taking of human life for whatever reason is diametrically opposed to the religious laws and values purported to be upheld by those states. By contrast when human life was taken in the Maya court, it was done with integrity, being in complete adherence to the laws of the religion of the state. The medieval executioner was always masked. The modern administrator of capital punishment is always an unknown entity. The Maya Ahau is happy to have himself portrayed and named in an act deemed worthy of celebration.

In figure 7.1 the handsign of sacrifice displayed by the presiding Ahau defines the essence of the ritual being performed and symbolically embodies its content. The eyes of the participants are focused on the handsign, which, like the baton of a conductor, orchestrates the action and is a central element in the composition. The same mudra is the epicenter and focalization of another sacrificial ceremonial rite illustrated in figure 7.2 wherein Lady Six-Stone is seen conjuring an ancestral spirit. In the final stage of the rite, the sacred handsign is at the nucleus of the event, the median communicative signal that empowers the shamanness to manifest the material presence of the divine ancestor from the realm of the spirit world onto the plane of human existence. The recognition of the meaning of such mudra is a key that unlocks previously hidden principles lying at the very core of Maya art, allowing us to penetrate into deeper levels of symbolic meanings previously shrouded in a veil of mystery.

Lady Six-Stone does not gaze at the majestic Vision Serpent that rears up

Figure 7.2. **Lady Six-Stone Conjures the Vision Serpent,** *stone lintel*

vealing in that the mainsign is a hand stressing that the action is essentially performed through the agency of the hand, regarded as a powerful conduit of supernatural forces. The *ah* postfix places the verb in the past tense and the mainsign is further modified by *ca*, "fish," which acts as a phonetic complement but has further connotations as a symbol. Let us recall that the Hero Twins were resurrected after their voluntary sacrifice by being transformed into fish. *Ca* also alludes to a word meaning "to count" and by extension time itself. And conjuring the ancestral spirits indeed involves transcending time barriers.

The text in the panel on the right elaborates on the basic statement made in the initial text and, importantly, it provides us with a reference to the sequential unfolding of stages in the ritual portrayed. The first glyph is that of the Vision Serpent the lady has conjured through an act of blood sacrifice. The instrument used was the rope that now hangs from the woven basket she cradles in her arms. It was passed through her tongue to obtain blood, the currency of the gods and the price of admission that opens the portal to the spirit world. The blood was sprinkled on strips of bark paper, placed in the sacrificial vessel, and set alight. In the resulting plumes of smoke the shamanness is culturally and psychologically conditioned to perceive the astonishing image of the Vision Serpent. The sacrificial bowl is ritualistically placed in the northern or left sector of the panel. The ancestor emerges on the top, eastern or male sector, and the shamanness

out of the vessel of offerings nor at the face of the ancestor that emerges from its mouth. She stares fixedly at the handsign displayed by the ancestor which reciprocates her own mudra, the culminating instrumental factor in the manifestation of the divine presence. Here again there is a tight interlocking synchronicity between the pictorial subject matter in the composition, the handsign displayed in it, and the accompanying text.

The panel in the upper left succinctly describes the action beginning with the time—Four *Cauac*, Twelve *Zip* or A.D. March 28, 755—the verb, *tzakah*, "she manifested"—and finally the personified glyph of the ancestor who was conjured on that day. The verb is re-

kneels on the bottom, western or female sector. Based on traditional ordering principles, the performance of the ritual is an act of centering, a theme woven into patterns on the *huipil* she wears for the occasion. The glyph of the Vision Serpent is superfixed by a *nal*-sign, a direct reference to the glyph *xaman*, "north," and describes this particular Vision Serpent as coming from the north, the realm of the ancestors.

The second glyph describes the Vision Serpent as *u way*, "her animal-spirit companion" and also her "ancestral soul." At present I think that the third glyph titles the Vision Serpent as *Ox Chac*, a divine being who can transcend the three realms of the Maya cosmos. The fourth and central glyph in the panel reads *iwal tzak*, "and then she manifests," followed by three glyphs naming and titling the ancestor materialized in further detail. In the initial panel the *tzak* verb is followed by a head portrait of the ancestor superfixed by a *yax* sign, which can mean "green," the color of the center. The abstract version of his nominal in the second panel begins with the *yax* superfix but has *sac*, "white," the color symbolic of the north as its mainsign. Only after she has magically transformed her blood into her *way* can she evoke the ancestral spirit with her hand, the climactic moment dramatically depicted in the scene.

The glyphs in the central panel refer to Lady Six-Stone and begin with the verb *u bah*, "she goes" or "she did," followed by *Ch'ul Na*, which may be translated simply as the Divine Lady or Lady of *Ch'ul*, Holy Lady of the Life Force. Here it is obvious that the glyph also directly refers to the action taking place in the ritual. The upturned jar spills out the sacred spiritual life force essences that are echoed in the beads of *ch'ul* seen emanating in spiral patterns from the body of the rearing Vision Serpent. *Ch'ul* is the eternal soul stuff of the inner spirit residing in human blood that has been released through the sacrificial rite of bloodletting.

Below the verb is the nominal glyph *Na Uac Tun*, Lady Six-Stone, and the glyph *Na Ahau Ik*, Noble Lady of the Ik Polity. She is one of Bird Jaguar's four wives and probably a sister or close relative of Lady Six-Sky who she closely resembles and who comes from the same place. Their nominals are complementary. Six-Sky means "raised up sky" and refers to the *Wakah Chan*, the World Tree, with its roots below in nadir, passing through the middle world of the four directions and the celestial realms through the zenith, where it flowers in the spirit world. Six-Stone means "raised up stone," and erected stones are called trees!

We have previously discussed how the *tun* glyph combines symbols of the dry season and the rainy season and thus represents a year after which a stone is erected. The *tun* becomes a symbol of time itself and just as Six-Sky implies transcending spacial realms, Six-Stone implies transcending cycles of time. The last two glyphs in the panel are *Na Bacab*, Lady Stood-Up Person, the title of an adept whose magical skills have reached above and beyond the limitations of time and space.

Figure 7.2 is a detailed and penetrating glimpse into Maya ancestor wor-

Figure 7.3. **The Ahau of Calakmul Enters the Spirit World,** *cylindrical vase*

ship. We peer into a world wherein death does not make a person cease to belong to a social unit and a great deal of attention is lavished on the royal dead. Ancestral spirits living in the sky are viewed as having a larger share of divine favor and influence than the living and they are called on as kindred beings to assist the community of the living and intercede with the gods. A close relationship exists between the ancestral soul of an Ahau and beings that are the *wayob* or co-essences of the Ahau.

All religion is concerned with postmortem security—whether it be achieved by ritual magic, divine assistance, or mystical enlightenment. Besides using all of these methods the Maya placed particular emphasis on the ability to transform into one's *way*, a crucial act performed by the Hero Twins in the mythology and an ability

well documented in their art in rituals performed by historical personages, as is exemplified vividly in figure 7.3.

The vase painting I have entitled *The Ahau of Calakmul Enters the Spirit World* integrates glyphs with the pictorial matter to the extent that the painting becomes an extension of the writing. An abbreviated P.S.S. on the far right reads *y-uch'ab ta tsih te'el cacao*, "his drinking vessel for tree-fresh cacao," followed by the glyph *Chahtan Uinic*, Person of the Dark Place, which appears on the far upper left of the illustration and means that the vase belongs to a deceased person. Although finally interred with him, it is also a ritual object that was used in ceremonial rites performed by the living in order to aid and guide the soul to the spirit realm of the ancestors. By portraying the precise moment that the deceased Ahau triumphantly emerges

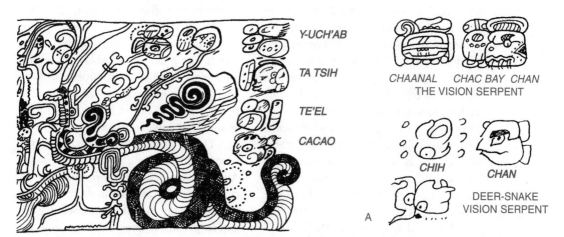

CALAKMUL   BA K(U)

Y-UCH'AB

TA TSIH

TE'EL

CACAO

CHAANAL   CHAC BAY CHAN
THE VISION SERPENT

CHIH   CHAN

DEER-SNAKE
VISION SERPENT

A

from the mouth of the Vision Serpent and is about to pass through the portal to the Otherworld as an actual event, the artist utilizes techniques we term sympathetic magic or creative visualization to induce the actual realization of the event depicted.

The painting is an invocation of some of the most potent forces known to the Maya shaman in dealing with the adversities of death: It calls forth and reminds the Ahau of his *way*, the traditional means through which generations of adepts extending back into mythological time have overcome the dark terrors and hazards of Xibalba and emerged into the light and security of the holy land of the ancestor.

As if leaping out of the *Chahtan Uinic* glyph, a fish nibbles on the waterlily in the headdress of the frog. The fish is an allusion to the transformation and resurrection of the Hero Twins in the waters of Xibalba. Below the fish the text continues with the phrase relating

to the frog, *Nen Uo Anab Way Ahau Te*, Lord Frog, He of Water, his Animal Co-essence Spirit, He the Tree Lord. The *Uo* glyph is attached to the tail piece composed of plumes of *ch'ul* that trails in the wake of the Vision Serpent. The *way* glyph is used to describe all three animals in the painting as guardian spirits of the deceased Ahau and it requires special attention as it conveys spiritual concepts that are fundamental to the Maya worldview.

Way has a counterpart in the Nahuatl word, *nagual*, which is derived from *nahualli*, meaning "animal disguise" and also "something that is hidden or veiled." It is applied to the animal forms magically assumed by sorcerers. To receive the guardian spirits an adept traditionally goes to an isolated spot where the *nagual* will appear in a dream or will be the first animal to confront the vision seeker upon awakening. The roots of these practices must extend far back into the very remote beginnings of shamanism itself. Anticipating the *Kauil* ceremony, the first creature that leaves its footprints on ashes spread before a newborn baby becomes that child's *nagual*. The belief system has variations from region to region. In some areas only the most powerful male leaders possess a *nagual* while in others all or most of the people have personal animal guardian spirits. The fundamental concept is so deeply embedded in Native American consciousness that it has variations in tribes throughout the entire continent.

Way is derived from Maya words meaning "to sleep" and "to dream," and this aspect of the animal companion spirit was also widespread, appearing in many tribes on a continental scale. As Native populations in North America generally carefully cultivated and attended to their dreams, and recalled dreams were given priority in the final decisions made by councils, early colonial writers stated: "The dream is the God of the country." The *way* glyph expresses the idea of "transformation" and in doing so it penetrates into the fundamental nature of the dream. Transformation is the basic characteristic of the manner in which the elements in the dream world unfold.

By joining the *Ahau* and jaguar glyphs the written word achieves communicative powers that go far beyond the limitations of the spoken word. The two glyphs are the emblematic symbols of the Hero Twins. Their exploits in the *Popol Vuh* not only represent the communal dream of the people, but supply the model for human behavior in the Otherworld that ultimately concedes the paramount need for postmortem security in the afterlife. Thus in the vase painting the Ahau is seen entering the portal to the sacred realm of the ancestors in the guise of *Hunahpu* accompanied by *Xbalanque* in the form of Baby Jaguar. Among the many transformative powers of the Twins is their ability to change into one another.

The concept of transformation is inherent in the *way* glyph in other ways. All the twenty daysigns represent aspects or "faces" of the Sun; in fact, they are the *way* of the Sun. In particular *Ix*, the jaguar glyph, is the nighttime sun assigned in the time-space mandala to the north. *Ahau*, in the south, represents the daytime sun and as a composite the glyph represents the transition of time in the continual transformations between day and night. Also, the *Ahau* part of the sign on the left carries a numerical value of four. *Ix*, on the right, has a value of nine. Together these add up to thirteen, the sacred number of transformation. Superficially the Maya appear to be preoccupied with time itself as a fundamental reality but actually time is perceived as an illusion in a dream world and the persistent quest is for the eternal present, which is timeless.

The eye in the frog glyph has the mirror sign that perceives the material world as but a reflection of the spirit world. The dismembered eye in the offering vessel raised by the frog symbolizes the sacrifice of external vision in order to obtain the inner vision capable of penetrating the hidden reality behind outward forms. The Vision Serpent emanates from the sacrificial bowl. The vessel also contains a cleverly personi-

*Figure 7.4. Funerary disk showing **Chac-Xib-Chac** sacrificing his hand*

fied bloodletting instrument and a dismembered hand. Self-sacrifice is the primary means of advancing on the
spiritual path. The dismembered hand
appears in similar scenes showing the
manifestation of the Vision Serpent. In
a funeral ritual object shown in figure
7.4, *Chac-Xib-Chac* is seen sacrificing
his own hand, paralleling the sacrifice of
the foot of *Kauil* in lieu of a superior
foot that can transform into the Vision
Serpent. We have seen that *kab*,
"hand," is also the verb "to make," and
it is the ultimate offering of the hand
that symbolizes the creative and gener-

ative power of sacrifice. It is doubtful
that an actual amputated hand is represented by the artist; probably the intent
is purely symbolic.

The hand is superimposed over the
final glyph in the phrase that titles the
deceased Ahau as Tree Lord. The tree
referred to is both the ancestral tree and
the World Tree that *Xaman Ek* is in the
center of. The frog's offering not only
generates the Vision Serpent but it manifests *Xaman Ek* on his back as the portal of the North Star opening to the
sanctuary of the ancestor. In a circular
chain of events the Ahau emerges from

the mouth of the Vision Serpent and is about to enter the portal with the assistance of his *wayob*, the most powerful in the pantheon. The frog's potency as a *way* is derived in part from the observation that amphibian skin can change color; thus the frog becomes a venerated symbol of the enabling of transformation as well as being a stalwart ally of humanity as the harbinger of the life-generating rains.

Besides assuming a simultaneous existence between an animal and a person, a *way* can represent a close bonding between a person and a natural object such as thunder, a tree, a planet, or a star. A difference exists between Maya and Western thought regarding what is classed as animate and what is considered inanimate. In the Maya world the sky is alive with celestial objects that are considered not only animate but very active in human affairs. The animal spirits depicted in the vase painting present a veritable skyscape representing in animated form the *wayob* of some of the most prominent features of the heavens. *Uo*, the frog, is the *way* of *u*, the Moon, and is a symbol of the *uinal*, the computational month of twenty days, which is related to the word *uinic*, "person," referring to the twenty digits of the human being's fingers and toes, the fundamental root of Maya counting and the calendar. The Monkey God personifies the North Star and Baby Jaguar, whose starry body markings surround an enormous sun emblem in his belly, is the night sun whose nocturnal passage through the underworld is here equated with the journey of the soul of the deceased Ahau. *Chiih*, the deer, is written

in the text as the *chi*-hand so that the painting celebrates the dawning of the Sun as a metaphor of the rebirth of the Ahau in the spirit world.

Baby Jaguar is seen to be stepping into the portal in the sky. He is named in the text before him as *Ch'ul Tan Ch'aktel Ix*, Holy Center Ax-Wielding Jaguar, the *way* of *Ch'ul Ahau Calakmul*, the Divine Lord of Calakmul. The text above the Vision Serpent names him as *O Chi Chan* referring both to the deer-snake vision quest rite and the verb *och*, "to enter." The glyph ending both of these phrases is a composite containing two of the most widely used glyphs in the writing system. Besides being daysigns, they have the phonetic values of *ba* and *ku* and this combination suggests a number of possible intended readings. Presently my leading contention is that *ba* here means "first" and *ku* is "god," and it is a title. If it were a nominal it would precede the topographical title. It may read *bak*, "bone," which often forms part of Maya titles and refers to both the ancestor and the center. Note the clever melding of signs in the *Ahau* symbol above the jaws of the Vision Serpent. The artist inserts the eyes at such an angle that they can be read simultaneously as the death "percentage" sign and as a qualifying glyph that can be read right into the text. The text forms a continuous circuit around the disk, beginning again where it ends with *y-uch'ab*, "his drinking vessel. . . ."

The similarity between the Maya version of an after-death experience and that described in *The Tibetan Book of the Dead* is remarkable. In Tibetan traditions the deceased is addressed directly and urged to continue on "a Great Perpendicular Path" in order to eventually experience "the Radiance of the White Light of Pure Reality." This corresponds very closely with recorded near-death experiences of individuals from various cultures. The two most consistent factors in recollections are a passage through a dark tunnel and emergence into brilliant white light. As renowned experimenters in the extremes of human consciousness, the Maya certainly paid careful attention to such phenomena, knowing that the interior of the Vision Serpent is the dark tunnel. Emergence from the tunnel is in the heavenly abode of the dead in the north, characterized by the color white, primarily because of the practically universal experiencing of radiant white light after death.

The daily emergence of the Sun at dawn readily becomes a continual reminder of the triumph of life over death and its most obvious metaphor seen in the patterns of natural phenomena. For the Sun to accomplish its journey through the underworld, the Maya assumed that it transforms into its *way* as the Jaguar of the Night Sky and consequently the jaguar is regarded as one of the most powerful of all the *wayob*.

In a drawing from a funerary vase shown in figure 7.5 the jaguar *way* is seen framed in a water cartouche as it struggles ferociously through the waters of the underworld. Using precisely the same formula that was used in the vase from Calakmul—ten miles to the north of Seibal—the text states, "the Waterlily Jaguar, His *way, Seibal Ahau.*" This is

Figure 7.5. Balam, the Waterlily Jaguar, and accompanying text, detail from a funerary vase

not the *way* of the Sun going eastward to dawn but the *way* of the deceased Ahau on the journey northward to the holy ground of the ancestor. In these vases there is a notable consistency in the *way* imagery, the text formation, and most remarkably in the strict adherence to the cosmographic underlying principle that north is to the left of a composition.

The schematic organization of sacred

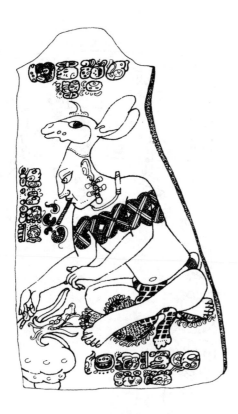

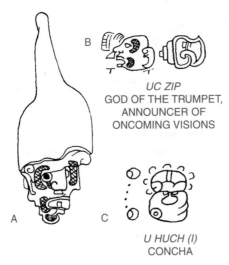

UC ZIP
GOD OF THE TRUMPET,
ANNOUNCER OF
ONCOMING VISIONS

U HUCH (I)
CONCHA

Figure 7.6. **A Shaman Invokes a Vision Serpent**, *incised conch shell, private collection*

space is again evidenced in the incised conch shell shown in figure 7.6 wherein a shaman conjures a Vision Serpent seen emerging from a conch-shell trumpet positioned in the north or left side of the composition. In order to accomplish the magical feat the sorcerer dons the headdress of a deer, the *way* of the Deer God known as *Uc Zip* who is also the god of the conch trumpet, the announcer of oncoming visions. The imagery and the text imply that the Ahau is impersonating the Deer God to perform the ceremony. Although incised on a hard surface the lines exhibit the flowing grace and flexibility of a brush painting.

The dark half-moon facial markings characteristic of *Uc Zip*, diagrammed in A, are engraved on an actual conch shell trumpet from the Early Classic period (A.D. 300-500). The glyphic nominals of the god shown in B are engraved on the trumpet and variants of these glyphs are found in the first and last positions of the opening line of text on the plaque. The *Uc Zip* introductory glyph is followed by a glyph containing the phonetics *ta* and *na*, which can be read *tan*, "center," followed by a glyph that strongly resembles the *ahk'ot*, "dance," glyph, with "centering" and "dancing" being related ideas closely associated with conjuring visions from the spirit world. The last glyph in the upper text reads *yi-lak*, "his flat object," referring to the hand-held plaque itself.

The first glyph in the middle text is prefixed by the general preposition *ti* meaning "to," "in," "on," "from," and so on, and its mainsign is the *chi*-hand subfixed with a *hi* phonetic to render *chiih*, the Cholan word for deer. The glyph is positioned in close proximity to the deer headdress, and coupled with the following glyph *u huch*, "his con-cha," an object closely associated with the deer in Maya art, serves to describe the ceremony being enacted. Both glyphs employ the *chi*-hand as a phonet-ic. They are followed by the name and a title of the person who is portrayed per-forming the rite. The nominal has *Balam*, Jaguar, as its mainsign and it is followed by the title, He of the Blood, which concludes the middle text.

Next comes that most interesting innovative technique that we have previ-ously observed in which the artist uses the handsigns employed by the actor portrayed, directly integrating them into the text so that they can be read as glyphic verbs serving to link two sets of glyphic statements. The right hand dis-played by the sorcerer is the *yalhiya*-hand meaning "he manifested it." The glyph beginning the bottom text is *yal*, which I am sure is a reference to this ac-tion. With his left hand he employs a sign that means "to beckon, to call forth." I do not know the meaning of this sign from the handsign language of the Plains Indian but I have often seen it used by Indians during my travels in Mexico. I remember being at first baf-fled by it: Rather than resembling our gesture meaning "come here," it bears a resemblance to our "goodbye" hand-sign with its fluctuating movement of the fingers. Gradually I came to realize that it means "come hither."

The first glyph in the very bottom line describes the sorcerer as a *Ch'ul* Ahau of the Xultan polity. The enthroned

Ahau is elegantly seated smoking a thinly rolled cigar that in all probability contains a narcotic or hallucinogenic substance of some kind. Across his arms and chest is body paint or tattoo mark-ings that are emblems of the center. The incised plaque has much in common with a stela from Xultan drawn in figure 7.7. Here an Ahau is portrayed in the act of conjuring Baby Jaguar and *Chac-Xib-Chac* in their dwarf forms. *Chac* has the serpent foot usually attributed to *Kauil*.

Speech scrolls emanating from the mouth of the Ahau represent mystical or magical utterances that accompany his handsign to induce a vocal response from Baby Jaguar whose elaborate speech scroll is composed of a *sac*, "white," "pure," glyph, indicating that these are sacred words that come from the spirit world. The handsign em-ployed closely corresponds to that dis-played by the deer sorcerer incised on the conch-shell plaque: It invokes, coax-es, and elicits a response from a divine being. As a public monument the stela serves to convey the idea that the Ahau is capable of communicating with pow-erful forces from the Otherworld and has influence and control over powerful supernatural beings—therefore it is an assertion of the right to rule.

From head to foot the Ahau is in-vested in attire infused with cosmologi-cal symbols, sky imagery, and emblems of the center. In the crest of his head-dress a quadrant containing four circles is the insignia of Venus. The three *Ahauob* in his pectoral identify him as a traveller through the three realms of the cosmos. His apron contains the image

Figure 7.7. **An Ahau Conjures Baby Jaguar and Chac-Xib-Chac**, *stela from Xultan*

glyphs ending the first line of the bottom text on the conch-shell plaque. There a glyph is prefixed by the number six, *wak*, a homonym of "stood up," and a glyph with an *ac* mainsign prefixed with an emblem of the Sun. The turtle referred to is the first sky image that appeared in the constellation Orion at the dawn of Creation. In order to manifest supernatural beings from the spirit world the shaman returns to conditions that were present at the beginning of Creation.

A comparison between figures 7.6 and 7.7 clearly reveals the underlying format inherent in Maya art in which the concealed but apparent presence of *Hunab Ku*, although invisible, manages to dominate the spacial orientation and visual organization of the compositions. The final product of the rites portrayed—the manifestation of the Vision Serpent and the voice of Baby Jaguar—emanates from the north, the divine realm of the hidden god and the sacred space where the shamans focus their attention.

A vivid portrayal of a complex ceremony involving some of the most prominent *wayob* in Maya shamanism is shown in the vase rollout in figure 7.8. Again the primary method of contacting the divine, the chief means used by the worshiper to approach the sphere of the heavenly gods, is through the medium of magical manipulations of the hands in symbolic gestures that communicate with and manifest beings from the sacred realms. A deer adorned with the crossed-bones symbol of sacrifice is ushered before an altar fashioned in the image of a personification of the World

of *Xaman Ek*, the god of the portal at the center of the night sky, and his footwear assumes the form of *moan* birds, the owl messengers of the underworld. The throne he stands on is composed of six *ac* or turtle heads, a device that may be compared with the two

Figure 7.8. Deer ceremony (above) and related glyphs, cylindrical vase

Tree, portal to the spirit world.

The high priests who lead and direct the ceremony do so through sacred handsigns. They are the caped shamans who sit on top of the altar and are numbers 1 and 2 in the diagram. A focal point in the composition is the *chi*-hand displayed by the sorcerer in 1. The mudra formed is the graphic daysign that symbolizes *chiih*, "deer," as a *way* of the Sun. The shaman in 2 raises his left hand above the side of his head in a gesture indicating deer horns and meaning "deer" in American Indian Sign Language. His right hand forms the *yalihiya* or "manifesting" handsign as if instructing the deerhunter in 7 to bring forth a deer. This begins the action depicted in which the culmination is the manifestation of the *Ahau Can*, a form of the Vision Serpent seen descending from the heavens by way of the Cosmic Tree in the altar. The ceremony is a variant of the ancient and widespread shamanistic rite of "bringing down the sun," the key elements

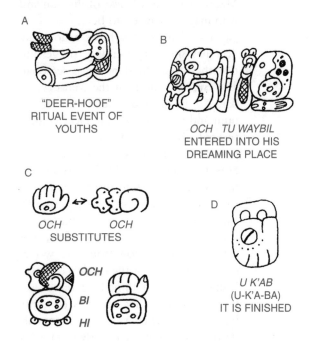

being the waterlily plant and the animals—the snake, the deer, and the jaguar—all of which are daysigns and therefore *wayob* of the Sun.

The shamans in 3 and 4 are magicians, "wearers of the jaguar skin," and they have snake-spot body markings indicating that they are impersonating deities. The shaman in 3 raises the conch-shell trumpet that announces oncoming visions. In front of the trumpet a descending celestial bird echoes the descent of the Vision Serpent. It is curious that in the Maya calendrical system each daysign has a patron usually in a pattern that presents a pairing of opposites. The patron of the day *Muluc*, Water, for example, is *Kauil*, a fire god. The god of the day *Chiccan*, Snake, is the celestial bird, *Kak Mo*, the Fire Macaw who is also a *way* of the Sun and who may be referred to here.

The shaman in 4 raises a horn the deer has shed in moulting, suggesting that the ceremony depicted is seasonal. The twelfth month of the Maya calendar, *Ah*, is devoted to divinities of the hunt and in it *Ah Ceh*, the Deer God, is revered. In some Maya dialects this month is known as *Tziquin Kih*, the Season of the Birds. The ability of certain animals to transform themselves through moulting, such as the snake's shedding of its skin or the butterfly's metamorphosis from its cocoon, the frog's transformation from the water-dwelling tadpole or the turtle's birth on land preceding an immediate immersion into the sea, readily suggests concepts inherent in nagualism. These animals become not only particularly suitable as *wayob* but symbols of the very fabric of life itself—changes and transformation.

A shaman is one who can ally with the transformative powers in nature and hence perform seemingly magical acts such as changing sickness into health.

Animism, as employed by the Maya, is a chief means of accessing spiritual powers and it is used to bridge a gap between the experience of human consciousness and its deeper roots, which are implanted in our animal origins.

Deer sacrifices are a frequent feature of rites of passage ceremonies of social transformation that signal changes in religious status and confer prestigious elevation within the tribe through induction into age-graded societies. The deer is the guardian spirit in coming-of-age rites that were widespread throughout North and South America. The *Maso* or deer dance was a central feature of the puberty rituals of the Yaqui tribe of Sonora, Mexico in which the trance-inducing rhythms of the dance were kept in time to the beat of deer-hoof rattles.

The Maya glyph shown in A represents such a life-cycle ceremony recorded as taking place in the youth of Maya kings. The glyph consists of a hand displaying the deer-hoof rattle and it expresses two salient features of the use of the hand in glyph formation. Firstly, the presence of the hand itself in a glyph can symbolize the performance of a ritual or communication with the spirit world. Secondly, when the ritual involves spiritual power or authority conferred from the ancestors, the hand will be shown as extending from the left or northern sector in the structure of the glyph. We will expand on these two principles later in this chapter and in the next, as they not only reveal fundamental formal patterns in the architecture of the language of signs but they have a central significance in formats that govern the principles of composition in Maya pictorial art in general.

That principles inherent in glyph formation are also applied to the compositional organization of pictorial formats is evidenced in the depiction of the altar surrounded by the shamans in 1, 2, 5, and 6. The altar constitutes the meeting place of gods and humanity, heaven and Earth, and it is the natural site of sacrifices for the divine and the human to express and create communication between these realms of existence. As we have seen, in Maya shamanism, the creation of an altar is the equivalent of "opening a road" to the spirit world. The glyph *be*, "road," is composed of four cardinal or solstitial points with the Cosmic Tree in the center, which is exactly the format utilized in the altar scene in which the artist has further elaborated on the theme by showing the Vision Serpent descending down the World Tree. The shamans in 5 and 6, dressed in the disguise of their deer *way* have "opened up a road," as expressed by their hand gestures, which allow the divine serpent spirit "to enter." In emphasizing the rattles or *och* of the snake (black tail) the artist refers to the word *och*, "to enter."

Let us examine the elements in the language of signs that are incorporated in the phrase, *och tu waybil*, "he entered into his dreaming place," shown in B, to see how the symbolic meaning of a sign can extend far beyond its phonetic value. The *och* glyph contains the snake rattles prefix in the lower left, a *chi*-hand superfix and a stepped pyramid mainsign that is infixed with a tree sign. The Maya pyramid is a temple contain-

ing a World Tree and it is regarded as a portal to the spirit world. The *way* mainsign in the phrase is infixed with a *be* sign which not only provides a phonetic value but represents the road to the spirit world that is opened up and entered into. *Way* also means "to dream." In dreaming the physical body sleeps and the person transforms into the dream state which awakens, then subsequently sleeps when the physical body awakens. The *way* glyph aptly expresses these alternating transformations.

It is interesting that the artist has placed the *be* sign at the mouth or entrance of the *Ahau* daysign that forms part of the *way* glyph. The *Ahau* daysign represents the blowgunner, who is sometimes depicted wearing the deer-hunter's hat, and it is associated with *Hunahpu*, as the jaguar daysign is associated with *Xbalanque*. Another characteristic of *Hunahpu* is the *hun*, "one," spot that is a godsign adorning his body or cheek. It seems that the shaman in 7 is an impersonator of *Hunahpu* and that the vase painting depicts a ritual that brings mythological beings into play as so much Maya culture serves to do.

In this respect another variant of the "to enter" verb shown in C is of interest and relevant to the descending bird in the vase painting. *Och* is here rendered by a *chi*-hand. Besides the phonetic values however, the symbols carry further implications as the hand represents ritual performance; therefore the meaning of the verb here is to enter into the portals of the spirit realms.

The Maya artist transforms already potent signs into symbols with extended

O CHI   CHAN   U WAY   KAUIL

Figure 7.9. Cylindrical vase

meanings by incorporating them into a hand as shown in D. The *Imix* or Waterlily daysign has a phonetic value of *ba* and combined with *ka*, "hand," subfixed by an *l(a)*, the phonetic reads *u k'ab*, "it is finished." As the first daysign, the waterlily or *Imix* glyph also carries connotations of "beginning" and "entering," and waterlilies are a notable feature of the altar in the vase painting.

The *Chi-Chan*, Deer/Snake glyphs of the Vision Serpent appear on an entering scene shown in figure 7.9. The artist is probably the painter of the cylindrical vase diagrammed in figure 7.3 and the subject is likely to be the same Ahau of Calakmul.

In figure 7.3 the Ahau is seen facing left or north, thereby entering the realm of the ancestors. Here the Ahau faces the opposite direction as if he is being materialized from the spirit world and magically manifested on the earthly plane. Glyphs on the lower right indicate the event took place on Seven Snake on the eighteenth day of *Sac*.

The shaman extends a ceremonial bar toward the heavens through which the Vision Serpent is seen entering, descending, and emerging from the ground at the other end. In Maya art ceremonial bars are recognizable by the characteristic crisscrossed *pop*, or "mat,"

A   B   C

Figure 7.10. Cylindrical vase

markings. These refer to "those of the mat," or rulers. The bars generally appear in portraits of rulers and are displayed as symbols of authority. Here is an instance wherein the ceremonial bar is used in a ritual that manifests an ancestral ruler.

The magician/shaman on the right is seen gazing into the Smoking Mirror glyph of *Kauil*, the Lord of Lineages. What happens is a uniquely fascinating interplay between the pictorial matter and a glyph in the text in which the artist unites art and writing and reveals that glyphs themselves are regarded as having sacred and magical powers.

We have seen that the mirror is a ritual implement central in rites invoking ancestral spirits. Here the glyph of the Smoking Mirror is substituted for an actual mirror. Not only does the magician focus on the glyph but the artist has embellished the interconnection with an *ik* or "spirit" sign. Peering into the mirror the shaman sees the supernatural emergence of the ancestor from the mouth of the Vision Serpent. The artist is painting those images seen by the shaman through the magical powers of the sacred mirror. This kind of interplay

between magician and glyph, man and deity, pictorial matter and writing is highly imaginative, unique, and unparalleled in the annals of art history.

The Vision Serpent is a god represented by a combination of deified animal forms that also appear as daysigns in the calendar. In this space-time sequence the Day of the Snake appears in the east followed by *Cimi*, a transformation deity and God of Death in the north and then *Manik* in the west, symbolized by the *chi*-hand alluding to *Chiih*, the Deer God or the deer aspect of the Sun. It is hard not to recognize in the deer/snake relationship echoes of the union of opposites expressed by the mythological Hero Twins.

Three pairs of magicians are seen communicating with the spirit world in the vase painting diagramed in figure 7.10. In A a *Xbalanque* impersonator displays a *yi*-hand, a sacred gesture related to the glyph *yi* meaning "to reveal" or "to show." A live snake held by the actor in B is intently focused on this hand. Native American cultures take animals existing in their environment and weave them into their elaborate pantheons as gods represented in animal

D   E   F

form. The deer cult is commonly associated with puberty rites from California to South America. The cult of the snake is widespread and especially important, the serpent being a recurring figure in religious beliefs, mythology, and rituals. The cult of *Quetzalcoatl*, the Feathered Serpent, is evidence of direct worship of the snake. Fundamental to practically all agricultural Native American cosmologies is the idea that celestial serpents reside at the four corners of the world and cause rainfall. In the famous Snake/Antelope Dance of the Hopi of Arizona, for example, snakes are released in the four directions to seek rain.

In the painting the character in B displays the *chi*-hand prominently entwined around the snake. The resulting image alludes to the glyphic representation of the Vision Serpent and thus through the handsigns and images in A and B we may read "he reveals the Vision Serpent." I have not yet completely translated this text but it is highly likely that within the hieroglyphic panel between A and B this statement acts as a verb, once again interweaving visual content with text.

The undulating snake in B flows into the deer headdress of the person in C who also displays a *chi*-hand, as does the one in D who wears the headdress of *Cimi*, the Death God and an agent of transformation. The Deer God is closely associated with *Hunahpu* and also the daysign *Ahau* symbolized by the deer-slayer as a blowgunner. The sequence of daysigns is regarded as transformations of the Sun. The snake/death/deer relationship within it is echoed in the imagery of the painting in which we see

magicians utilizing their transformative powers to render the spirit world visible. Through the sacred power of handsigns, the actors manifest visible images on the ground, generated from the invisible spirit world in the heavens.

Beginning the text panel between C and D is the familiar *ti ahk'at* glyph, which as we have seen means literally "to dance" and in actuality "to commune with the gods." The text flows down from this and ends in a curious glyphic object, manifested by the magician in D, resembling *Imix*, the waterlily daysign, which can symbolize water or liquid. The reference here is not to ordinary liquid but to the precious nectar of the gods, known to the Maya as *itz*, which has been universally sought by shamans from time immemorial and is procured from the heavens. The *Bacab* impersonator in E opens his left hand, which extends from a sky-band belt, to reveal the curlicue symbol of water altered by dots to indicate the precious liquid of the heavens. His right hand extends into the text panel wherein, directly above, is a glyph containing the all-pervasive *chi*-hand. The last two glyphs in the panel are *yal*, meaning "child of the mother," and finally the nominative meaning "Lady Venus." As the *yal* glyph appears in the same position at the end of each of the three panels of text, we can safely assume that the last glyph in each panel identifies the mother of a participant named or portrayed in the painting and demonstrates a concern with firmly establishing matrilineal ancestral descent.

It is known that not only the Maya but the Aztecs and the Pueblos, among others, evolved codified ceremonial sign languages using traditional gestures which were incorporated into various sacred dances. These rites were frequently enhanced by vision-inducing communal drinking ceremonies. It is therefore not surprising to find that numerous Maya ceremonial drinking vessels are adorned with depictions of these very rites. In these, as we have seen, the Maya artist brilliantly confronts the problem of showing a moving sequence of handsigns on a two-dimensional surface. In the vase illustrated in figure 7.11, a simple sweep of the hand is shown. Above, substituting for the usual P.S.S., a sky band is painted. In A the shaman's open hand, with fingers pointing toward the heavens, is extended in a gesture of blessing. In B the extended hand is moved downward in a gesture of giving or presenting. The shaman serves as a connection between heaven and Earth, the spiritual and material realms of the cosmos.

As a ritual object, the vase itself aids in communicating with the Otherworld —it contains the vision-inducing cacao drink that provides access to the spirit world. It also serves as a doorway to the realm of the ancestors. In the central panel of the diagram, ancestor cartouches appear in mirror images. Inside the cartouches, bones indicate that these are entrances to the realm of the dead. Framing them are liquid signs referring to the sacred *itz* that emanates from the heavens through these portals. By showing a simple movement of the hand, the artist portrays a shaman magically opening up a path between heaven and Earth.

A vase showing a fertility dance is illustrated in figure 7.12. We have seen that the "breaking" handsign represents a separation of Earth and sky on the horizon through which the Sun enters. The sign means "dawn" and by extension "birth." In the performance of ceremonies it refers to giving birth to the gods through dancing. The dance is presided over by the shaman in C who wears the ceremonial hat of the deer-hunter, crowned with an emblem of

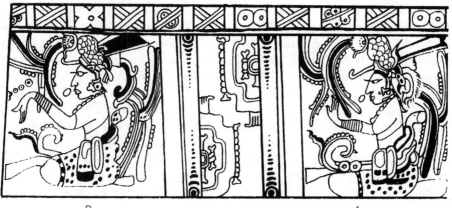

B   A

Figure 7.11. Cylindrical vase

TSIH   TE'EL   CACAO   SAC   AY-A   TZUC   Y-ICH   HOY-I   CACAO   TS'IB   NA HA   Y-UCH'AB

A   B   C   D   E

Figure 7.12. **The Dance of the Ah Nab,** *cylindrical vase*

the supernatural deer/snake motif. The lady and lord shown in A and B are depicted again in D and E. These ancient Maya "break-dancers" are shown performing sweeping gestures with their arms; the subtle movements of their hands express motion. The lady in A and D lifts her foot, a device artists use to indicate dancing. In A her hand extends upward, and in D her hand is reversed in the same motion the shaman utilizes in figure 7.11. The lord in B displays two right hands, another device conventionally used by artists to convey motion. In E the lord's right arm has a left hand and his left arm has a right hand.

The text consists of the usual P.S.S. written across the top rim, and panels of a curious cursive style of writing, interspersed among the figures, which has unfortunately come to be known as "pseudo-glyph." This widely accepted interpretation holds that the painter of the P.S.S. is a highly skilled calligrapher, but the painter of the pictorial matter is an illiterate artist who decorates the scene with the meaningless "pseudo-glyphs" for purely decorative purposes.

I at once became doubtful of this interpretation. Such a procedure would not be in keeping with the ideals of the Maya artist whose quest was to make visible spiritual realities and truths, albeit symbolically and imaginatively but never artificially or frivolously. Secondly, one does not need to be an expert handwriting analyst to recognize that the painter of the P.S.S. and of the pictorial matter and its accompanying text are one and the same artist. This can be readily seen by observing the use of the *Imix* glyph. In the P.S.S. the phrase *ts'ib naha*, "it was painted," utilizes the glyph phonetically as *b (a)*. The same glyph repeated in the text below means *nab*, "water." The glyph in the P.S.S. is done in a very formal style and the glyph below is done in a looser, more cursive manner—but they are rendered by the same hand!

Finally, far from being meaningless, the glyph repeated in the text below is prefixed by the phonetic *Ah* and can be reread as the honorific title *Ah Nab*, He of Water. Following the *ts'ib naha* phrase in the P.S.S. is the *y-uch'ab* glyph meaning "his vase." The owner is not named but is portrayed by the artist in B and E. It is by no means proven but I am currently exploring the possibility that the cursive style of writing is indicative of singing or chanting—and here represents the repetitious chanting of an honorific title of the owner of the vase—that accompanies the dance. The lady in D especially seems to be uttering this chant.

The most ingenious and elaborate depictions of sacred handsigns and gestures incorporated into dance and ritual were done in the late eighth century A.D., and occur in the murals of Bonampak in eastern Chiapas, Mexico. For many years I had recognized that the handsigns in these murals were not only extensive but carefully orchestrated and synchronized. They surely represent what is perhaps the Maya artist's greatest achievement: exploiting the communicative power of the sacred sign language. However, in interpreting handsigns in art, highly accurate and definitive renditions of the original paintings are required, as the subtle movement of a single digit of the hand sometimes changes the entire meaning of a sign. During this time that I was realizing the full importance of the majestic Bonampak murals in reference to my research, no reproductions of such quality existed.

About a decade ago, Mexican archaeologists began carefully cleaning the Bonampak murals by removing deposits of calcite. The true beauty and splendour of the art began to emerge from the walls, unveiling a veritable Sistine Chapel of the Americas.

In 1992 color photographs were taken by Enrico Ferorelli. In 1993 Doug Stern, a computer artist, reconstructed the line art. A combination of infrared photography, the original Ferorelli photographs, and Stern's line art produced final computer-generated reconstructions of extremely high resolution and accuracy. Some of these were reproduced in the February 1995 issue of *National Geographic* magazine. The article, entitled "Maya Masterpieces," was written by Mary Miller, who chairs the Art History department at Yale University.

By the time the article appeared, I had already uncovered the basic vocabulary of the Maya sacred sign language. With these readable reproductions of the signs at Bonampak, I quickly realized that the artists had created new ways of depicting moving hands in which these were intended to be read in sequence like a hieroglyphic text. At first I was concentrating on the enormous influence handsigning had in the development of writing. At Bonampak we see another continuous process unfold, wherein the sequential nature of writing had a tremendous impact on the Maya artist's ability to render the silent language as a series of meaningful and highly communicative handsigns brought to life by being set in motion. The remaining drawings in this chapter were inspired by the computer reconstructions that appeared in the *National Geographic* article.

The diagram in figure 7.13 represents what is widely regarded as Bonampak's most cherished scene. In it Maya actor-dancers, deity and animal impersonators, and an orchestra of musicians reenact a corn dance in celebration of the installation of a new heir to the throne. The actor in A had already been tentatively identified as representing the Corn God. We can now confirm this, as the handsigns displayed express simply and with extreme brevity the myth of the Corn God.

The Sun God dies and is resurrected as the Corn God. Beginning an anticlockwise sequence, the impersonator in A raises his right hand in the *chi*-sign, which here retains its primary meaning, "Sun." His left arm extends further upward, the handsign transforming into the *uaxac*-hand, which we now know has the numerical value of eight and is the sacred mudra of the Corn God, who personifies that number. The Corn God represents underlying principles in nature that enable the generation of corn and out of which corn evolves. He is re-garded as the creator of corn. He initiates the process by which the actual harvested corn materializes—corn that is presented by the *Bacab* impersonator in the final sequence in F.

The inception of corn begins as the Corn God touches the waterlily extending from the headdress of the *Bacab* impersonator in B. Glyphically the waterlily can mean "beginning" and also "water." It emerges from the ear ornament of the alligator mask worn by the actor. Within the ornament are three triangular dots, which form the ancient symbol of fire. These are symbols of the basic elements in nature that nurture growth. The *Bacab* impersonators in B, C, and D are imitative of river-dwelling creatures that symbolize water, while those in E and F resemble wind gods. The *Imix-Ik* glyph between F and E, which can be read as "water-wind," also appears between D and C. These *Bacabob* are "the nourishers" stationed in the four cardinal directions.

The action of the handsigns continues to flow upward to the gesture displayed by the actor in B. In American Indian Sign Language this gesture means "to grow." The open hands are held upward, palms facing the body. The signer raises the hands in a jerking motion imitating the growth of a tree. The logic of the handsign is quite natural and therefore practically universal. The maize plant is now shown to be emerging from the ground.

The hands of the actor in C are engaged in playing a musical instrument but we have learned that, in Maya art, hands that grasp or manipulate objects can sometimes also relate to specific

F   A   **E (BEHIND)**   B   **D**   C

Figure 7.13. **The Corn Dance**, *Room One, North Wall, Bonampak mural, detail*

handsigns. The left hand forms the familiar *chi*-sign as the right hand moves downward in a gesture that means "rain" in the sign language. Here the Sun and water nourish the plant as it springs forth from the ground. The Corn God stares intently at the *Bacab* in C, as does the *Bacab* in B who opens his mouth widely as if to receive the nourishing substances.

The results are demonstrated by the upright actor in D who extends his arms wide in imitation of the fully grown maize stalk. The last sequence in E and F shows the blossoming of the plant and its final fruition—the materialization of a harvested ear of maize. The person in E opens his hands in a natural and universal gesture that opens, presents, or manifests as the character in F triumphantly displays the precious cob of harvested corn. The artist has juxtaposed the actual corn with the elaborate glyphic representation of corn that is the headdress of the Corn God. When we recognize the sequential relationship of the characters and their gestures, we perceive that the artist has vividly created a circle of dancers whose movements express the drama of the agricultural cycle.

The corn dance shown on the North Wall of Room One at Bonampak was part of elaborate and extraordinary ceremonial arts that served to install an heir apparent, a procedure that was lavishly painted on the South Wall. The displaying of the heir apparent is shown in the

Figure 7.14. **The Presentation of the Heir Apparent**, *Room One, South Wall, Bonampak, mural, detail*

detail illustrated in figure 7.14. In the ceremony the heir apparent is presented to the nobles of the court but more importantly he is introduced to the ancestral spirits. He is therefore shown being presented to the left or symbolic north. The entrance of Room One faces actual north, the realm of the ancestors and the portal to the Otherworld.

The heir apparent in E extends the small finger of his left hand. In the Maya hierarchy of fingers the little finger represents the youngest child and the thumb represents the great-grand-father so the heir apparent may be indicating his youthful status. His right hand is raised in the *chi*-sign signifying that the ruler is the living embodiment of the Sun.

The left hand of the attendant in F echoes the handsigns in the writing system which display or present. The noble in D raises his right hand to his shoulder in a gesture expressing reverence. With his left hand he displays the *hom*-sign. We have seen this handsign and its corresponding glyph used in the destructive sense in war activity where it means

Figure 7.15. **The Apparition of Kauil**, *Room Three, East Wall, Bonampak mural, detail*

"bringing down" or "destroying buildings"; and we have seen it used frequently in terms of "bringing down" or "manifesting." In this context it means "to bring down" or "come down from a temple or pyramid," which in Maya terminology is descriptive of the rite that confirms the heir apparent—he is brought down from the temple and introduced to the lords and nobles of the court.

The noble in C also displays this sign with his left hand and with his right he commences a series of *chi*-hands. In a flowing rhythmic pattern the noble in B raises the *chi*-hand as if to express the rising Sun. The noble in A closes his right hand in the death fist, symbolizing the setting Sun, and completes the circuit by opening his left hand in the *chi*-

sign. The artist has utilized the gestures of multiple characters in a sequential arrangement to describe a dance of hand-signs that closely relates to the pervasive rites of "bringing down the sun."

On the East Wall of Room Three, drawn in figure 7.15, the young heir apparent is seen in a subsequent ceremony that serves to seal the heir ascension event. This too is a form of "bringing down the sun," and a variation of the rite which "brings down" the apparition of *Kauil*, Lord of Lineages. Apparently the youth has now been invested with spiritual powers that enable him to manifest the divine presence of *Kauil* with the assistance of female relatives and a male attendant who kneels at the right. The heir stares intently into a rectangular object that presumably contains the

Figure 7.16. **The Capture**, Room Two, South Wall, Bonampak mural, detail

maize flour known to be a part of the ritual. As he displays an open hand meaning "to show" or "to reveal," his right hand forms the *chi*-sign, closely associated with this ritual; a ghostly image from the Otherworld appears in the box. The ladies are engaged in bloodletting rites that enable communication with ancestral spirits. In this scene the heir is facing north. The blood of the participants has been sprinkled on paper and is seen burning in a ceremonial pot on the dais. Fire, blood, and the numerous *chi*-hands that permeate this scene are closely associated with *Kauil*.

The heir apparent never was to be seated in rulership at Bonampak, which was abandoned soon after the murals were painted. The city's last known

ruler has been identified as Chaan Muan; he can be seen in a battle scene on the South Wall of Room Two, illustrated in figure 7.16. In these murals warfare can be seen as an extension of Maya religious practices (nagualism) in which a simultaneous existence is assumed between an animal or a guardian spirit and a person. Chaan Muan, who grasps the hair of a falling captive, is arrayed in the guise of the Jaguar Protector, a war god and probably the *way* of the ruler during battle. The recent cleaning has revealed a thin line before his face which indicates that a mask aids in the transformation. The attire of the warriors is intended to awe and terrorize the enemy into submission. The flayed faces of enemies hang from the

Figure 7.17. **The Presentation of the Captives**, *Room Two, North Wall, Bonampak mural, detail*

warriors' shoulders. The warrior on the left brandishes the shrunken body of an enemy that displays the closed fists of death. The falling captive raises his right hand in this sign of defeat.

On the North Wall of Room Two, illustrated in figure 7.17, we witness the outcome as the prisoners are presented to Chaan Muan in a bloodletting ritual. Their expressive hands plead for mercy in contrast to the assertive *hom*-hand of Chaan Muan which here indicates destruction. In the center, and dominating the composition, is the spear firmly grasped in the death fist of Chaan Muan. The entire composition is focused on the ritual implement. It is interesting to note the position of the spear in relation to the architecture of

the temple—it is placed directly over the northern entrance, the portal to the land of the dead and the ultimate destination of the captives.

Just a few decades ago, the rulers of these empires of the Sun were dark shadows, unnamed and unknown. Now with the unveiling of the writing system we have records of their deeds, including such details as dates, genealogy, and political affiliations. The once-unfathomable and murky waters of this pre-Columbian history are now coming into the light. In the forefront of this unfolding scenario stride some of the most remarkable personages ever produced by any civilization—in the guise of the Maya Ahau.

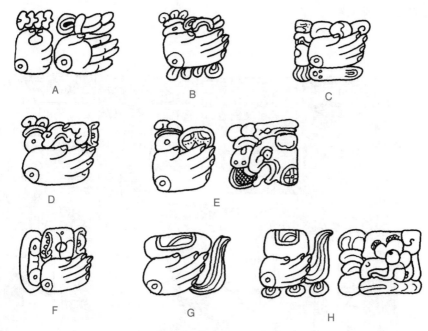

Figure 8.1. Accession glyphs

RULERS OF THE
EMPIRES OF THE SUN

Rulership in the ancient kingdoms of the Maya was indeed a sacred thing as expressed in both imagery in the art and hieroglyphs in the writing system. Glyphs expressing the coronation rites of Maya kings all feature the presenting hand as a mainsign signifying the ritual nature of these events as shown in figure 8.1. As mentioned this hand is shown as being extended from the northern or left sector in the formation of the glyphs, as kingship is believed to be the gift of ancestral gods who dwell in the north. The king represents god on Earth and partakes of transcendent heavenly powers through the rites of accession, which are regarded as an entering. This is expressed by the *och* glyph preceding the accession glyph in A.

The glyph in B reads *tzukhiya sak hunal*, "the white headband was closed." The royal white headband is named the White Paper and the Resplendent One, referring to the crown itself as a living personification of the god *Sak Hunal. Sak*, "white" or

Figure 8.2. **Tablet of the Captives**, Palenque

"pure," refers to the color associated with the north and *hun* means "one" and "eternal" or "perpetual" in Yucatec, as well as the paper made from bark cloth bleached or painted white. The glyph in C states *u tzuk hunal*, "he closed the headband." The presenting hand in F is postfixed with a *na* sign.

The glyph in E reads, *tzuk sak hun tubah*, "the white headband was closed or displayed for him." In a variant glyph shown in F an upturned frog head reads *hu* and is postfixed with an *n(a)* phonetic to render *hun*. The glyph in G substitutes a *tzuk*, "mirror," for the headband and the positional suffixing—*wan*—rendering *tzukwan*, "he took the mirror" is an accession glyph. H is an heir designation phrase, *Tzukwan ta ochte-le(l)*, "he took office on entering tree-ship."

As we know a Maya king or member of the ruling class is considered to be a *Ch'ok*, "sprout," of the ancestral tree, and the divine right to legitimate rulership is founded upon the heir's status as a lineage member. Consequently establishing and defining this status becomes a preoccupation of Maya rulers and a recurring theme in art depicting accession rituals. Coronation ceremonies are performed to secure the continuity of the sacral power of rulership and frequently the successor is shown being brought into physical contact with the ancestral predecessor. Such a strategy is employed in the accession rites performed in the *Tablet of the Captives* illustrated in figure 8.2.

To establish the legitimacy of his inauguration the ruler first of all links his accession to that of the greatest king in the history of the Palenque polity, the Great Sun or *Mah K'ina Hanab Pacal*. The text begins in 1 with the date *Ho Lamat, Hun Mol*, the day Five Venus, the first of the month Jade or A.D. July 29, 615, the day upon which Pacal the Great acceded to the throne to commence a reign that was to extend for over 68 years. Pacal's nominal in 2 describes him as an *Ahau Tun*, Lord of the Year, or by extension Lord of Time; and its mainsign is *pacal*, "shield."

The Sahal is depicted at the moment of being invested with the proper insignia of authority from his parents. His focus is on the headdress, a war helmet emblazoned with the image of *Sac Hunal* and containing the divine power through which the lord rules. It is being presented by his father, Pacal, on the left. In strict adherence to established tradition and in accordance with principles inherent in glyph formation, this action will invariably extend from the north, the seat of the ancestral spirits. The young man is named in the panel numbered 3, which ends with the honorific title *Ch'ok*, as does the nominal of his mother in the panel numbered 4.

His mother presents a ritual object that consists of a personified eccentric flint on a shield of a flayed human face. The flint head contains *cuauc* signs that can be read phonetically as *cu*, "god," and from the forehead protrudes an all-seeing eye. The mother is seated on the throne of the Deer God, her *way* or ancestral animal guardian spirit.

The ruler sits on a throne of two bound captives whose hair is tied up in a manner indicating that they will be sacrificed to seal the power of the accession ritual. They have already been subjected to bloodletting rites as evidenced by the paper strips piercing their ears; in fact they have been procured by the heir specifically for this purpose. We know from various texts that bloodletting rites were enacted during accession ceremonies. An example is the phrase shown in A which states *iwal tzukah*, "and then the mirror was presented," followed by the bloodletting verb, *tzak*, "to conjure (spirits, *wayob*, or ancestors)." As we shall see, ancestors that appear in depictions of accession rites are not necessarily physically alive at the time of the performance of the ritual. Their divine presence is conjured from the spirit world through bloodletting, but they are frequently portrayed by the artists as living beings.

A central feature common to most pictorial representation of accession rituals is the display by the heir of a particular handsign that signifies the precise

Figure 8.3. **The Accession of Pacal**, *tablet, Palenque*

tors from the spirit world and prowess as a warrior in procuring captives, the essential requirements of Maya kingship.

In texts written on the walls of the pyramids of Palenque, ancient kings went to extraordinary lengths to establish the undeniable legitimacy of their right to rule. The historical content of these proclamations traces the lineage of the Palenque dynasty back to the founder, Balam-Kuk, who was born in A.D. 397. From there the great tree is extended back into the ages of legend in the time of the Olmec with the birth of U Kix Chan in 993 B.C.; then it leaps back again into the mythological time of the gods, placing the birth of the mother, *Na Sac Kuk*, Lady White Quetzal, in the year 3121 B.C., or in a divine age prior to the present Creation. The message conveyed is threefold: The king possesses the right to perform the official act of ascending to the throne of the state; the sacral character of the kingdom is revealed as having its roots in the holy realm of the gods; and the ruler's powers are supernatural forces dwelling within the Ahau and allowing mediation between the people and the gods, the heavens and the Earth.

In Maya mythology Lady White Quetzal is the First Mother, the ancestral mother of gods and the Moon Goddess who gives birth to sun gods and to the Hero Twins (also known as the Headband Twins since they are frequently depicted wearing the elaborate knotted white cloth headbands of royalty). The Ahau is regarded as a living manifestation of the Hero Twins and, as in other Maya rituals, accession

moment of accession to the throne. To sign "good" in American Indian Sign Language, the flat right hand, back up, is briskly raised in front of and close to the left breast. The meaning of the sign is "it is level with my heart," which is the idea conveyed when it is used in accession rites. It communicates the acceptance of the crown but it also implies that the heir is capable of performing the numerous responsibilities that rulership entails. He is "up to" the performance of these tasks because they are "level with his heart," so to speak. In the *Tablet of the Captives* the ruler has embellished the meaning of the handsign by demonstrating both spiritual power enabling him to conjure ances-

rites reenact events that happened at the very beginnings of Creation.

Maya art is an extension of ritual as it participates in striving to connect the spirit realm of the divine with the material world of humanity, the central impetus of Maya culture itself and the driving force underlying it. In recording the accession of Pacal, illustrated in figure 8.3, the artist manages to unify a historical event with elements deeply rooted in mythology. In it we see Pacal's mother, dressed in the jade net skirt and cape of the Moon Goddess, kneeling as she presents the war helmet crown to her son. Not only has she donned the attire of the Moon Goddess, but in the text above her portrait she has assumed the name of the First Mother, *Na Sac Kuk*. She wears the *Sac Hunal* headdress, as she acceded to the throne on A.D. October 22, 612, after the death of Pacal the First on March 9 of that year.

Pacal, portrayed in the elegant manner in which an artist would render the Hero Twins, also wears the *Sac Hunal*. The throne he sits on is an image drawn from creation texts wherein it is stated that in the beginning of this age three stones were born or set up at the "place of the first dawning" by the Paddlers. The first of these stones was the Jaguar Throne. By linking the historical event of A.D. July 29, 615, directly to symbolism derived from the remote mythological past, the artist emphasizes that the rites of accession signal a cosmic new beginning while still retaining the all-important continuity in the transmission of ancestral sacral power.

Pacal, born on Eight *Ahau*, Thirteen *Pop*, or A.D. March 26, 603, was only twelve years of age at the time of his accession. His mother had only been ruling for nearly three years and it is assumed that because of his tender age she continued to serve as regent. She must have foreseen that politically she was at the apex of her power and it was an opportune time to install Pacal as king. Internal conflicts may have led to situations that would make it not so advantageous later. The fact that Pacal exerted so much effort to establish the legitimacy of his right to rule, in public monuments and by emphasizing the descent of the ancestral sacral power through maternal lineage extending back to events prior to the present Creation, strongly suggests that his status as heir apparent was disputed and that it was being challenged along these lines.

Historically the time of Pacal's accession was one of great stress both internally and externally for Palenque, which was then just beginning to emerge as a prominent polity. It had recently come under attack from the city-state of Ponoma. During Pacal's illustrious reign of 68 years, Palenque became a major power dominating the southwestern region of the Maya lowlands and expanding its rule over the surrounding region. By the time of Pacal's death on A.D. August 31, 683, Palenque had emerged as one of the great centers of the Maya world.

In portraying Pacal's accession to the throne the artist emphasizes through handsigning that Pacal is the living manifestation of the Sun on Earth. In presenting the crown Lady *Sac Kuk*'s right thumb and index finger touch to form the *chi*-hand, the great mudra of the Sun. The honorific glyph ending her nominal, *Ch'ul Na*, Holy Lady, which appears directly above the crown, refers to this as it contains the upturned celestial jug emblazoned with the emblem of the Sun, symbolizing spiritual power or *itz* descending from the Sun. The handsigns here are utilized to communicate a message to the general public and to the gods. It is not presumed that all the gods could read glyphs, which are very much a human endeavor, but it is assumed that everyone including divinities would understand the handsigns and they are therefore prominent. Ironically, in the rereading of Maya texts modern epigraphers began to comprehend the hieroglyphs long before they began to realize the meaning of the handsigns that accompany and complement them.

Pacal wears an elaborate pendant that contains the sacred *Ik*, Spirit, glyph indicating his divinity. Note that in Pacal's headdress there is a mirror emblem out of which comes a *chi*-hand, the sacred symbol of the lineage deity, *Kauil*. In his nominal, the second glyph of three on the right, the mainsign *Pacal*, Shield, is prefixed by *Mah K'ina*, Great Sun. Following it is a title that has as its mainsign one of the emblematic placenames of Palenque prefixed by *Ch'ul*, Divine, and superfixed by an *Ahau* sign. The handsign he displays denotes his acceptance and ability to maintain the divine power inherent in the crown. It is also subtly altered to include the sacred mudra of sacrifice as if stressing that although only a boy of twelve years of age he is yet a sacrificer, initiat-

ed into the chief means through which the Maya shaman draws down the sacred power of the Sun.

Pacal makes an extraordinary supernatural appearance in *The Accession of Xoc* illustrated in figure 8.4. This event, written as Eight *Ahau*, Eighteen *Xul*, occurred in the year A.D. 734 and happened on the same daysign as Pacal's birthday. We know that Pacal died in A.D. 683 and had been physically dead for over 51 years at the time of Xoc's accession, but Pacal was conjured from the ancestral spirit world in order to present the crown to his son. In his headdress Pacal wears the fish nibbling on a waterlily, the symbol of rebirth derived from the mythological resurrection of the Hero Twins through their *way* as fish. I think that this symbol is also a play on the honorary title *Bacab*, Stood-up Person, as the waterlily has the phonetic value *ba*, and the fish has the phonetic value or is the god of the sound, *ca*.

Some epigraphers, such as Linda Schele, whom I have a great deal of respect for otherwise, have identified the heir in this scene as being Kan Xul, the second son of Pacal. I have three rather weighty objections that argue strongly against this conclusion. First of all the nominal glyph in C, which follows the accession glyph in B, is that of Xoc and clearly not that of his older brother Kan Xul. Secondly, the introductory date of the text in E is followed by a birth glyph in F that has *sih*, "birth," an upturned frog, as its mainsign postfixed by an *ah* sign, which puts it in the past tense. The title in G is that of Xul, the same honorific title that follows his name in D.

Figure 8.4. **The Accession of Xoc,** *detail, tablet, Palenque*

The date of birth given in E is Three *Ahau*, Three *Uayeb*, which occurred in the year A.D. 678. Xoc was Pacal's last known son and this birth date comes after the birth date of Kan Xul on Eleven *Ahau*, Eight *Mac*, in the year A.D. 643. Finally, the date of this accession is given as the year 734 A.D. It is clearly not that of Kan Xul, whose accession is recorded in other texts as having occurred on Five *Lamat*, Six *Xul*, in the year A.D. 702. (Note that the daysign of Kan Xul's accession was carefully chosen; it is the same daysign as for Pacal's accession and occurs in the month bearing Kan Xul's name.)

The glyphs in H, I, and J record a distance number that counts the individual days that have elapsed between Xoc's birth and his accession to the throne. They add up to over 56 years, Xoc's age at the time of his coronation. In A, the day of the month reached, Eighteen *Xul*, is correct as is the daysign *Ahau*, but the daysign number eight is incorrect and should be ten. Either the artist has consciously manipulated the date to be a reflection of Pacal's birthday or has made an error. The Maya artist is capable of making such manipulations; and errors in Maya texts, like those in ancient Chinese writing, also seem to have been regarded as divine interventions and as such are not only left uncorrected but are reverenced.

In regard to date manipulations, the reader has probably noticed that an unusually high proportion of birth daysigns of kings occurs on *Ahau* days. It is both extremely advantageous for a prospective heir to have been born on an *Ahau* day and unlikely that so many rulers were actually born on this precise day. In birth episodes described in the *Popol Vuh* the mother goes to a secluded place outside of the house for a period of time before and after giving birth. I believe that this tradition is at least partly a strategy that allows the mother certain leeway in which she can claim a favorable birth date for her child. Birth under this daysign would be a strong concluding argument for designating that child as an heir apparent. The word *Ahau* is Yucatec; in Quiché it is *Hunahpu,* and in Nahuatl it is *Xochitl,* Flower, lords being the flowers of the ancestral ceiba tree. Contemporary Maya daykeepers refer to an *ahau* day as Ancestor's Day.

In the accession scene Pacal sits on the Jaguar Throne, a reference to the first stone set up at the dawn of Creation and reflected as a star in the sky. The roaring jaguar depicted on the altar here is specifically the Waterlily Jaguar, the *way* of the Sun in its nocturnal passage through the underworld and simultaneously Pacal's *way* in his triumphant journey through the realm of Xibalba. This mimics the adventures of the Hero Twins and is the very means by which Pacal has overcome the perilous hazards of the underworld and so can reappear quite intact on the plane of the living, conjured as an active participant in the performance of an accession ritual that magically transfers the ancestral sacral power to his son.

Xoc wears the pendant of the ancestral cruller-eyed Jaguar Protector spirit. Behind him is the oval palace tablet illustrated in figure 8.3 which is situated in a place called *Lac Nuc Nah,* White Big House. He sits on a throne that represents the second stone set up at the Creation. Mythologically it was erected at a place named "earth-center." It bears the image of an unidentified snaggle-toothed deity. It is the same throne that is personified in figure 8.2.

At the time I illustrated the palace tablet in figure 8.2, I was focused on the significance of the north direction and the function of handsigns in accession rites. I therefore produced a detail (figure 8.4), neglecting to include the third actor in the cultic drama, Pacal's wife, Lady *Ahpo Hel,* who had been dead for 61 years at the time of the accession. It is indeed fascinating that she presents the heir with an eccentric flint shield identical to the one she presented in figure 8.2. She sits on the Serpent Throne, the third stone set up at the Creation. Therefore the complete palace tablet, partially illustrated in figure 8.4, represents the three stones that were set up at "the place of first dawning;" once again accession rites were symbolic of a cosmic new beginning.

The text accompanying the accession rites shown in figure 8.5 opens with the Sun God as the personification of the number *Chan,* Four, and the daysign *Muluc,* Water, in 1A. In 1B is the Goddess of the Number Two, *Ca,* a personification of flint, prefixing the month sign *Sac,* White. The date expressed is A.D. September 11, 683. The glyphs compounded in 2A state, "He was seated on the Jaguar Throne as Ahau." Tentatively I have translated the glyphs in 2B as reading, "He the Ahau of the Bonampak polity," although the

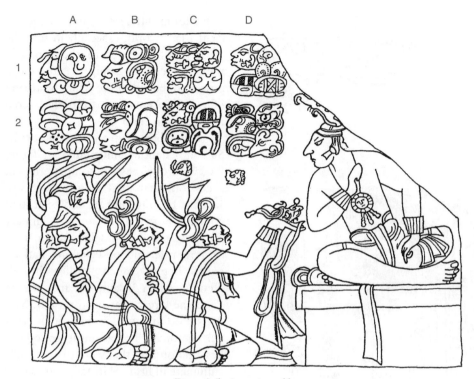

Figure 8.5. Accession tablet

actual placename of Bonampak is a modern appellation. Glyphs in 1C and 1D record a distance number that leads to the day Eight *Ahau* in 2C, or A.D. March 12, 692, which ended a *Katun* or twenty-year period. The daysign precedes a *tun*, "year" or "stone," glyph superfixed above a shell sign that expresses the passage of time. The text ends in 2D with a placename, Black Earth, which probably names the palace in which the event took place. As the three Ahauob performing the rite are all named in the respective glyphs written above their heads, I take it that the *Chan Ahau*, Snake Lord, glyphs in 2D are nominal title glyphs of the Ahau being installed in rulership.

The *Ahau Ti Ahauob*, Lord of Lords, strikes an elegant pose as he signs the mudra of accession. He extends the small finger of his left hand in a dignified gesture that expresses the release of cosmic energy that flows down from the heavens upon the occasion, a divine force that the artist emphasizes and echoes in the graceful downward flow of the king's apron. One of the Ahauob presents a vividly animated *Sac Hunal* with the mirror emblem in its forehead. The ritual headdress seems to be alive, exuding vibrant spiritual energy. The two other Ahauob have folded their arms in a gesture expressing respect. The scene demonstrates a remarkable uniformity in the performance of acces-

A   B   C   D   E

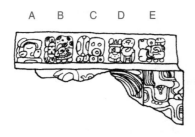

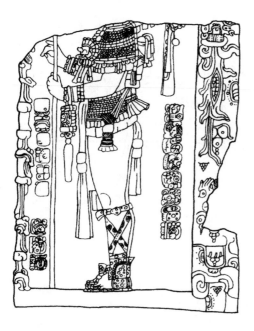

F

Figure 8.6. Tablet, Temple of the Sun

sion rites in different polities of the ancient Maya world, especially in that the artist rigidly adheres to the compositional principle stressing that the sacral power contained in the white headband of rulership emanates from the sacred northern direction.

In a tablet from the Temple of the Sun at Palenque, illustrated in figure 8.6, we are witness to complex rites of accession that had begun on A.D. January 10, 690, and are shown at their conclusion ten days later on January 20. Preparations for Chan Balam's ascent to rulership of Palenque had already begun much earlier in his lifetime. Chan Balam, the first son of Pacal the Great, was born on A.D. May 23, 635. On June 17, 641, at the tender age of six, he had undergone heir-designation rites that were to eventually culminate in his final installation as king of the illustrious city-state.

The text begins in A on the upper left of the tablet, appropriately opening with the *Ch'ul*, Divine, glyph showing *Xaman Ek*, the North Star Monkey God appearing above a mirror subfix. In B, Chan Balam's nominative glyph, Snake-Jaguar, is prefixed with *Mah K'ina*, Great Sun. The title *Bak Ahau*, Bone Lord, appears in C, followed by a title in D that contains *Ah Pits*, "he the adorned . . ." and finally in E he is proclaimed *Ch'ul Ahau* of the Palenque polity.

Although his father and mother are not physically portrayed in the ritual, texts referring to them are positioned in strict accordance with established tradition. The glyphs to the north or front of Chan Balam, although by now almost completely obliterated by the vicissitudes of time, clearly end with the nominal glyph of his father, *Mah K'ina Pacal*, in the lower left. On the right or southern sector the text begins with the manifesting hand *Yal* in a glyph meaning Child of the Mother followed by *Ch'ul Na Po Hel*, naming Chan Balam's mother and describing her as divine. A frame at the right of the panel balances what remains of a bone frame, referring to the ancestral spirits and appropriately positioned on the left. These frames create a portal through which we peer at Chan Balam, attired in battle armor as a warrior, in the final act of sealing his ascent to rulership. Distinguishable in the frame on the right are *cuauc* throne stones at the top and bottom, mirror signs surrounded by *itz,* glyphic representatives of fire and water, and in the very center of the frame kernels of corn appear in a vulvalike emblem within a foliated maize plant. Noteworthy is the presence of an open hand. This range of symbols links the accession rites with the elemental roots of Maya cosmology: the rebirth of the First Father as the Corn God and the miracle of Creation itself.

Of paramount importance is the handsign raised by Chan Balam that finally concludes these rites. The seeds of this action appear in glyphs excerpted from texts in the Temple of the Sun shown in F. Herein it is stated that on the fifth day after performing his heir-designation rites—that is on A.D. June 21, 641, the summer solstice—Chan Balam became a living manifestation of the Sun. The exact phrase used is *Och Te' K'in K'in*, literally, "He entered the Tree, the Sun" or simply, "He became the Sun." Here therefore is an intensive correlation between the use of a handsign representative of the Sun, accompanying text referring to the king as being a living manifestation of the Sun, and a nominal title glyph proclaiming him as a Great Sun, all of which simultaneously appears in a pyramid called the Temple of the Sun.

The last two glyphs in the excerpted text are of extreme interest. *Yichnal Ahau K'in* means "accompanied by or in agency with the Sun God or the First Father." The *chi*-hand in the *yichnal* glyph is not merely a phonetic; it is the same hand that Chan Balam raises in the accession tablet and it links him directly to the First Father, tying the kingship to conditions that existed prior to the present Creation. In extending its origins beyond the genesis, Maya cosmology boldly ventures into some unexplored areas of human consciousness and establishes for itself a rather unique and special place in the cosmologies of the world, in the past and most significantly in the present.

In 1913 when Vesto Slipher noticed quite accidentally that about a dozen galaxies in our vicinity are moving away from the Earth at extremely high speeds, up to two million miles an hour, he stumbled on the first hint that the universe is expanding, which eventually led to a New Cosmology that has had an enormous impact on theology in the present century. Einstein published his equations of general relativity in 1917 and Willem de Sitter, a Dutch astronomer, almost immediately found a solution to them that predicted an exploding universe. Around 1930, models of an expanding universe derived by Alexander Friedmann and Georges Lemaitre became widely known at the same time that Edwin Hubble published his famous law on the expansion of the universe, one of the great discoveries in science. So both theory and observation pointed to an expanding universe and a beginning in time. About 1950 science solved the mystery of the birth and death of stars, acquiring further evidence that the universe had a beginning. The "Big Bang" theory, a scientific version of the Creation, became widely accepted over the old "steady" theory of an eternal universe by the majority of cosmologists, physicists, and astronomers.

Astronomical evidence for the creation of the universe was of course welcomed by theologians. The value of the New Cosmology for religion was summed up fairly well by Pope Pius XII in 1951 when he stated that science "has confirmed the contingency of the universe and also the well-founded deduction as to the epoch when the cosmos came from the hands of the Creator. Hence Creation took place in time. Therefore there is a Creator. Therefore God exists."

With the new insight scientists came to share in something else that theologians had been grappling with for centuries: What came before the beginning? However, for the sake of brevity I would sum up the view of most scientists on this matter with a statement made by James Peebles of Princeton University: "What the Universe was like at day minus one, before the big bang, one has no idea. The equations refuse to tell us, I refuse to speculate." The attitude of most astronomers and physicists is in fact very close to that of theologians whose view is perhaps best summed up by that of Saint Augustine, who, asking himself what God did before creating heaven and Earth replied, "He was creating Hell for people who ask questions like that."

The general scientific picture leading to the Big Bang theory is now well known: The beginning of time came in a gigantic explosion, and we are witnessing its aftermath. The age of the universe, as determined by retracing the path of outward-moving galaxies backward in time, is about fifteen or twenty billion years, but as the astronomer Robert Jastrow has stated, "The important point is not precisely when the cosmic explosion occurred, but that it occurred at a sharply defined instant."

Ancient Maya cosmologists placed the date of Creation at dawn of Four *Ahau*, Eight *Cumhu*, or August 12, 3114 B.C. However they did something unique and very special in comparison to the rest of the world's ancient genesis mythologies. They placed the birth of the First Father on One *Ahau*, Eight *Moan*, or June 16, 3122 B.C., and the birth of the First Mother on One *Ahau*, Eighteen *Zotz*, or December 7, 3121 B.C.—that is, in a previous creation. The Maya cosmos therefore resembles the universe envisioned by some modern astronomers which eventually collapses, melts down, is remade in the caldron of another creation—except in the modern version no trace of the existing universe remains.

Both of these views manage to unite the scientific evidence for an explosive moment of creation with the concept of an eternal universe that oscillates forever, passing through an infinite number of moments of creation in an eternal cycle of birth, death, and rebirth. When Chan Balam raised his right arm in a display of the *chi*-hand on A.D. January 20, 690, he expressed his unity with the First Father, the Sun God, and linked the Maya kingship with an ancestral tree having its roots in realms extending beyond the limits of the present creation and into infinite dimensions of time.

The *chi*-hand emerges as the most highly revered and powerful of all Maya mudra and, not surprisingly, the most widely used. Understanding its full meaning and implications is a key that unlocks a far deeper and more comprehensive appreciation of Maya ritual as depicted in the art and opens up for the viewer paths to new and exciting perceptions that have been previously unknown and left unexplored. As such it deserves special detailed attention, not only as it appears in portrayals of rituals but also in its important role as a manograph in the formation of glyphs that frequently accompany and complement its appearance as an active agent in the performance of rituals.

A comment in reference to the drinking vessel illustrated in figure 8.7 states that it is "surely the finest ceramic object ever found at Copan." As the vase shows very little wear, it was probably deposited in the tomb of its owner very shortly after it was produced.

Figure 8.7. Funerary vase, Copan

Three other figures incised on the vase are gods so I draw the conclusion that the personage depicted is its original owner and, judging by his headdress with its mirror emblem, he was undoubtedly an Ahau or a noble of high standing.

Here once again the deceased lord equates himself with the Sun through a ritual performed by the hands. His extended right arm displays the *chi*-hand but the *chi*-hand held at his chest is also a right hand, indicating the movement of that hand in a sequence of ritual gesturing. Glyphs directly above this action are descriptive of the ceremony performed. In one a sun emblem prefixes a glyphic *chi*-hand and it is followed by the general verb *bah*, "he went" or "he did." Next the *a-ya* glyph introducing the P.S.S. is seen, so the portrait of the lord is at the end where a nominal glyph would be expected to be found.

In general the *chi*-hand is displayed on the right hand, considered to be

*Figure 8.8. **Bringing Down the Sun, 1**, cylindrical vase*

masculine. The moon handsign, which it closely resembles, is usually made on the left, considered to be feminine. The moon handsign displayed by the Lunar Goddess, which was discussed earlier, appears to be a right hand, although anatomically a left hand is depicted. In portrayals of rituals, however, very often the *chi*-hand will be displayed on the left hand, especially when the right hand is employed performing some very positive or highly powerful hand signal. In glyph formation however, the *chi*-hand is quite uniformly a right hand.

Graphically a left hand changes the phonetic value of the same handsign to *hu*. This is demonstrated in variations of the glyph *hulah*, "to have come," shown in figure 8.7A and B. In A the frog, *u(o)*, carries the *hu* value. As we have seen *u* means "Moon" in Maya languages. The variant in B substitutes a left hand, easily confused with the *chi*-hand, for the phonetic value, *hu*. The reader of Maya hieroglyphs must be aware of these distinctions. By way of comparison the glyph *u-hach*, "it is true," is presented in C. Here the right hand *chi*-sign provides a very different phonetic value.

In the vase rollout illustrated in figure 8.8 an Ahau seated on a dais in 1 performs the ceremony of "bringing down the sun," clearly expressed by his use of two sacred handsigns. Extending his left arm he displays the *chi*-hand as his right arm is brought downward in an emphatic gesture displaying the *yalhiya*-hand, "he manifested it." The primary action on the hands is continued as the assistant in 2 backsigns a right *chi*-hand to the assistant in 3 whose gesturing is depicted as two anatomical right *chi*-hands expressing the downward movement of the Sun or solar energy.

Enhancing the feeling of spiritual energy that exudes from this painting are signs related to speech scrolls emanating before the faces of the actors in 1 and 2. More than merely representing mystical or magical utterances, these signs are indicative of a divine energy, the sacred life force of prana, "breath," "air," "spirit," or the pneuma pervading the painting. They seem to float in an ethereal atmosphere and they are positioned near the central focus of the composition.

The *chi*-hand displayed by the Ahau is placed directly in the center of the composition, signaling the moment of contact with the spirit world. The ritual being performed is a very close relative of and a variant of ceremonies discussed previously in which the apparition of *Kauil* is manifested in a mirror. The elaborate pendant worn by the Ahau contains an *Ahau* emblem, but often such pendants display an obsidian mirror. As we can ascertain in a subsequent depiction of a ritual of this type, the participant in 2 wears such a mirror pendant. There is a clearly discernable alignment between the pendant, the central handsign, and the "speech" scroll along which the gaze of the Ahau is intently fixed. The viewer is meant to perceive that the shaman is communicating with the spirit world through the sacred language of handsigns reflected through the portal of a hidden mirror.

Plainly in view directly below the main handsign is another central ritual object, a ceremonial drinking vessel painted in a pattern correlated to the *chi*-hand. It has been known for some time that the "checkerboard" motif is emblematic of the Sun God, as demonstrated in the glyph *Mah-K'ina K'in Ahau*, shown in A. As this glyph contains the head portrait of the First Father, the Sun God, it is obvious to most epigraphers in the field that the matrix pattern is representative of the Sun. Over a decade ago, I began to question why the Sun would generate such a pattern as this symbol. A fascinating point about epigraphic problems is that a question posed may be contemplated for many years, then very often its solution appears suddenly in a momentary flash of insight. Just so, recently I came to the realization that hidden within the checkerboard motif is a repetitive pattern consisting of two fundamental glyphic signs generated by the repeated glyph in 4 as an extreme abbreviation of the P.S.S. The glyph can be read as a combination of *yax*, "fresh," and *te*, "tree," or "tree-fresh," which is very frequently found in the P.S.S. formula. However, the Maya hi-

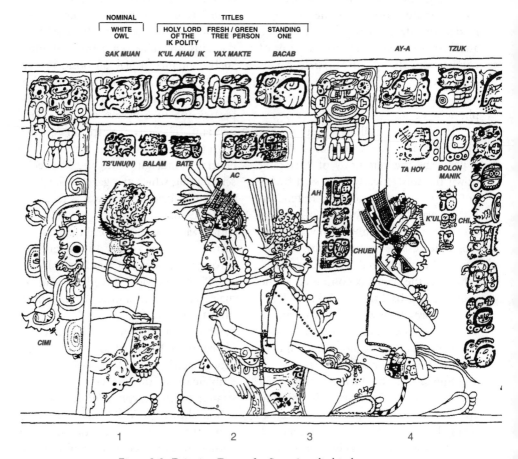

Figure 8.9. **Bringing Down the Sun, 2**, *cylindrical vase*

Sun. Both *k'in*, "sun," in B and *be*, "road," in C can be recognized interspersed within the pattern.

The vase painting presents some other interesting insights into glyph formation. Originally I had interpreted the eroglyph is capable of being interpreted and properly understood on various levels simultaneously and often will contain double meanings. In 5 the other glyph in the band introduces a deeper context for the interpretation of the main glyph, adding another dimension and directly relating the text to the ceremony enacted in the painting.

The glyph in 5 is the manograph *ye*, "to reveal," a sample of which is shown in D. It usually is infixed with a mirror

in Copan, shown in F, there is an intriguing combination of the *lo*-sign and the *ye*-hand. The glyph *lo* shown in E can refer to the sacred work of shamans. Maya artists are fond of making a play on the reverse sound of a word or its

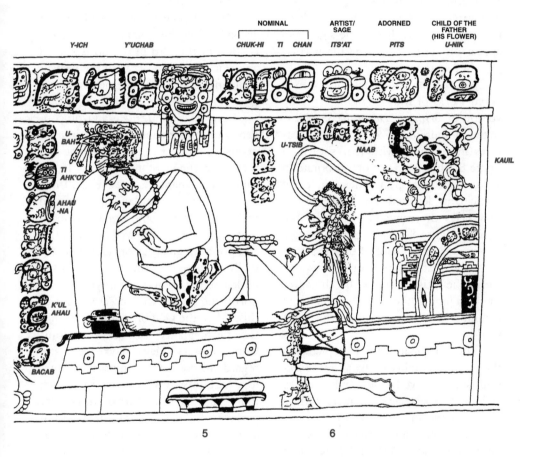

sign and in 5 it is also infixed with a *cuauc* sign, which we know can mean *cu* or *ku*, "god." The elements of hand, mirror, and god are expressive of the ritual portrayed.

In a detail from a ceremonial bench

mirrored equivalent, so *lo* becomes *ol*, "portal," and also Heart of Heaven. The heart of the thirteen heavens in the Maya cosmological scheme is the seventh or central realm; it is interesting that the artist repeats that glyph seven times in the glyph band.

In front of a remarkable altar composed of these glyphic symbols a headbanded shaman is seated performing a ceremony. Either from or into his mouth flow sacred beaded droplets of *itz*. Below these are *u*-signs, which signify water, blood, or liquids of any kind including *itz,* and these same signs also appear on apparel worn by the participant in 3 in the vase painting.

One of the most beautifully executed works of Maya ceramic art—the version of *Bringing Down the Sun* illustrated in figure 8.9—contains many features in common with that shown in figure 8.8 but it is far more elaborate in style, scope, texts, and the number of participants depicted. The high priest in 5 displays the same handsigns as the Ahau in figure 8.8 as he gazes into the unseen mirror pendant of the attendant in 4 who gestures in a sign of respect. Again the artist captures the climax of the ceremony, the exact moment of communicative contact with the spirit world.

The participant in 3 is depicted in the act of raising his left hand in the *chi*-sign, and here we become onlookers to an intimate spectacle of an ancient Maya occult drama in progress. In the portrayal of architectural space in the composition, the actors in 1 and 2 are not in the immediate presence of the high priest but appear in a room behind but within view of the participant in 3. Through his handsign this actor conveys the arrival of the divine presence conjured to the participant in 2. This individual then transmits the signal to the shaman in 1 who responds by raising a drinking vessel accompanied with a gesture of offering. The action is a sequential performance in the sacred language of mudra in which the participants communicate not only among themselves but in an interaction with divine beings in the Otherworld.

Each participant is named in text accompanying his portrait with the exception of the lord in 5 who is named above in the P.S.S. Between the participants in 4 and 5 is a statement that begins "On the holy day of Nine *Manik* . . ." The daysign *Manik* is a glyph consisting of the *chi*-hand, which is simultaneously a sign for the number nine and the central theme of the painting. In the time-space mandala of the 260-day sacred calendar, this day falls almost in the very center of the northern quadrant. The artist is very well aware of this and positions an ancestor cartouche, actually a segment of the mandala, in the far left of the composition, symbolizing north, the land of the deceased. Out of this, *Cimi*, the God of Death, peers into the performance of the ceremony. Contemporary Maya daykeepers still regard *Manik* days as important times for religious observances in which individual, clan, and town rituals are performed. These are days that permit access to the ancestors, who are regarded as being closer to the spirit world, thus able to assist in communicating with divine beings.

It is very clear in the text following the daysign that, in the verbal expression *u-bah ti ahkot,* "he goes or he went to dance," a literal meaning is not intended. Dancing is a metaphor for the act of bringing down the gods or opening up the portals of the material and spirit worlds, which is exactly what the participants are portrayed as doing. To do this properly and efficiently requires conjuring deceased ancestors who reside in the northern realms. In relation to this the P.S.S. on the drinking vessel is very carefully constructed.

The P.S.S. is divided into three parts separated by images of the Jaguar Protector God, who is the guardian of the ancestral lineage. The introductory *a-ya* glyph and its subsequent description of the vase itself is placed above the immediate central focal point of the ceremony. Following it the high priest is named and described as an *its'at* and the child or literally "the flower" of *Sac Muan*, White Owl. The name of the deceased father is positioned appropriately in the north near the ancestor cartouche. The P.S.S. reads in a circle uniting the father and the son and expressing their relationship in reference to the lineage tree of which the son is the flower. The father is titled *Yax Makté*, Tree Lord Person. I think that *yax* here refers to green, the color of the center and the tree is the *axis mundi* in the center of the cosmos in which the father is described as being a *Bacab*, a Stood-Up Person.

One reason why Maya painting is considered tribal art, not true fine art, is because it does not usually conform to the standard media of Western art. The rectangular canvas is an expression of the Western conception of time as being linear whereas the Maya artist's preference for a circular medium—the vase— is the result of a cyclical perception of time. Another reason is that fine art is

considered to be the personal expression of an individual who is expected to sign the work. Tribal art is a communal enterprise in which individual expression is subjugated to the requirements of the group and therefore is unsigned. These criteria would seem to be quite valid but they completely fall apart in view of the comparatively recent breakthroughs in the decipherment of Maya hieroglyphics.

Directly above the participant in 6 are three glyphs beginning with *u-tsib*, "his painting," followed by the name of the artist. The phrase appears to emanate from the mouth of the image of *Kauil*. It appears directly below the *its'at* glyph with its "eye" mainsign in the P.S.S. In certifying the painting as the personal expression of an individual the artist has gone a lot further than merely signing it: he includes a self-portrait. The *chi*-hand displayed mimics the artist holding a brush and the plate offered is a beautifully constructed metaphor of presenting the painting itself. The artist plays on the second glyph of the P.S.S., which states "it was presented." The vibrant image of *Kauil* implies that the work was done under the auspices of the God of Ancestral Lineages and is therefore sacred and proper.

In one of the great masterpieces of Maya art, the plate painting of the Sun God resurrected as the Corn God, illustrated in figure 8.10, it is again the *chi*-hand that predominates in the action portrayed. After defeating the Lords of Death in the underworld, the immediate task of the Twins became to bring their father, who had been decapitated, back to life. This was accomplished

A-YA   U-LAK   TI-OHAM   KAUIL   SAC OL WAY

Figure 8.10. **The Resurrection of the Sun God,** *plate painting*

largely through the magical power of mudra. In the painting the *chi*-hands displayed by *Hunahpu*, who is portrayed and named on the left, resonate with the *chi*-hand extended by the First Father, thus creating a magnetic tension in a field of energy. One is reminded of Michelangelo's depiction of Creation in the Sistine Chapel in which God brings Adam to life with a similar technique, symbolically utilizing the tension created by hand gestures.

Hun Nal Ye, One Maize Revealed, is another name for the First Father.

The death skull within the turtle carapace in the painting symbolizes the seed that must die to generate the living corn plant. Reflecting on death the artist reminds the viewer that the generative power of nature is such that one grain produces ten thousand, and that far from being an end death is a new beginning and an integral part of the process of Creation. *Cimi*, the Death God, is here portrayed as an ally in the production of life.

The First Father is positioned at the top or eastern sector of the composition. The emergence of life from the turtle carapace is compared to dawn, the *chi*-hands evoking the regenerative powers of the Sun and the triumphant appearance of the Sun after its perilous journey through the underworld. The carapace is an Earth symbol. In Maya cosmology the land is seen as the back of a gigantic turtle emerging from the waters of the world; hence, native inhabitants of the Americas refer to the continent as Turtle Island.

In order to generate life from the death skull, *Xbalanque*, who is named and depicted on the right, pours forth *itz*, the sacred essence of being, from a jar. The *Akbal* daysign on the jar is the sacred symbol of the Jaguar Night Sky God that is associated with the number seven, the heart of heaven itself. In Maya concepts of parallels, the night sky is viewed as a mirror image of the underworld. Besides being symbolic of the Earth, the turtle carapace can also be seen in the heavens—and the painting becomes a vision of the night sky.

The First Father, *Hun Hunahpu* is named in the two glyphs directly in front of him. The second glyph *Chan*, "snake," is a reference to him as a sky god. Within the ear of the snake is the triangular arrangement of three dots, which also appear on the cheeks of *Hunahpu* and *Xbalanque*. As we have seen earlier, this symbol represents the triangle of three stars in the Orion constellation—Alnitak, Saiph, and Rigel. These stars, known as *Yax Ux Tunal*, First Three Stone Place, were set up at the beginning of Creation and are representative of a reflection of a center, actually the three hearthstones of the

typical Maya kitchen fireplace. Alnitak forms part of what we see as Orion's Belt, three almost exactly aligned, perfectly spaced stars that are among the most luminous anywhere in the Milky Way galaxy. In ancient Maya hieroglyphic writing concerning Creation, the image of a turtle was seen in these stars. In a stela at Quirigua, it is stated that on the day of Creation—Four *Ahau*, Eight *Cumhu—ilahi yax koh Aac*, *Chak K'u Ahau*, "it was seen, the first image, Turtle, Great God Lord." It is this turtle that appears in the plate painting. In the tradition of the Maya shaman, in order to magically resurrect the First Father the Twins revert to conditions that were present at the dawn of Creation.

Within the triangular arrangement of the three "hearthstones," the Maya saw the Orion nebula as the fire. In a truly astounding insight that could hardly be coincidental, it is remarkable that the ancient Maya chose this particular nebula as a creation image. Current scientific investigation shows that the Orion nebula is in fact a gigantic "star factory," and of all the stellar nurseries scattered throughout our galaxy none is more vibrantly dynamic. C. Robert O'Dell, an astronomer at Rice University in Houston, has studied the Orion nebula for 30 years, most recently as the lead scientist for the Hubble Space Telescope observations. He has stated, "It has it all, it's the brightest nebula, the closest and the youngest," and also, "When we look at Orion we are seeing a star factory and what our solar system looked like in its infancy." He describes it as one of the most densely congested star clusters of any known region in our galaxy, "a violent, stirred-up place, where material is moving at supersonic velocities."

Supposedly the Orion nebula was first observed in 1610 by the amateur French astronomer de Peiresc using a telescope given to him by Galileo, who had somehow missed the nebula. In an instructive description of Orion's role as a star birthplace the British astronomer William Herschel in the 1780s called it the "chaotic material of future suns." It is truly amazing to consider that these observations were apparently preempted by intuitive ancient astronomers in Mesoamerica and that their awareness was embedded into Maya mythology and art.

Out of the left side of the turtle carapace emerges *Uo*, the Frog God who represents the Moon and is symbolic of the element water, as is *Hunahpu* who appears to spring from the Frog God's headdress. The frog's ear contains the sign of the God Seven, the Heart of Heaven. From the right side *Yahaute*, The Lord of the Tree, issues forth. Iconographic features in his image, especially the square eye, associate him with the Sun and consequently with the element fire, as is *Xbalanque* who springs from his headdress. The jaguar *way* of *Xbalanque* is particularly the night sun. *Yahuate* displays the *yalhiya-* or manifesting-hand, here symbolic of birth, which is metaphorically referred to by the Maya as "touching earth." He points to a waterlily emblem, the first daysign in the sacred calendar and therefore the roots of the cosmic tree of time, which is generated by the Sun. The last daysign, *Ahau*, is the flower of the tree and it is associated with *Hunahpu*. In fact, directly or indirectly the artist manages to allude to most of the twenty daysigns in the calendar.

The central theme of the painting is rebirth and the triumph of life over death. In rereading the P.S.S. starting with *a-ya*, "it came into being, it was blessed, its painting . . .", we come to the glyph *u-lak*. *Lak* means plate or any flat object. *U* is a possessive pronoun meaning that the plate is owned by someone. *Ti toham*, "for pozole," tells us that the plate was used for eating corn gruel. The Smoking Mirror glyph here is probably the nominal of the owner, and Kauil was a popular name among the classical Maya. *Sac Ol Way* describes him as a Pure Spirit of the Portal, a title applied to deceased persons. We may safely conclude that the plate is a ritual object specifically designed for use in ceremonies for the dead in which the theme of the resurrection of the Corn God was, as we have seen earlier, a highly favored subject, and regarded as being particularly appropriate in accompanying funerary rites.

The same theme is brilliantly explored in a magnificent drinking vessel diagramed in figure 8.11. Here the artist emphasizes that the goal of the deceased person's journey is to reach the land of the ancestral spirits, which lies beyond the Polestar in the north. Much of the text has been obliterated and I have not included it in the diagram. However, it can be ascertained that the text began with a date and the meaning of at least three of the remaining six

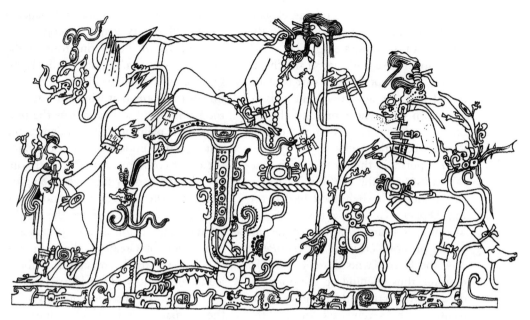

Figure 8.11. **The Resurrection of the Sun God,** *cylindrical vase*

glyphs can be discerned.

The date is followed by the verb *hulya,* "to arrive," and glyphs that refer to a place, in part named *Ho-Chan,* Five Sky. The number five is practically synonymous with *be,* "road." The last glyph is *xaman,* "north," so it can safely be assumed that a supernatural heavenly place is referred to, and the text leaves little doubt as to where it is located. The pictorial matter is a further confirmation of this.

The painting is usually interpreted as depicting the birth of a god but that is only in a vague sense true. We are dealing here with the fundamental theme, derived from mythology, that was frequently favored by artists producing funerary ritual objects. Much of the confusion arises because the *hulya* verb, "to arrive," is practically identical

to the verb *sih,* "to be born," and is closely related to it. It is only through the context in which the glyph is used that we can determine exactly which meaning is intended. The north is the Land of the Dead wherein the deceased hopes to arrive or be reborn. The artist compares this to the resurrection of the Sun God. In the original the background is completely black, which is indicative of the dark supernatural spirit world. For purposes of clarity and to stress other salient features of the painting I have eliminated the black background in the illustration.

The action is again performed by the hands but in this case the Hero Twins display the sacred *yalhiya*-sign, which manifests the Corn God. In interpreting these handsigns we should realize that the extended, curved small finger in each case is merely an elegant stylization and in no way affects the meaning of the mudra employed.

Also the usual format in which the top of the composition is east is abandoned here for a very specific reason. The Corn God who represents the deceased is shown ascending the cosmic World Tree or the Milky Way in order to use the portal in the north, which logically must be at the top of this particular painting. The beheaded bird is the Big Dipper, *Vucub Caquix* or Seven Macaw, who usurped the role of the Sun in the previous creation. In the *Popol Vuh*, the Hero Twins destroy this bird monster, thus opening up the portal to the ancestral spirit world as shown in the painting. The seven stars forming the Big Dipper are naturally associated with the portal of the Polestar and the Heart of Heaven. The gaze of the Corn God is intently focused on the hand gestures of *Xbalanque* who opens up the portal by a magical display of the handsign "seven" with his left hand.

Near the base of the World Tree are crossbands signifying the sky and representing the crossing of the Milky Way with the ecliptic. The World Tree itself is a cross formed by the upright Milky Way surmounted by the branches of the ecliptic upon which the Corn God reclines. The ecliptic of course is the path of the Sun and the planets through the sky. Along this flows the Corn God's jaguar tail symbolizing the nighttime journey of the Sun, another reference to a path taken by the deceased in the afterlife.

Before *Hunahpu* on the left is a flowing image of *Chac-Xib-Chac*, the deified incarnation of water. Balancing this is a highly stylized but recognizable head of *Kauil*, "fire," in front of the portrayal of *Xbalanque* on the right. Out of its Smoking Mirror emanates one of the cords that winds throughout the painting. In a band across the bottom of the painting the artist depicts the waters of the underworld out of which the other cord emerges. The intertwining of these cords symbolizes the union of all opposites including life and death. The artist succinctly states the fundamental Maya vision of the cosmos and conception of Creation, the grandiose idea at the root of Maya culture embodied in the identity of the Hero Twins.

The central obsession of the Maya is the human condition regarding the meaning of life and death. This concern even overshadows their intractable fascination with time or their obstinate insistence on establishing legitimate rights to rule. The Maya developed an intensively strong belief in an afterlife largely modeled on the diurnal rebirth of the Sun. At death they emulated this as a confirmation of the continuation of life beyond mortality. A distinctly recognizable result of this pattern is its enormous imprint on Maya art as exemplified by the ceramic incense burner illustrated in figure 8.12.

The two-part effigy was found at a burial site in Uaxactún. The lower half of the ritual object held burning copal incense. In the upper part, openings made in the eyes, nose, mouth, and the back of the head emitted light and smoke during funerary rites that took place in the tomb. The original is black and the incisions are filled in with white

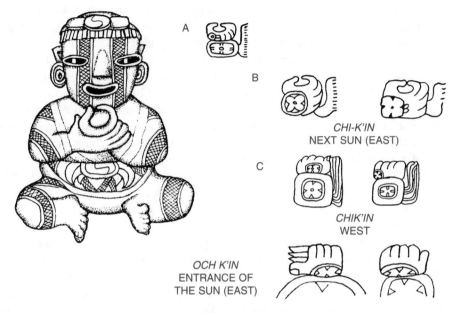

A

B

CHI-K'IN
NEXT SUN (EAST)

C

CHIK'IN
WEST

OCH K'IN
ENTRANCE OF
THE SUN (EAST)

Figure 8.12. Ceramic incense burner

pigment. An attempt to illustrate this would obscure many of the pertinent features of the figure so in the diagram I have omitted the black coloring of the object and marked the white incisions with black lines. The vertical striping on the effigy suggests god-marks. Cross-hatching is frequently used to indicate the color black so apparently the figure represents an unknown deity of the night or perhaps a personification of the nocturnal sky.

The deity seems to be wearing a cloak, perhaps the cloak of darkness out of which his hands protrude in the familiar *chi*-sign but here the gesture is strongly reinforced. It may be compared with variants of the glyph *k'inich*, "sun" or "day," shown in A. In these glyphs the *ni*-sign doubles as both a phonetic complement and an image of the rays of

the Sun or what the Maya refer to as its "cords." The handsign of the effigy is raised and presented by the benevolent smiling deity in a powerful gesture that mimics the Sun's emergence from darkness at dawn.

The *chi*-hand is sometimes used in variants of a glyph for east, *chi-k'in* or "next sun" as shown in B. Something interesting happens in glyphs expressing west, *chik'in* or *ochk'in*, "entrance of the sun." As shown in C the hand closes or "dies," as we have seen in Maya finger counting. These expressive movements of the hand as they appear in glyphs are extremely pertinent in analyzing what is probably the most famous of all Maya works of art, the monumental sarcophagus lid that covers the tomb of Pacal the Great, illustrated in figure 8.13.

The tomb lies deep within the recesses of a pyramid at Palenque known as the Temple of the Inscriptions. Born in A.D. 603, the great king probably started working on the sarcophagus some eight years before his death in 683, as he felt his end approaching. As an epitome of the *Ahau* ideal, Pacal—high priest, statesman, warrior, architect, and above all, an *its'at*—undoubtedly had a great deal to do personally with the design of his final statement in stone.

The work is very much the creative expression of an individual and yet it encompasses and summarizes the worldview of an entire culture, strictly adhering to the canons of an art steeped in tradition and fashioned on the anvil of the highly imaginative and visionary experiences of generations of shamans. In creating this masterpiece it would seem that Pacal was consciously intent on producing a graphic compendium skillfully stretching the virtuosity of the art form and the cosmological principles underlying it to their highest possible limits.

Pacal's life was filled with a rich variety of outstanding achievements in many fields but in his final encapsulating presentation he portrays himself in the act of accomplishing the supreme goal and highest development of human life. The representation of his apotheosis is a projection into the future. Utilizing art as a creative visualization he confidently illuminates the culminating event in his existence as a reality long before it has actually occurred. He shows himself as a human being in the act of triumphing over death.

Pacal's posture in this portraiture appears to be extremely awkward unless it is properly understood. Actually the body language is extremely eloquent. Underneath the lid, Pacal's body lies prostrate, his head positioned toward the north. On the lid however is the image of the same man in the act of rising from this supine position. His legs kick upward as his arching back jolts forward raising up his head. It vividly portrays the enactment of a resurrection from the dead, an awakening that commences the ascension into the divine spirit realm of the ancestors. Pacal's gaze is pointed fixedly toward the north. His right *chi*-hand is projected toward this sacred direction which flows along the path of an illuminated World Tree reaching upward into the highest levels of the heavens. Although probably the most famous of all the great works of Maya art, the sarcophagus lid is also simultaneously the most deeply misunderstood and widely misinterpreted. In interpretations of this work Pacal is universally described as falling into the maw of the underworld at the moment of death whereas in fact quite the opposite meaning is intended. Pacal has risen. He is shown as having already overcome the perils of the underworld and he is now commencing the process of ascent into the heavenly realms.

Pacal sited the Temple of the Inscriptions along an alignment connecting it with the center of the Palace of Inscriptions and the position of the setting Sun at the winter solstice. This line runs directly through the tomb. At winter solstice the Sun sets at its southernmost point on the horizon after which it begins its journey northward.

NORTH

MOON
WEST

SUN
EAST

SOUTH

Figure 8.13. **The Ascension of Pacal**, sarcophagus lid, Temple of the Inscriptions, Palenque

The architecture of the sacred precinct is manipulated in such a way that there is a correlation between the Sun's northward movement and Pacal's spiritual journey in the same direction. In death as in life Pacal has identified himself with the Sun.

As in so many other works of Maya art that we have discussed, the central action is expressed by the hands. Here Pacal's handsigns are positioned precisely in the geometric center of the composition. They concisely summarize the grandiose assertion expressed in the macrocosmic scheme that was constructed in accordance with the movements of the universe. The message they proclaim is now quite evident: "The Sun has died." The implication of course is that the Sun will rise again. Pacal makes this assertion from a throne that is a personification of the Sun. The fleshless lower jaw of this image symbolizing death contrasts with vibrant eyes, foliating forms, and dynamic symbols expressing life. Through his own death Pacal has penetrated into the unity of all existence as he rises into the plane of *Hunab Ku*, the God of Oneness.

After the completion of elaborate funerary rites the tomb was sealed. The stairwell leading down through the interior of the pyramid was then filled with rubble as well as with deposits of jade, shells, and pottery. Ultimately Pacal's final statement was meant to address a supernatural audience in the dark silence of the spirit world.

In 1952 the archaeologist Alberto Ruz Lhuillier uncovered the passageway and reached the inner sanctum of the tomb, revealing what is perhaps the most precious treasure of Maya art. *Hunab Ku*, the invisible god, is called the Hidden Maya. But more than any other known human individual who has ever lived it is Pacal who is most deserving of the title, *Balan Maya*, Hidden Maya.

APPENDICES

APPENDIX 1

Garrick Mallery

After graduating from Yale in 1850, Garrick Mallery studied law and was admitted to the bar in Philadelphia. Had it not been for the outbreak of the Civil War he would have become an obscure jurist like his father. He was wounded and taken prisoner at the battle of Peach Orchid, Virginia. He was commissioned as a lieutenant colonel of the 13th Pennsylvania Cavalry after his exchange. After the war, he became acting signal officer in a branch of the Army that was to become the United States Signal Corps, the first of its kind in the world.

The signal system of the Army and Navy was in fact directly adopted from the Indian system which was an extension of the sign language. To communicate over wide distances in the vast plains, the Indians used coded movements of horses, smoke signals and fires at night, and flags. Major Albert Myer, an expert on handsigning, observed the Apache system and then worked out a complete visual alphabet which is still in use today.

While on duty at Fort Rice Dakota in 1876, Mallery, like many other soldiers, quickly became interested in the sign language and pictography of the Indians. "A Calendar of the Dakota Nation" (1877), a paper originating from his observations among the Indians was to foreshadow his future work on picture writing. "Introduction to the Study of Sign Language Among the North American Indians as Illustrating the Gesture Speech of Mankind" (1880) established him as easily the foremost student of the subject. This was followed by "Sign Language among North American Indians Compared with That of Other Peoples and Deaf Mutes" (1881). A discussion of the origin of the communication of ideas by the vehicle of sign language symbols was an important feature of this study. His culminating treatise, "Picture Writing of the North American Indians," has been described as a monumental storehouse of well classified and digested data without peer. His influence in promoting scientific methods in the formative period of the branch of anthropology was notable. He was an active member of many scientific societies, known to have been a pleasant associate and deeply appreciated by his scientific equals.

APPENDIX 2

Trade Trails into Old Mexico

It is now well established that extensive trading took place between Mesoamerica and various regions in what is now the United States. In Chaco Canyon, New Mexico, evidence for such Mesoamerican high-status imports as macaws and copper bells has been found. A petroglyph in Indian Petroglyphs State Park, New Mexico, is informative and revealing. It clearly shows two macaws. These birds do not migrate; they must have been transported from Mesoamerica. One of the macaws is depicted in a cage complete with a handle, telling us how they were transported.

The most indisputable evidence of systematic contact between the two regions was produced in an article—written by German Harbottle, a senior chemist at Brookhaven National Laboratory, and Phil Weigand, an anthropologist—entitled "Turquoise in Pre-Columbian America" (1992). They explain that virtually all the turquoise mines on the North American continent extend in a great arc from California to Colorado. By using a technique called neutron-activation analysis, they traced turquoise found in Mexico to specific mines in New Mexico, Arizona, and Nevada, more than 1000 miles away. Not only did they prove the existence of systematic trade, but they were able to determine how extensive and well established the trade had become and what trade routes were probably used.

The earliest known use of turquoise in Mexico was found in Mezcala, Guerrero, and dates to 600 B.C. Isolated occurrences of the gem are found in western and central Mexico dating to 200 B.C. By 50 B.C. extensive use began in Oaxaca. By A.D. 1000 turquoise was popular throughout Mesoamerica outstripping its competitors' gem and jade in consumption. By A.D. 1050 evidence has been found for extensive use among the Maya. Only small amounts were used by the people of the American Southwest; the gem was chiefly mined for export to Mesoamerica.

Harbottle and Weigand trace an Early Postclassic trade route that begins in Chaco Canyon in northern New Mexico and extends south into Mexico as far as Tula. From there it sweeps eastward way out across the Yucatan Peninsula finally arriving at the great Maya metropolis of Chichén-Itzá. The transshipment of the gem over such vast distances must have involved many intermediaries. In order to maintain a system of intertribal and international trade, it was necessary for the Indians of the Americas to develop a general trade language independent of their numerous spoken languages and dialects. Without doubt the *lengua franca* used was the hand-sign language.

APPENDIX 3

Coatlicue

Coatlicue has inspired what has been described as one of the most curious remains of American antiquity, illustrated in figure 1.23. Indeed this astonishing monstrosity deserves a special place in the history of art, for although grotesque and enigmatic, it is yet among the most sublime and haunting images ever fashioned by human hands. When the monolith was first unearthed from beneath the Zócalo, the cathedral square in Mexico City, in 1824, the excavators took one awestruck look at it and promptly reburied it. It eventually came to rest in the National Museum in Mexico City.

The site in which the statue was originally found was the famed Aztec capital of Tenochtitlan. It was one of a pair that stood in the courtyard of the great temple. When the temple complex was destroyed, one of the statues toppled over and broke into pieces. This one fell over and was found covered with the burnt timbers and rubble of that last terrible battle of the Aztec Empire.

Coatlicue is a goddess symbolizing both life and death as aspects of the same thing. She is a consort to the Lord of the Dead and is known by a litany of names. She is Mother of the Gods, Mother Goddess, Mother Earth, Lady of Serpents, Goddess of the Serpent Skirt, Goddess of the Earth. Her *huipil*, or skirt, is decorated with writhing rattlesnakes, human hearts, and feathers. The rattlesnake was held in affectionate veneration because of its links with the Earth. It was regarded as a symbol of the underworld because it crawls from holes in the ground. The feathers represent the heavens. The heart is the precious jewel symbolizing the meeting place of opposed principles. The number five, alluded to by the hands, represents the center, the point where heaven and Earth meet.

The plan of the great temple at Tenochtitlan is known from codices. Its central theme is the unity of opposing forces in the cosmos. Although the statue is a detail, it is an integral part of a highly inspired whole, containing in itself all the major concepts in the vast poem of which it is a part.

In the eastern sector of the great temple precinct an enormous pyramid was constructed surmounted by two temples, one dedicated to *Huitzilopochtli*, the Sun as God of War and the other dedicated to *Tlaloc*, the Rain God. The juxtapositioning of these two temples represents a basic underlying theme fundamental to Mesoamerican religious thought and cosmology in general—the union of the opposing primary elements, fire and water. As the Mother Goddess, *Coatlicue* had given birth to *Huitzilopochtli*, the Sun, and to *Coyolxauhqui*, the Moon. Eventually she gave birth to all the gods and all the stars.

A ball court was set in the western sector of the ceremonial precinct. The "games" performed there were considered acts in the drama of cosmic union. In the struggle of opposing forces the ball represented the movement of heavenly bodies.

Rather than being done as games, the rites observed in this sanctuary were theoretically destined to offer souls to the Sun. The losers, who were promptly sacrificed, were usually captives of war who had been considerably weakened before the contest. The spectacles may have surpassed in their excesses the gory events that took place in the coliseums of ancient Rome. The victims would have been very much aware of the fate which awaited them. A prominent rack for skulls, the *tzompantli*, was placed just above the ball court. Before being led up the stairs of the great pyramid, the last sight they witnessed in this world would have been the monstrous image of *Coatlicue*—then painted in brilliant colors. In the ritual eating of the limbs of the sacrificial victims, the hands—because they were regarded as being particularly tender—were reserved for the nobles.

Much of the bizarre imagery contained in the statue can be understood in reference to the context in which it was found. It is carved in the form of the eagle vase into which sacrificial hearts were thrown. The terrifying visage stands over eight feet in height and was probably carved when the New Fire was kindled for the last time in A.D. 1508. Fire is yet another symbol of sacrifice. The two-fanged snakes that emerge from the severed neck of the Earth Goddess are fertility symbols. In the great Maya ball court at Chichén-Itzá in the Yucatan, which was built around A.D. 1000, an elaborate scene shows defeated ballplayers being decapitated. From the severed neck of one player, six snakes and a grandiose tree emerge, symbolizing the fertility that such a sacrifice would bring.

BIBLIOGRAPHY

Amon, A. *Talking Hands*. Garden City, NY: Doubleday & Company, 1968.

Atkinson, M.J. *Indians of the Southwest*. San Antonio, TX: Naylor Co., 1973.

Aveni, A. *Skywatchers of Ancient Mexico*. Austin, TX: University of Texas Press, 1980.

Barrera Vasquez, A. *Diccionario Maya Cordemex, Maya-Español, Español-Maya*. Mérida: Ediciones Cordemex, 1980.

Beetz, C. and L. Latterthwaite. *The Monuments and Inscriptions of Caracol, Belize*. Philadelphia: University Museum, University of Pennsylvania, 1981.

Bolio, A. *Libro de Chilam Balam de Chumayel*. San José, Costa Rica: Sauter and Co., 1930.

Brennan, M. *The Boyne Valley Vision*. Dublin: Dolmen Press, 1979.

____. *The Stones of Time*. Rochester, VT: Inner Traditions, 1994.

Brinton, D. *Annals of the Cakchiquels*. Philadelphia: Library of Aboriginal American Literature, 1885.

Caesar, J. *The Conquest of Gaul*. London: Penguin Books, 1982.

Cambell, J. *The Hero with a Thousand Faces*. Princeton, NJ: Princeton University Press, 1968.

Campbell, P. *Astronomy and the Maya Calendar Correlation*. Laguna Hills, CA: Aegean Park Press, 1992.

Caso, A. *Codex Nuttall*. Cambridge, MA: Peabody Museum, 1902.

Catlin, G. *Letters and Notes on the Manners, Customs, and Conditions of the North American Indians (1844)*. New York: Dover Press, 1973.

Cody, I.E. (Iron Eyes). *Indian Talk*. Healdsburg, CA: Naturegraph Publishers, 1970.

Coe, M.D. *Breaking the Maya Code*. London: Thames and Hudson, 1992.

____. *Lords of the Underworld: Masterpieces of Classic Maya Ceramics*. Princeton, NJ: Princeton University Press, 1978.

____. *The Maya*. London: Thames and Hudson, 1966.

____. *The Maya Scribe and His World*. New York: The Grolier Club, 1973.

De Sahagun, B. *Historia general de las cosas de nueva Espana*. Mexico City, 1938.

Duran, F.D. *The Aztecs: The History of the Indies of New Spain*. London: Cassell, 1964.

____. *Book of the Gods and Rites and the Ancient Calendar*. Norman, OK: University of Oklahoma Press, 1971.

Edmondson, M. *The Book of Counsel: The Popul Vuh of the Quiché Maya of Guatemala*. New Orleans: Tulane University, Middle American Research Institute Publication 35, 1971.

_____. *The Ancient Future of the Itza: The Book of Chilam Balam of Tizimin.* Austin, TX: University of Texas Press, 1982.

Eliade, M. *Shamanism: Archaic Techniques of Ecstasy.* Princeton, NJ: Princeton University Press, 1970.

Fash, W. *Scribes, Warriors and Kings: The City of Copan and the Ancient Maya.* London: Thames and Hudson, 1991.

Feldman, S., MD. *Mannerisms of Speech and Gestures in Everyday Life.* New York: International Universities Press, 1959.

Fox, J. and J. Justeson. *Phoneticism in Mayan Hieroglyphic Writing.* Albany, NY: Institute for Mesoamerican Studies, 1984.

Freud, S. *Moses and Monotheism.* London: Hogarth Press, 1964.

Friedel, D., L. Schele, and J. Parker. *Maya Cosmos.* New York: William Morrow & Company, 1995.

Fronval, G. and D. Dubois. *Indian Signals and Sign Language.* New York: Bonanza Books.

Gelb, I. *A Study of Writing.* Chicago: University of Chicago Press, 1952.

Gomez, A. *La Leyendas del Popol Vuh.* Buenos Aires: Espasa-Calpe, S.A., 1951.

Grove, D. *Ancient Chalcatzingo.* Austin, TX: University of Texas Press, 1986.

Hofsinde, R. (Grey Wolf). *Indian Sign Language.* New York: William Morrow and Company, 1956.

Hunbatz, M. *The Secrets of Mayan Science/Religion.* Santa Fe, NM: Bear & Company, 1992.

Johnson, R. "Two Vases: Suggested Readings of the Secondary Texts." *U Mut Maya* magazine, 1989 edition.

Kerr, J. *The Maya Vase Book* (vols. I and II). New York: Justin Kerr, 1989.

Lumholtz, C. *Unknown Mexico.* New York: Charles Scribner & Sons, 1902.

Mallery, G. *A Calendar of the Dakota Nation.* Washington, D.C.: Bulletin of the Geological and Geographical Survey, vol. III, no. 1, 1877.

_____. *Introduction to the Study of Sign Language Among the North American Indians as Illustrating the Gesture Speech of Mankind.* Washington, D.C.: Smithsonian Institution, Bureau of Ethnology, 1880.

_____. *Picture Writing of the American Indians.* Washington, D.C.: Tenth Annual Report of the Bureau of American Ethnology, 1893.

_____. *Sign Language among North American Indians Compared with That of Other Peoples and Deaf Mutes.* Washington, D.C.: First Annual Report of the Bureau of American Ethnology, 1881.

Martineau, L.V. *The Rocks Begin to Speak.* Las Vegas, Nevada: KC Publications, 1973.

McClintock, W. *The Old North Trail or Life, Legends and Religion of the Blackfeet Indians.* Lincoln, NB: University of Nebraska Press, 1992, 1910.

Megged, N. *El Universo del Popol Vuh.* Mexico City: Editorial Diana, 1991.

Morley, S.J. *An Introduction to the Study of the Maya Hieroglyphs.* Washington, D.C.: Bureau of American Ethnology, 1915. [also avail. as *Maya Hieroglyhics.* New York: Dover Press, 1975.]

____. *The Ancient Maya*. Stanford, CA: Stanford University Press, 1946.

Nuttall, Z. *The Codex Nuttall: a picture manuscript from ancient Mexico*. New York: Dover Press, 1975.

Pagden, A. *The Maya: Diego de Landa's Account of the Affairs of Yucatan*. Chicago: J. Philip O'Hara, Inc., 1975.

Pius XII (Pope). *The Proofs for the Existence of God in the Light of Modern Natural Science*. Vatican: Tip. Poliglotta Vaticana, 1951.

Preuss, M. *Gods of the Popul Vuh*. Culver City, CA: Labyrinthos, 1988.

Recinos, A. *Popol Vuh: The Sacred Book of the Ancient Quiché Maya*. Norman, OK: University of Oklahoma Press, 1950.

Reents-Budet, D. *Painting the Maya Universe: Royal Ceramics of the Classic Period*. Durham, NC: Duke University Press, 1994.

Roys, R. *The Book of the Chilam Balam of Chumayel*. Norman, OK: University of Oklahoma Press, 1967.

Sarabia, A. *Popul Vuh: Antiguas Historias de los Indios Quichés de Guatemala*. Mexico City: Editorial Porrúa, 1975.

Schele, L. and M. Miller. *The Blood of Kings*. New York: George Braziller, 1986.

Schele, L. and D. Friedel. *A Forest of Kings*. New York: William Morrow & Company, 1990.

Schele, L. *Notebook for the XVth Maya Hieroglyphic Workshop at Texas*. Austin, TX: Art Department, University of Texas.

Schellhas, P. *Representation of Deities of the Maya Manuscripts*. Cambridge, MA: Harvard University Press, 1904.

Seler, E. *Collected Works in Mesoamerican Linguistics and Archaeology*. Culver City, CA: Labyrinthos, 1992.

Séjourné L. *Burning Water*. Berkeley, CA: Shambala Publications, 1976.

Smith, M.E. *Picture Writing in Southern Mexico*. Norman, OK: University of Oklahoma Press, 1973.

Spinden, H.J. *A Study of Maya Art, Its Subject Matter and Historical Development*. Cambridge, MA: Harvard University Press, 1913.

Tedlock, B. *Time and the Highland Maya*. Albuquerque, NM: University of New Mexico Press, 1982.

Tedlock, D. *Popol Vuh*. New York: Simon and Schuster, 1985.

Thompson, J.E. *A Catalog of Maya Hieroglyphs*. Norman, OK: University of Oklahoma Press, 1962.

____. *Maya Hieroglyphs Without Tears*. London: British Museum, 1972.

____. *Maya Hieroglyhic Writing: An Introduction*. Washington, D.C.: Carnegie Institution of Washington, 1950. [reissued under same title by University of Oklahoma Press, 1971.]

____. *Rise and Fall of Maya Civilization*. Norman, OK: University of Oklahoma Press, 1963.

Tompkins, W. *Indian Sign Language*. New York: Dover Press, 1969.

Wiegar, L., Dr., S.J. *Chinese Characters: their origin, etymology, history, classification and signification*. New York: Dover Press, 1965.

Zavala, M. *Gramatica Maya*. José Díaz-Bolio, 1974.

INDEX OF HANDSIGNS

INDEX OF GODS AND HEROES

ABOUT THE AUTHOR

Martin Brennan grew up in New York where he discovered his profound fascination with the relationship between writing and art. He later trained in visual communication at Pratt Institute. His life-long interest in Maya culture and Mesoamerica took him to Mexico, where his interests in prehistoric rock inscriptions, ritual, and traditional art developed. For many months Martin lived with an Indian family deep in the mountains of Jalisco, where he conducted extensive field work on local art and religion. He realized that in all forms of ancient Maya art and artifacts an abundance of mysterious handsigns are prominently displayed.

Martin went on to study Oriental art and calligraphy at Shotokugi Zen Monastery in Japan. He also spent more than a decade in Ireland, the land of his parents, engaged in active research on megalithic art. In Ireland, he deciphered Stone Age petroglyphs at New Grange, a principal prehistoric mound in the Boyne Valley, many of which he demonstrated to represent the oldest sophisticated calendars in the world. His findings had international significance. He tapped into some of the earliest methods of recording numbers and the fundamental beginnings of writing, and reported these startling discoveries in his critically acclaimed *The Stars and The Stones*, later reissued as *The Stones of Time*.

Returning to America, Martin turned his attention to ancient American petroglyphs, and realized that much of the rock art on this continent is derived from American Indian hand sign language. A study of this art revealed its origins could be traced to Mexico. His research utilizes the known sign language of the Plains Indians to unlock the enigmatic Maya handsigns of Mexico, and continues to reveal unexpected and rather spectacular insights into the Maya and other early Mesoamericans.

Martin currently lives and teaches in Boulder, Colorado.

BOOKS OF RELATED INTEREST
BY BEAR & COMPANY

MAYA COSMOGENESIS 2012
The True Meaning of the Maya Calendar End-Date
by *John Major Jenkins*

THE MAYAN FACTOR
Path Beyond Technology
by *José Argüelles*

THE MAYAN ORACLE
Return Path to the Stars
by *Ariel Spilsbury and Michael Bryner*

MEDICINE OF THE CHEROKEE
The Way of Right Relationship
by *J.T. Garrett and Michael Garrett*

THE PLEIADIAN AGENDA
A New Cosmology for the Age of Light
by *Barbara Hand Clow*

SECRETS OF MAYAN SCIENCE/RELIGION
by *Hunbatz Men*

SURFERS OF THE ZUVUYA
Tales of Interdimensional Travel
by *José Argüelles*

STARWALKING
Shamanic Practices for Traveling Into the Night Sky
by *Page Bryant*

Contact your local bookseller or write:

BEAR & COMPANY
P.O. Box 2860
Santa Fe, NM 87504